The PRINCIPAL ASSESSMENT LEADER

Edited by **Thomas R. Guskey**

CASSANDRA ERKENS

WILLIAM M. FERRITER

TAMMY HEFLEBOWER

TOM HIERCK

CHARLES HINMAN

SUSAN HUFF

CHRIS JAKICIC

DENNIS KING

AINSLEY B. ROSE

NICOLE M. VAGLE

MARK WEICHEL

Solution Tree | Press

a division of
Solution Tree

555 North Morton Street
Bloomington, IN 47404
800.733.6786 (toll free) / 812.336.7700
FAX: 812.336.7790
email: info@solution-tree.com
solution-tree.com

Visit **go.solution-tree.com/assessment** to download other materials associated with this book.

Printed in the United States of America

13 12 11 10 09   1 2 3 4 5

Library of Congress Cataloging-in-Publication Data

The principal as assessment leader / edited by Thomas R. Guskey ... [et al.].

     p. cm.

   Includes bibliographical references and index.

   ISBN 978-1-934009-48-2 (perfect bound) -- ISBN 978-1-935249-10-8 (lib. bdg.) 1. School principals--United States. 2. Educational tests and measurements--United States. 3. Educational evaluation--United States. I. Guskey, Thomas R.

   LB2831.92.P719 2009

   371.2'012--dc22

                              2009019012

President: Douglas Rife
Publisher: Robert D. Clouse
Director of Production: Gretchen Knapp
Managing Editor of Production: Caroline Wise
Proofreader: Elisabeth Abrams
Cover Designer: Amy Shock
Text Designer: Raven Bongiani
Compositor: Amy Shock

Table of Contents

Introduction
  Thomas R. Guskey, Editor 1

Part One
Laying the Foundation of Assessment Literacy 7

  Chapter 1
  Paving the Way for an
  Assessment-Rich Culture

    Cassandra Erkens. 9

  Chapter 2
  Build, Promote, Guide, Provide, Monitor:
  Action Words for Principals as Instructional
  Leaders in Assessment

    Susan Huff. 31

  Chapter 3
  A Principal's Guide to Assessment

    Chris Jakicic 53

  Chapter 4
  Building Assessment Expertise Through
  Twenty-First-Century Professional Development

    Dennis King. 73

Chapter 5
A Seven-Module Plan to Build Teacher
Knowledge of Balanced Assessment

   Tammy Heflebower 93

Part Two
Collecting, Interpreting, and Reporting Data . . . 119

Chapter 6
Plug Us In, Please: Using Digital Tools for
Data Collection

   William M. Ferriter. 121

Chapter 7
Finding Meaning in the Numbers

   Nicole M. Vagle 149

Chapter 8
The Courage to Implement Standards-Based
Report Cards

   Ainsley B. Rose 175

Part Three
Assessing Students at Risk. 201

Chapter 9
Lowering High School Failure Rates

   Mark Weichel 203

Chapter 10
Assessing the Student at Risk: A New Look at
School-Based Credit Recovery

   Charles Hinman 225

Chapter 11
Formative Assessment, Transformative
Relationships

Tom Hierck 245

Index 265

THOMAS R. GUSKEY

Thomas R. Guskey, PhD, is professor of educational psychology in the College of Education at the University of Kentucky. A graduate of the University of Chicago, he served as director of research and development for Chicago Public Schools and was the first director of the Center for the Improvement of Teaching and Learning, a national research center.

Dr. Guskey coedited the *Experts in Assessment* series (Corwin) and was a contributor to the assessment anthology *Ahead of the Curve: The Power of Assessment to Transform Teaching and Learning* (Solution Tree, 2007). He has been featured on the National Public Radio programs *Talk of the Nation* and *Morning Edition*.

Dr. Guskey is listed in the National Staff Development Council's *Leaders in Staff Development*. He is the only person to have won the Council's Book of the Year Award twice and the Article of the Year Award three times. His work has been honored by numerous organizations, and his articles have appeared in prominent research journals, as well as *Educational Leadership, Phi Delta Kappan,* and *The School Administrator.* He served on the policy research team of the National Commission on Teaching and America's Future, the task force to develop the *National Standards for Staff Development*, and was recently named a Fellow in the American Educational Research Association, which also honored him in 2006 for his outstanding contribution relating research to practice.

Introduction

Thomas R. Guskey

The use of assessments to guide improvements in teaching and learning has a long and rich history in education. In fact, the value of "formative" assessments was identified nearly four decades ago by true giants in the field of education. In their 1971 book *Handbook on Formative and Summative Evaluation of Student Learning*, Benjamin Bloom, Thomas Hastings, and George Madaus described the benefits of offering students regular feedback on their learning progress through classroom formative assessments. Bloom went on to outline specific strategies teachers could use to implement formative assessments as part of regular classroom routines, both to improve student learning and to reduce gaps in the achievement of different subgroups of students (Bloom, 1971). It was Bloom who initiated the phrase *formative assessments* and who provided practical guidance for their use in modern classrooms (Guskey, 2006, 2007).

Although it has taken a while, education leaders at all levels today are coming to recognize the importance of assessment results in efforts to enhance student learning. They understand that assessments *for* learning can help guide improvements in teaching quality and spur advances in a variety of student outcomes (Stiggins, 2008). Many have been impressed by the work of Paul Black and Dylan Wiliam (1998), who verified what Bloom and his colleagues told us decades ago: regular formative assessments paired with well-planned corrective activities offer one of the most powerful tools teachers can use to help all students learn well (Bloom, Madaus, & Hastings, 1981; Guskey, 2008).

This book is designed to offer education leaders, especially school principals, practical ideas on how to initiate, lead, and sustain such improvement efforts. But unlike other books whose authors base their ideas on opinions or conjectures, the authors of each of these chapters derived their ideas through hard-earned experience. Their perspectives have been shaped by the successes and failures they have known in real school settings. They are not writing from an ivory tower or from the comfort of a research center, but from the front lines, where they have learned firsthand about the real challenges and difficulties that school leaders face in their efforts to improve the learning outcomes of all students.

Part 1 of this volume focuses on "Laying the Foundation of Assessment Literacy." We begin with "Paving the Way for an Assessment-Rich Culture" by Cassandra Erkens. In this chapter, Cassandra sounds the call for change in assessment policy and practices, provides evidence to support the need for such change, and demonstrates the vital importance of strong leadership in this change process. Emphasizing that formative reflection on the part of teachers is an essential first step in developing high-quality formative assessment for students, she describes how school leaders can create effective pathways for such sharing and reflection to take place.

In "Build, Promote, Guide, Provide, Monitor: Action Words for Principals as Instructional Leaders in Assessment," Susan Huff stresses that while efforts on the part of individual teachers to enhance the quality of their assessments can yield significant gains in the learning outcomes of students in their classrooms, principals hold the key to schoolwide improvements. She then describes five categories of practices essential to such leadership: (1) building supportive structures, (2) promoting a focus on learning, (3) guiding teacher teams, (4) providing and managing data, and (5) monitoring improvement efforts.

Chris Jakicic's chapter on "A Principal's Guide to Assessment" offers practical advice on how to establish a balanced program that combines formative assessments and summative assessments in meaningful ways. Her discussion about whether, early in the change process, teachers' assessments should be common or individual is particularly interesting.

Professional development issues provide the focus for Dennis King's chapter on "Building Assessment Expertise Through Twenty-First Century Professional Development." Starting from the foundation of a sound response to intervention model, Dennis describes how curriculum mapping can be used to facilitate high quality professional development that helps teachers improve their own assessment literacy. He then illustrates one school's successful journey to success using this process.

Good ideas make no difference if they are not implemented well. So in "A Seven-Module Plan to Build Teacher Knowledge of Balanced Assessment," Tammy Heflebower explains how principals can guide teachers in creating a balanced assessment system within a school or district. Building on experiences gained through programs such as Nebraska's School-based Teacher-led Assessment and Reporting System (STARS), she shows how to make assessment development meaningful by keeping it close to the classroom interests of teachers.

In Part 2 we turn to "Collecting, Interpreting, and Reporting Data," beginning with a chapter by William Ferriter titled, "Plug Us In, Please: Using Digital Tools for Data Collection." Through detailed descriptions of several successful programs, William describes how education leaders can facilitate the appropriate and meaningful use of new forms of technology in schools. He then outlines the specific steps that principals must take to help teachers use new forms of technology to gather data on student learning quickly, efficiently, and with relatively little effort.

Nicole Vagle's chapter on "Finding Meaning in the Numbers," examines the challenges that school leaders must meet to appropriately interpret assessment data and samples of student work. Based on evidence gathered in one study, she then identifies a series of strategies and protocols principals can use to create a culture of collaborative inquiry and build "data literacy" in practical school settings.

How to report information accurately on students' performance to parents and others through standards-based report cards is the challenge that Ainsley Rose takes on in the next chapter, "The Courage to Implement Standards-Based Report Cards." Based on experiences gained through work with a school district in Quebec, Canada, Ainsley describes the importance of careful planning, thoughtful leadership, broad-based collaboration, and guided implementation in these essential change efforts.

Part 3 on "Assessing Students at Risk" begins with Mark Weichel's chapter on "Lowering High School Failure Rates." Mark emphasizes that improving assessment scores and reducing high failure rates take commitment to ongoing collaboration, the implementation of high-quality assessment practices by all teachers, schoolwide intervention plans, and continual follow-up by school leaders. He then presents six steps principals can take to significantly lower failure rates among high school students.

In "Assessing the Student at Risk: A New Look at School-Based Credit Recovery," Charles Hinman describes a program designed to reduce the number of students who drop out of high school. The highly successful program he describes engages students in intense instructional interventions paired with targeted counseling, and then allows them to show basic proficiency in content areas through alternative means.

We conclude with Tom Hierck's chapter on "Formative Assessment, Transformative Relationships." Tom explains how school leaders can facilitate teacher growth and promote positive assessment relationships between teachers and their students by modeling positive relationships with teachers. He also examines the vital role of clear learning goals, descriptive feedback, self-assessment and goal setting, and communicating about learning.

In going through these chapters, some readers will likely be distressed by the complicated nature of the issues involved and the lack of consistency in the authors' responses to these issues. In the midst of these differences, however, I believe readers will be deeply impressed by the authors' insights, the diversity of their perspectives on improvement, and the creativity and breadth of their proposed solutions. They will see that leadership in using assessments *for* learning is not about one particular set of strategies or activities, but rather about a range of strategies and activities—formal and informal—that must be adapted to the unique contextual characteristics of a school. What works in one setting may not work equally well in another. To be successful, leaders must adapt strategies and activities to individual school settings where particular teachers teach particular students from particular communities. Effective leaders recognize that teachers working in different contexts have unique needs that must be addressed in unique ways. Just as a "one size fits all" approach does not work in teaching, it does not work in leadership, either.

The hope shared by the authors of these chapters and me is that the ideas and strategies presented on these pages will spur leaders to action. Given the recognized power of assessment practices to improve student learning, we cannot wait for their slow and gradual evolution into modern classrooms. Far too many students will be lost if we do, abandoned by an educational system that holds the key to their success but does not use it. Instead, we need bold and courageous leadership that presses hard for broad-based implementation, armed with the established knowledge base of effective practice. Although the precise paths school leaders take in these challenging endeavors may be different, we believe that such action is absolutely necessary in order to ensure that all students learn well and gain the many positive benefits of that success. Our hope is that this book provides guidance to those willing to take on that challenge.

References

Black, P., & Wiliam, D. (1998). Inside the black box: Raising standards through classroom assessment. *Phi Delta Kappan, 80*(2), 139–144.

Bloom, B. S. (1971). Mastery learning. In J. H. Block (Ed.), *Mastery learning: Theory and practice* (pp. 47–63). New York: Holt, Rinehart & Winston.

Bloom, B. S., Hastings, J. T., & Madaus, G. (1971). *Handbook on formative and summative evaluation of student learning.* New York: McGraw-Hill.

Bloom, B. S., Madaus, G. F., & Hastings, J. T. (1981). *Evaluation to improve learning.* New York: McGraw-Hill.

Guskey, T. R. (Ed.). (2006). *Benjamin S. Bloom: Portraits of an educator.* Lanham, MD: Rowman & Littlefield Education.

Guskey, T. R. (2007). Formative classroom assessment and Benjamin S. Bloom: Theory, research, and practice. In J. H. McMillan (Ed.), *Formative classroom assessment: Theory into practice* (pp. 63–78). New York: Teachers College.

Guskey, T. R. (2008). The rest of the story. *Educational Leadership, 65*(4), 28–35.

Stiggins, R. (2008). *An introduction to student-involved assessment for learning* (5th ed.). Upper Saddle River, NJ: Merrill, Prentice Hall.

PART ONE

Laying the Foundation of Assessment Literacy

CASSANDRA ERKENS

 An independent consultant and recognized leader in education, Cassandra Erkens shares her knowledge with teachers and administrators throughout the United States and Canada. She is the president of Anam Cara Consulting, Inc., and an adjunct faculty member at Hamline University, where she offers Master of Arts in Education courses and facilitates a learning community for educators engaged in the two-year MA Ed extended degree program. Cassandra has served as a high school English teacher, district-level director of staff development, and state-level educational effectiveness regional facilitator. She is author and coauthor of several formal education-based training programs and contributed chapters to *The Teacher as Assessment Leader* (Solution Tree, 2009), *The Collaborative Administrator: Working Together as a Professional Learning Community,* and *The Collaborative Teacher: Working Together as a Professional Learning Community* (Solution Tree, 2008).

ONE

Paving the Way for an Assessment-Rich Culture

Cassandra Erkens

In recent years, there has been an explosion of information regarding the power of and the need for formative assessment. The data are compelling. Researcher Dylan Wiliam (2007/2008) examined five reviews of the research in this area (Black & Wiliam, 1998; Crooks, 1988; Kluger & DeNisi, 1996; Natriello, 1987; Nyquist, 2003), which synthesized more than four thousand research studies undertaken during the last forty years. According to Wiliam, "The conclusion was clear: When implemented well, formative assessment can effectively double the speed of student learning" (2007/2008, pp. 36–37). These studies and others like them have laid the groundwork for a plethora of educational books, journals, and articles dedicated to defining and exploring the use of formative assessment in the classroom. The data are so compelling, in fact, that many experts today are calling us to action.

In his anthology *Ahead of the Curve: The Power of Assessment to Transform Teaching and Learning* (2007a), Douglas Reeves affirms that each of the book's contributing experts "call for a redirection of assessment to its fundamental purpose: the improvement of student achievement, teaching practice, and leadership decision-making. The stakes could not be higher" (p. 1). In his assessment manifesto *A Call for the Development of Balanced Assessment Systems* (2008), assessment expert Richard Stiggins states, "We have reached a tipping point in the evolution of our schools when we must fundamentally reevaluate, redefine, and redesign assessment's role in the development of effective schools" (p. 2). Likewise, Robert Marzano asserts in his vision document *Getting Serious About School Reform: Three Critical Commitments* (2008) that the very first commitment schools must make in their reform efforts is to invest in developing "a system of individual student feedback at the district, school, and classroom levels" (p. 8).

But a call for change alone will not suffice. Indeed, these resounding proclamations require significant changes at every level—from the instructional designers in our classrooms to the policy designers in our legislatures. The experts' arguments are compelling, but they alone will not get the job done. We need leaders to make the difference in our schools.

As leaders, we must provide teachers with the research, knowledge, skills, and job-embedded practice that will eventually generate change locally and thus provide trusted evidence that using formative assessment is integral to teaching well and does, in fact, increase student achievement. While outside expertise might be required to redirect our understanding of assessment literacy, traditional forms of professional development alone are not sufficient to share the content knowledge required to understand the *what* and *how* of formative assessment. They are merely a starting point. As Wiliam (2007) tells us,

> if we are to have any chance of really changing teacher practice, we have to take seriously that implementing minute-to-minute and day-by-day formative assessment is not primarily a matter of providing teachers with new knowledge. . . . The crucial thing is to change habits, and traditional teaching structures do not change habits. (p. 196)

Leaders must create a culture of learning and create pathways for sharing expertise (DuFour, DuFour, & Eaker, 2008; Elmore, 2004; Fullan, Cuttress, & Kilcher, 2005). In very focused ways, we need to model and monitor for formative assessment practices in the classroom.

It can be hard for teachers—entrenched in an assessment culture heavy with summative assessments, normed scoring, and grades used for ensuring compliance—to recognize the flaws in a system that they themselves have respected for many years and worked to perfect. It is somewhat akin to asking fish to see the waters in which they swim. And it is difficult to trust that the waters in a different pond might be better. Teachers struggle to employ quality formative assessment practices most often because they cannot conceptualize how these practices could possibly work in their classrooms. How, for example, might a teacher truly get increased student motivation, productivity, and achievement if homework and quizzes are not graded and then included in the final score? Would learners even do the work? Such dramatic proposals, counterintuitive to the very systems in which we ourselves grew up as learners, are suspect and overwhelming.

It is unfair for us as leaders to simply tell teachers to trust us because the research says it is the right thing to do. While books, workshops, and other modes of professional development will be required to alter our understanding and application of the accurate design and effective use of assessments, nothing will be more powerful than our ability to create a learning culture, model the strategies we promote, and support—*with monitoring*—the work that teachers must do to implement new practices. Daily, we must be willing to practice what we preach and learn alongside our teachers regarding what works best in creating balanced assessment systems that honor the natural learning process. The changes required in our assessment practices are as much cultural as procedural. We must create an environment rich with learning for *all* of our learners—including teachers.

Creating a Culture of Assessment Literacy

Formative assessment works because it honors the natural, iterative learning process for learners of all ages:

- It identifies the gap between where learners are now and where they are going (learning targets).

- It offers descriptive feedback to support learners in closing the gap.

- It facilitates processes and provides tools to involve learners in addressing their learning needs. (Hattie & Timperley, 2007; Heritage, 2007; Stiggins, Arter, Chappuis, & Chappuis, 2007; Wiliam & Thompson, 2008)

Rick Stiggins, Judith Arter, Jan Chappuis, and Steve Chappuis (2007) identify seven practical classroom strategies to involve students in their learning with focus and deliberation. Applied at the adult level, these seven strategies model the process of formative assessments minute-by-minute and day-by-day and allow adults to learn by doing in their classrooms:

1. Provide an understandable vision of the learning targets for assessment literacy.

2. Use models of strong and weak assessment work.

3. Offer descriptive feedback instead of evaluation regarding assessment practices.

4. Help teachers self-assess, keep track of their learning, and set goals for their own assessment literacy.

5. Design professional development mini-lessons to focus on one aspect of quality at a time.

6. Engage teachers in focused revision of assessment materials.

7. Engage teachers in self-reflection and sharing what they know.

When we model these seven strategies for student learning at the adult level, we move traditional professional development to job-embedded, integrated learning. Equally important, we create a formative assessment culture in which all learners can thrive.

Provide an Understandable Vision of the Learning Targets for Assessment Literacy

While our efforts to conduct meaningful professional development have dramatically improved, in truth, we still most often see the standard workshop occurring with little attention to follow-up support or tools to measure implementation of initiatives. Often, teachers are required to attend a professional development event by topic ("We're focusing on math because our scores are low") or title ("How to Teach Nonfiction Reading Strategies in the Social Studies Curriculum"). Teachers often express frustration that these professional development events have little relevance to their individual and specific learning needs. And even when the event seems highly relevant to our participants, it is rare that administrators clarify the learning targets for our participants' learning, and even more rare that we maintain and monitor those targets with buildingwide focus and ongoing support until there is sufficient evidence that the required learning has occurred and the desired practices have become habits for our teachers.

Our ability to integrate the best practices of assessment would be richly enhanced if we identified the learning targets for assessment literacy, posted them on our staff lounge walls, tied our professional development efforts and on-the-job discussions to those targets, and monitored for evidence of implementation and mastery of the targets.

We must begin by answering the question, What is it that an assessment-literate staff should know and be able to do? Using Stiggins and Chappuis' materials on sound assessment practices as a starting point (2006, p. 12), we might generate a list of teacher statements such as the following:

- I can design classroom-level learning targets for students in student-friendly language.

- I can match learning targets with appropriate assessment methods.

- I can write assessment questions of all types well.

- I can create assessments and supporting assessment tools such as rubrics to generate sufficient and accurate evidence of student learning.

- I can accurately interpret the assessment results I generate.

- I can use assessment results effectively to promote and enhance student learning.

- I can offer descriptive feedback in a manner that empowers learners to make necessary changes.

- I can involve students in assessing, tracking, and setting goals for their own learning.

There is so much to know about assessment literacy that this list could continue. It is ideal when teachers and leaders work together to study best practices in assessment design and use and then create, as a cumulative product of their attained knowledge, a list of agreed-upon learning targets for the next step of application.

But identifying the learning targets is simply the first step. It is important to understand up front how we will assess each of those targets. Just as teachers design the assessments for standards before beginning instruction in the classroom with students, leaders must also begin with the end in mind. Knowing what we would examine to see our learning targets in action offers definition and clarity to the vision of assessment literacy for teachers. For each target, we must ask, How will we know we have learned it? Again, best is when we work together to explore what competency of each learning target might look like (see table 1.1).

Table 1.1 Teacher Learning Targets for Assessment Literacy

Targets for Assessment Literacy *What do we want to learn?*	Targets in Action *How will we know we have learned it?*
I can design classroom-level learning targets for students in student-friendly language.	Each teacher has posted student-friendly learning targets in easily accessible locations: on classroom walls, on teacher webpages, in parent communications, and so on. Teachers use student-friendly targets as the starting point for the design of all assessments, and those targets can readily be found within the assessments themselves. Students can name their learning targets and identify their strengths and opportunities for growth based on the targets.
I can match learning targets with appropriate assessment methods.	Teachers work collaboratively to evaluate and refine the assessments they are using with a given rubric (such as Rick Stiggins' rubric on Five Keys to Assessment) for target/method match. The evidence generated in student samples of the work is an accurate reflection of the intended learning targets.

Evaluation measures need to be named for each identified assessment-literacy learning target. This is not to suggest that we are creating high-stakes tests for teachers. Rather, it ensures that we work together to watch ourselves grow by monitoring what matters in our efforts. Change expert Michael Fullan (Fullan et al., 2005) states, "A culture of evaluation must be coupled with a culture of learning for schools to sort out promising from not-so-promising ideas and especially to deepen the meaning of what is learned" (p. 56). The very practice of collaborating with our peers to answer questions about our learning targets and measures for assessment literacy deepens our understanding as we apply the concepts we have been exploring in our professional development efforts. It likewise helps us experience the very same process we must use in our classrooms.

Use Models of Strong and Weak Assessment Work

Students better understand their learning targets when they can examine anonymous samples of work, make decisions about what quality is and is not, co-create rubrics regarding quality, and practice using their rubrics on additional samples of work and eventually their own samples of work (Stiggins et al., 2007). The same can be said for adults. When using assessments created and published by others—especially anonymous or commonly used textbook assessments to get started—we employ a critical eye to review the materials, make decisions about quality, co-create rubrics to monitor quality on our own assessments, and so on. Eventually, with experience in the process, confidence in our developing assessment literacy, trust in our capacity to support each other, and in keeping our students' best interests at heart, we begin to use the process of reviewing and evaluating the assessments we create for use in our classrooms. Fortunately, this process can happen fairly quickly if we work to create a culture of safety, exploration, and collaboration from the beginning. The best way to discover if our own assessments meet the standards of quality is to gather descriptive and supportive feedback from those with whom we work closely.

Offer Descriptive Feedback Instead of Evaluation Regarding Assessment Practices

It is a common phenomenon cited in educational literature but most often observed directly with our own peers that master teachers are seldom able to define their craft. While they understand that learning is happening in their classrooms and they are keen to observe it and respond accordingly when it is or is not occurring, many master teachers cannot seem to isolate the specifics of what they themselves are doing to create the "magic" of learning. Often operating intuitively, master teachers associate teaching with more of an art than a science. But teaching is both an art and a science. A master teacher's effectiveness can be replicated consistently and confidently only if and when we can isolate and describe the strategies and variables worth replicating. We have a tremendous need to identify and articulate the characteristics of a master teacher's effectiveness for both the master teacher and his or her peers: the research on effective teachers indicates that master teachers can teach in six months' time what it might take less successful teachers up to a full year to teach (Wiliam & Thompson, 2008).

Traditionally, our teacher appraisal systems have been predicated on and limited to the notion of evaluation. It is a mirror image of how we have limited the work of classroom assessment to the discrete practice of testing for the sake of evaluation and data in classrooms. While evaluation might help a teacher answer the critical question, Where am I relative to where I need to be? as far as an administrator is concerned, it does little to help teachers understand the assessment *for* learning question of what they can begin to do to close the gap between where they are and where they need to be. If we employed the practice of descriptive feedback, we could inform our understanding of the science of teaching, helping everyone, including master teachers, see and hence solidify their own craft knowledge. With such specific, informational feedback, we can better support all teachers trying to master their craft.

Efforts to shape our collective craft knowledge with descriptive feedback should not be a task exclusive to administrators. If we create a culture of collective inquiry and shared practice regarding effectiveness, everyone can participate in generating feedback with and for each other on what works as we implement assessment *for* learning practices in our classrooms. Identifying assessment practices that work can be done in the vein of public learning and celebration. Imagine, for example, that a team working to improve their assessment understanding and practice gathers to co-create an assessment and during that meeting, one teacher turns to another and offers the following feedback as a means to launch the team into writing thought-provoking and rigorous questions:

> *When we were learning about item development on our tests, we talked about the idea that we could assess knowledge beyond the recall level. In reviewing each other's assessments, I have noticed that when you develop assessment questions and materials for your students, you consistently engage your learners in one or more of the following activities regarding their knowledge:*
>
> - *Exploring how what they already know came to be understood by others before them*
>
> - *Defining the criteria or evidence used to evaluate what makes their understanding true today*
>
> - *Problem solving with what they know today to be a solution to an existing or projected problem of tomorrow*
>
> - *Identifying how it's possible that what they know today might be false tomorrow or how the solutions we have today with our current knowledge might become tomorrow's problems*
>
> - *Constructing their own explanations for how what they have learned will be relevant and meaningful in their world outside of your classroom*
>
> *In each of these cases, I can see that you are still able to understand what they know while engaging them in rigorous and*

relevant applications of their learning. You are really moving beyond knowledge for the sake of knowledge and into applying knowledge in meaningful ways. You really make your learners think!

Our specific feedback informs practice. Our celebrations change culture. As leaders, we must work to create a collaborative environment where peer-to-peer feedback can be shared openly and frequently. When we create the conditions for staff to share powerful feedback with each other, we shift the individual fixed mindset from what works in *my* classroom to a more productive and collective growth mindset: what works for *our* students. According to Carol Dweck (2006),

> this *growth mindset* is based on the belief that your basic qualities are things you can cultivate through your efforts. Although people may differ in every which way—in their initial talents and aptitudes, interests, or temperaments—everyone can change and grow through application and experience. (p. 7)

We can create a growth mindset in and among our staff when we create a culture and an expectation of shared professional and descriptive feedback. On a professional level, individual teachers become learners; on the system level, we become a true learning organization.

Help Teachers Self-Assess, Keep Track of Their Learning, and Set Goals for Their Own Assessment Literacy

The idea of personal goal setting is not new to professional development. We have evolved and improved the process over time, increasing success with each attempt, but we are still missing the mark on the power of this strategy.

In the beginning, we asked teachers to set goals for their own learning, but the process was loose, and individuals selected interest-based areas of focus. Not only that, the responsibility for finding the books or training opportunities that would help teachers meet their needs was the responsibility of the individual teacher. In this scenario, end-of-the-year goal reports were summaries of activities accomplished during the year and submitted to a principal for reading and/or storage in a file somewhere.

We then moved to tying individual teacher goals to a buildingwide focus of interest, and then we improved yet again to tie teacher goals to student achievement needs and building SMART goals (Strategic and Specific, Measurable, Attainable, Results-oriented, and Time-bound per O'Neill & Conzemius, 2006). Still, the process of self-assessing, goal setting, and self-monitoring was confined to teachers submitting a goal in the fall and a summary report in the spring with an added clarifying requirement of sharing a practice or two they were now implementing in their classrooms with conclusions—sometimes involving student achievement data—about how it was working.

In all of these cases, the system, while striving for increasing capacity, was aimed at *individual* teacher competence. Moreover, the process of moving to mastery was left in the hands of people who were already doing the very best they knew how. It is akin to telling a struggling learner to set a goal for him- or herself and close his or her own achievement gap. In essence, we answered the questions, Where are you now? and Where are you going? without offering any support or feedback to teachers regarding the critical question, What can you begin to do to address the gap?

The self-assessing, goal-setting, and self-monitoring process has since moved to teachers creating team goals defined by building-level SMART goals and specifically tied to the student-achievement needs in their classrooms. This has brought the process as close to success in building capacity as it has ever been. While this is better, it is still not best. Teams can still set goals in the fall, work hard all year to make a difference, and wait for the data in the spring to see if it worked, nervously chewing their fingernails while their students are testing. What is missing? *Self-monitoring*—specifically, our ability along the way to answer the question, How are we closing the gap? Working together as a professional learning community, teams must agree to apply an identified strategy; evaluate its effectiveness by examining its impact on student learning with the results from their common measures; document their decisions to keep, modify, or delete that strategy; share their results and discuss their conclusions along the way with the entire staff; and then begin the cycle again (DuFour et al., 2008). We ourselves *experience* formative assessment as we define and refine our practice with each iteration. In this way, we inform our professional knowledge of our craft and increase our collective capacity to impact student learning in positive ways.

It would be an error for teams to keep their results to themselves; likewise, written reports regarding whether or not we feel we met our goals will not suffice, even if those reports are distributed buildingwide. We must keep the conversation about increasing our assessment literacy alive throughout the school year with whole-faculty discussions about the effectiveness of our efforts based on specific student achievement results. It is the only way we will know we have developed our assessment literacy and are fully integrating sound assessment practices beyond the confines of a workshop on the topic.

Design Professional Development Mini-Lessons to Focus on One Aspect of Quality at a Time

If teachers are monitoring their own progress along the way, misunderstandings or hurdles become immediately clear and should not have to wait until the next available professional development day to be addressed. In addition, learning needs are specific to the learning targets of the teachers involved. One-size-fits-all professional development will *not* fit all. We would radically transform the current practice of professional development if we designed mini-lessons to focus on one aspect of quality at a time, *responding in time, as needed.* Imagine, for example, that one team discovers that they need to spend more time improving the quality of their questions on selected-response assessments, while another team realizes that they need to spend time examining student work together so that they can calibrate their scoring to be alike on their commonly shared rubric for the assessment task. Two questions naturally emerge: (1) When? and (2) How?

First, if we direct our attention to one aspect of quality at a time, we create a laser-like focus on a narrowed topic, and it is likely that an entire day of professional development will not be needed. Sometimes we can find our answers in as little as fifteen to thirty minutes. Given that, leaders work with teachers to "find" time in creative ways:

- Renegotiating time—*The third-grade team has some helpful ideas on how we can help young children self-assess. If we stay for a thirty-minute session after school today, we can all leave thirty minutes early on Friday.*

- Freeing up time—*I will step into your classroom for the next hour so you can work with the English department on rubric development.*

- Creating common time—*I'll send the agenda items from our upcoming staff meeting out in note form this week so we can use staff meeting time to hear from the fifth-grade team regarding the way they are organizing their common assessment data.*

- Purchasing time—*I am hiring some reserve teachers to float throughout the day next Tuesday. The PE department will have the first hour of the day to refine their health and wellness performance assessments. Please bring to your meeting the information you have been gathering from area PE teams on their learning targets and performance criteria for the health and wellness standard. The math team will have the second hour to work on . . .*

Leaders are working creatively to find time for their teams. In addition, leaders are helping their teams maximize the collaborative time they already have by sharing meeting tools such as planning templates, meeting agenda formats, student work protocols and rubrics to assess the quality of teacher-created assessment products, and so on.

The "how" involves learning teams both seeking outside expertise and openly sharing their expertise internally. To return to the earlier example, the team seeking guidance on improving the quality of their selected-response questions might review the literature, seek the outside counsel of an expert, write practice items, and collaboratively evaluate those items for quality. The team seeking to calibrate their scoring to be alike, however, might only need the time to put their student work on the table and begin scoring it with their shared rubric. Neither team should be "trapped" in another workshop that does not help to further their immediate work. Likewise, neither team should be keeping their team learning hidden from the rest of the building. Instead, teams should make a deliberate effort to share their new insights, practices, and results to increase assessment literacy. Professional development should not be limited to an outside speaker, or even the principal or a district administrator for that matter: "One of the most powerful drivers of change involves learning from peers, especially those who are further along in implementing new ideas" (Fullan et al., 2005, p. 55). In this way, we again highlight local best practices through the venue of celebration.

When we design mini-lessons to focus on one aspect of quality at a time, we create a professional development system that is responsive, timely, and differentiated for the various learning needs in our buildings. In addition, we build a culture of shared learning and an expectation of continual improvement.

Engage Teachers in Focused Revision of Assessment Materials

If we are doing all of the work outlined so far, revision is already happening naturally within teams on their individual materials. Like good teachers, however, leaders can continue to check for understanding on the staff-generated assessment-literacy targets (two noted earlier were "I can design classroom-level learning targets for students in student-friendly language" and "I can match learning targets with appropriate assessment methods," for example). Only through monitoring can leaders identify the targets that are already being addressed and introduce the targets not yet fully addressed for more developmental work.

As we all play a role in developing a culture of assessment literacy, it would be appropriate for leaders to collect artifacts (test questions, prompts, rubrics, and samples of student work, for example) for discussion on how to improve them. The principal might say, for example,

> *When we looked at our state data, we agreed that our students were not performing well on the extended written response items. In addition to creating more essay assessments so that our students can practice, I know we need to do more work as a staff on improving the quality of our prompts. To help, I've gathered some information from national testing companies and a few assessment articles from leaders in the field. Let's see what the experts advise, and then let's examine and refine some of our own extended written response items in our teams. When we are ready, we'll begin sharing our prompts with each other and analyzing them for quality based on what we learned from the experts.*

Teams can then practice essay prompt development and make recommendations for improvement for each other's examples.

When teams share their recommendations with the entire staff, yet another collective conversation emerges to help inform teacher thinking and practice; over time and with trust, teachers begin to bring their own work to the table for group discussion and revision. In a process such as this, we develop confidence in the quality, validity, and comprehensiveness of our own assessment tools.

Engage Teachers in Self-Reflection and Sharing What They Know

Reflection is one of the most powerful ways to integrate learning and achieve mastery. As Doug Reeves (2007b) notes,

> reflective leaders take time to think about the lessons learned, record their small wins and setbacks, document conflicts between values and practice, identify the difference between idiosyncratic behavior and long-term pathologies, and notice trends that emerge over time. (p. 49)

With reflection, we move from "lucky" to "learning" and "leading" (Reeves, 2007b).

While learning can be done privately, we are working to build individual competence and collective capacity. We must share our insights and inform the craft knowledge of all. Engaged in reflection, a teacher might say, "I have found that it is not enough to name learning targets for my students; I achieved even better results when I engaged learners at the end of each lesson in describing how our learning that day tied to the learning targets posted on our classroom walls!" That reflection shapes understanding and improves the collective practice of a learning community committed to implementing and further investigating the best practices identified by the experts and affirmed by their peers. Imagine how different our profession would be if new teachers could hear master teachers reflect on how their own research, tied to the findings of national research, impacted the quality of their instruction and assessment practices. Better still, imagine how different our profession would be if we created a venue for collective reflections connecting research to our local data proving student gains in learning.

One teacher, reflecting on his efforts to model formative assessment practices for his peers, captures the essence of employing the seven strategies for student-involved learning with adults:

> To my surprise, the best practices of professional development and adult learning connected with the best practices of formative assessment. Adults need to receive descriptive feedback, interact with others discussing new topics and relating them to their current teaching situation, and receive ample time to reflect and self-assess. Essentially, adults have the same needs as students. Adults need to see what they are supposed to achieve, identify where they are in relation to the learning topics, and determine how to close that gap. (Overlie, 2007, pp. 129–130)

Paving the Way

Strong leaders model the very practices they value, but they do not trust success to modeling alone, hoping that others will simply "notice" their good work. Strong leaders make their efforts explicit and engage the entire system in exploring possibilities and assessing effectiveness. As we do this work, we inform our own craft knowledge about leading effectively and creating a true learning organization. Engaged in our own application of formative assessment processes, we ourselves begin to understand the complexities, the barriers, the successes, and the opportunities. The truth is that when we model publicly that which we want from others, we have the opportunity to find our own gaps between where we are and where we would like to be. And we create a public and safe environment in which we can gather feedback from our staff on how we can best close the gap that might be evident in our own efforts. We learn by doing. In the spirit of formative assessment and with our own growth mindset intact, we approach each experience—even our failures—as an opportunity to improve. We must create an environment rich with learning for *all* of our learners—including ourselves as leaders.

References

Black, P. J, & Wiliam, D. (1998). Inside the black box: Raising standards through classroom assessment. *Phi Delta Kappan, 80*(2), 139–148.

Crooks, T. J. (1988). The impact of classroom evaluation practices on students. *Review of Educational Research, 58*(4), 438–481.

DuFour, R., DuFour, R., & Eaker, R. (2008). *Revisiting professional learning communities at work: New insights for improving schools.* Bloomington, IN: Solution Tree.

Dweck, C. (2006). *Mindset: The new psychology of success.* New York: Random House.

Elmore, R. F. (2004). *School reform from the inside out: Policy, practice, and performance.* Cambridge, MA: Harvard Education.

Fullan, M., Cuttress, C., & Kilcher, A. (2005, Fall). Eight forces for leaders of change. *Journal of Staff Development, 26*(4), 54–64.

Hattie, J., & Timperley, H. (2007, March). The power of feedback. *Review of Educational Research, 77*(1), 81–112.

Heritage, M. (2007, October). Formative assessment: What do teachers need to know and do? *Phi Delta Kappan, 89*(2), 140–145.

Kluger, A. N., & DeNisi, A. (1996). The effects of feedback interventions on performance: A historical review, a meta-analysis and a preliminary intervention theory. *Psychological Bulletin, 119*(2), 254–284.

Marzano, R. (2008). *Vision document. Getting serious about school reform: Three critical commitments* [Pamphlet]. Bloomington, IN: Marzano & Associates.

Natriello, G. (1987). The impact of evaluation processes on students. *Educational Psychologist, 22*(2), 155–175.

Nyquist, J. B. (2003). *The benefits of reconstruing feedback as a larger system of formative assessment: A meta-analysis.* Unpublished master's thesis, Vanderbilt University, Nashville, Tennessee.

O'Neill, J., & Conzemius, A. (2006). *The power of SMART goals: Using goals to improve student learning.* Bloomington, IN: Solution Tree.

Overlie, J. (2007). *How can a formative assessment professional development program be developed to model best assessment practices?* Unpublished MA Ed graduate capstone, Hamline University, St. Paul, Minnesota.

Reeves, D. (2007a). From the bell curve to the mountain: A new vision for achievement, assessment, and equity. In D. Reeves (Ed.), *Ahead of the curve: The power of assessment to transform teaching and learning* (pp. 1–12). Bloomington, IN: Solution Tree.

Reeves, D. (2007b). *The learning leader: How to focus school improvement for better results.* Alexandria, VA: Association for Supervision and Curriculum Development.

Stiggins, R. (2008). *Assessment manifesto. A call for the development of balanced assessment systems* [Pamphlet]. Portland, OR: ETS Assessment Training Institute.

Stiggins, R., Arter, J., Chappuis, J., & Chappuis, S. (2007). *Classroom assessment* for *student learning: Doing it right—using it well.* Princeton, NJ: Educational Testing Service.

Stiggins, R., & Chappuis, J. (2006, Winter). What a difference a word makes: Assessment FOR learning rather than assessment OF learning helps students succeed. *Journal of Staff Development, 27*(1), 10–14.

Wiliam, D. (2007). Content *then* process: Teacher learning communities in the service of formative assessment. In D. Reeves (Ed.), *Ahead of the curve: The power of assessment to transform teaching and learning* (pp. 183–204). Bloomington, IN: Solution Tree.

Wiliam, D. (2007/2008). Changing classroom practice. *Educational Leadership, 65*(4), 36–42.

Wiliam, D., & Thompson, M. (2008). Integrating assessment with learning: What will it take to make it work? In C. A. Dwyer (Ed.), *The future of assessment: Shaping teaching and learning* (pp. 53–82). New York: Lawrence Erlbaum Associates.

SUSAN HUFF

 Susan Huff, EdD, is principal of Spanish Oaks Elementary in Spanish Fork, Utah. During her former principalships at Westside Elementary and Santaquin Elementary in the Nebo School District, she developed innovative solutions to daunting challenges. Westside was the lowest performing school in the district, with mobility rates, the highest number of English language learners, and the highest poverty level. During her eight years at Westside, Susan led the staff in changing the culture of the school through engaging in weekly team collaboration, following team-made curriculum maps, using common assessments, and learning by observing their colleagues. Westside students now perform well on standardized and criterion-referenced tests. Dr. Huff began the same cultural shifts at Santaquin in her two years there, before her transfer to Spanish Oaks. In addition to the principalship, Susan enjoys working with other principals and teachers to assist them in their school improvement efforts. Dr. Huff is a contributor to *The Collaborative Administrator: Working Together as a Professional Learning Community* (Solution Tree, 2008).

TWO

Build, Promote, Guide, Provide, Monitor: Action Words for Principals as Instructional Leaders in Assessment

Susan Huff

When principals act as instructional leaders in their schools, they assume a role as leaders in assessment. The administrative, moral, and political support of the principal makes the difference in *schoolwide* improvement and learning using assessments; otherwise, professional learning is limited to individual endeavors (Scribner, Cockrell, Cockrell, & Valentine, 1999). The leadership capacity of the principal is critical in identifying a shared focus for improvement and in guiding the school staff to develop a collective vision for the entire school (Morrissey, 2000). Effective assessments measure progress toward the school's vision, drive classroom instruction, and measure individual student progress.

Like me, many principals became principals before No Child Left Behind; they may not have personally participated as a teacher in the kind of assessment work that is now required of schools to make adequate yearly progress under NCLB. Principals can still confidently lead this work, however; in fact, principal leadership in assessment is critical in moving a school forward. This leadership work is both challenging and rewarding. A principal functions as an instructional leader in assessment by implementing specific, concrete practices. Analyzing assessment data, for example, helps schools identify which of their improvement efforts are making a difference and by how much. Principals also facilitate the work of collaborative teacher teams in using assessments to improve teaching and learning. This chapter describes five categories of principal practices that help principals effectively work with teachers in assessment. Principals as assessment leaders build supportive structures, promote a focus on learning, guide teacher teams, provide and manage data, and monitor improvement efforts through the use of assessments.

Principals Build Supportive Structural Conditions

The goal of improving teaching and learning through assessments is best accomplished as a collaborative activity with teams of teachers. Richard Elmore (2004) found that in the most successful schools, teachers do not work in isolation; collective work is the norm. Principals support collaborative assessment work by building both supportive social and structural conditions (Bryk & Schneider, 2003). Supportive structural conditions include collaboration time for teachers to develop, use, and refine assessments.

Build Trust and Respect Among Colleagues

Trust and respect are the foundation of collaborative teamwork in building and using assessments. If principals are to effectively lead assessment work, they must foster trust and respect among teams and between teachers and administration. Trust promotes collegial relationships, a willingness to accept feedback, and conditions for continuous critical inquiry and improvement. By its very nature, assessment work can be risky business for teachers. As they begin the collaborative work of building assessments and sharing assessment results, teachers may feel vulnerable as their data are displayed with their teams.

Teachers depend on administrators for support and the resources they need to do assessment work. Administrators depend on teachers to monitor student learning through effective assessments. When any stakeholder takes deliberate action to make the other party feel safe and secure, thus reducing a sense of vulnerability in others, trust builds across the community (Bryk & Schneider, 2003). *Principals build trust with teachers by never making formative assessment data evaluative.* Teachers must feel safe that principals will use their formative assessment data only to help improve their instruction and monitor student learning along the way to meeting the standard, not to evaluate their performance for official purposes.

We discern the intentions of others through their actions; we consider the history of previous interactions with a person and weigh whether new interactions match or conflict with our expectations for that person. In their research, Anthony Bryk and Barbara Schneider (2003) organize these discernments around the four topics of respect, personal regard, competence, and personal integrity. *Respect* results when parties genuinely listen to each other and then take these views into account in subsequent behavior. *Personal regard* is demonstrated by a willingness and openness to reach out to others. *Competence* builds trust because desired outcomes result. *Personal integrity* builds trust as stakeholders keep their word. When teachers risk by extending an element of trust as assessment work begins, that trust may be fragile and should be carefully guarded. As teacher teams and principals model respect, personal regard, competence, and personal integrity in their assessment work, trust grows.

Trust and respect are preconditions for collaborative work using assessments, but they are also outcomes of this work. When principals model risk taking, when they promote safety in examining formative assessment data without making it evaluative, when they teach, monitor, and celebrate teachers using data, they build trust.

Build an Interdependent Work Structure

An interdependent work structure among teams recognizes that teams of teachers have the potential to be more powerful in selecting and designing assessments and in analyzing the data that results from assessments than individual teachers who work in isolation: "When groups, rather than individuals, are seen as the main units for implementing curriculum, instruction, and assessment, they facilitate development of shared purposes for student learning and collective responsibility to achieve it" (Newmann & Wehlage, 1995, p. 38). An interdependent work structure builds from the synergy that occurs as teachers discover they can do much more as teams than as individuals: "My success depends on you, and your success depends on me."

At Santaquin Elementary, we promoted an interdependent work structure by building time for teacher collaboration into the school schedule, and then expecting teachers to work collaboratively on assessments and data analysis through the following process. Teams followed a school collaboration agenda with a focus on assessment. A scribe took notes on the agenda; the notes were submitted to me for review. I required assessment products from each grade-level team, which then held teachers accountable for their collective assessment work. Teams selected or produced common formative assessments for their essential learning outcomes, which they administered to students within the same week. Teams then met to analyze their assessment results, to review the test's effectiveness for the next time it would be given, and to determine how to provide additional time and support to students who had not yet mastered the content. School leaders provided job-embedded professional development for collective learning, with training on assessment and with common reading and discussion materials for all teachers. I also attended weekly team collaboration, alternating among teams to mentor teachers in their assessment work.

Principals Promote an Unwavering Focus on Student Learning

Assessment work supports the fundamental purpose of schools—student learning. The purpose of assessments is to improve learning. When schools have an unwavering focus on student learning, assessments become valued tools to measure success and indicate areas for improvement. Principals can guide their school staffs in looking at school characteristics and practices that help students achieve at high levels. There are specific practices related to assessment work that principals model to make this happen.

Promote Precise Academic Standards

Effective assessments are carefully aligned with curriculum standards and instruction. Grant Wiggins and Jay McTighe (2005) describe the first step in this alignment process as identifying desired results: What do we want students to know and be able to do? Stephen Covey (2004) describes this thinking as beginning with the end in mind. From precise academic standards, teachers then determine acceptable evidence that learning occurred—they design assessments to measure student learning. Finally, teachers plan learning experiences and instruction that align with the assessment and standards. Thus, before designing or selecting assessments, teacher teams must first have precise academic standards.

A school system with too many standards promotes curriculum by default. When there is too much to teach, it is left to the teacher to determine which standards are taught and which ones are not. In contrast, curriculum by design reflects decisions made by teacher teams before the school year starts (Reeves, 2005). Teachers map out the curriculum for the year in advance and determine essential standards. Then teacher teams design or select assessments linked to those standards.

Principals lead this work by providing teams with state, district, and local standards. Principals then provide *time* for teams to unpack the standards, map the curriculum, and select assessments that reflect the standards. Santaquin Elementary provided paid time for teachers to discuss state standards, determine power standards, map the curriculum, and select team-made common formative assessments. Teacher teams submitted copies of their curriculum maps and common assessments to the principal. As I attended weekly grade-level collaboration, I could observe if teams were indeed referring to their curriculum maps and using their common assessments.

Promote High Expectations

Principals set the tone for expectations within the school. Students have higher performance in schools where there is an expectation that all students will work hard and meet high academic standards, where homework is expected (particularly at the high school level), and a high priority is placed on learning (Newmann & Wehlage, 1995; Scribner & Reyes, 1999). Harris Cooper's (2007) review of studies on homework found that for adolescents, the effect of homework on student achievement was impressive. The achievement for high school students doing more than two hours daily homework was no different, or perhaps even worse, than those doing about two hours, suggesting that there is such a thing as too much homework. The correlation in Cooper's research review between homework and achievement for children in grades K–6 was unclear. Principals with high expectations resist the pattern of some low-performing schools to select the easiest solutions to accountability problems: teaching to the test or focusing only on the students who are closest to meeting standards, rather than those who are furthest away (Elmore, 2004). Principals who promote high expectations insist that expectations and standards apply to *all* students. This requires examining assessment data on individual students in all classrooms and then focusing on the specific problems of low-performing students. Success in such a school is measured not solely based on averages, but on the achievement of individual students and subpopulations.

At Santaquin Elementary, I modeled high expectations in the way I talked about students in faculty meetings and staff development. I spoke positively about students and expressed a belief in their ability to learn. I shared anecdotal stories with teachers about students succeeding. I probed teachers about struggling students, asking, "What interventions is the student receiving? Are there any additional resources you need? How did individual students perform on a particular assessment? How are you providing more time and support for struggling students to meet the standard?" Because we expected all students to complete homework assignments, we started a homework lab before and after school and during lunch recess where students can come to finish uncompleted homework. Students could self-select or teachers could require students to attend. As a school, we expected all students to complete assigned work. As a school, we held all students accountable through assessments.

Promote a Common Curriculum

Assessment leaders promote a common curriculum. A common curriculum precedes the collaborative work of teacher teams of designing and selecting assessments. A common curriculum unites teacher teams and promotes collective responsibility for student learning (Lee, Smith, & Croninger, 1995). A common curriculum eliminates the instructional lottery that results when teachers are free to teach whatever they want (McLaughlin & Talbert, 2001). Without a common curriculum, any individual student's chance of receiving standards-based curriculum depends on which teacher he draws in the lottery of class or teacher assignments (McLaughlin & Talbert, 2001). At Santaquin Elementary, all grade-level teams are required to map their state standards in a curriculum map that each team member agrees to follow. When principals promote a common curriculum among teachers teaching the same content or grade level, the natural progression is for teacher teams to then produce team-made common formative assessments. Common formative assessments are only effective when teams pace together and teach the same content at the same time. A common curriculum and common assessments support collective responsibility among team members for all student learning.

Promote Team-Made Common Formative Assessments

Principals increase the effectiveness of assessments when they promote team-made common formative assessments. Common assessments guide the work of collaborative teams as they use assessment results to improve their individual and collective results. A common assessment holds all students (and teachers) to a common standard, which is set and agreed upon before instruction begins (Fisher, Lapp, & Flood, 2005). Then the team compares results of the assessments to identify students who may need more time and support to meet the standard, to determine strengths and weaknesses of individual teachers or programs, and to revise instruction and/or assessment. Common team-made formative assessments make teachers mutually accountable to each other. These assessments result in collective responsibility for individual student learning for all students within the team and ensure high levels of learning for all students because teachers agree on a mutual proficiency standard (Huff, 2007).

During my first year as principal at Santaquin, teacher teams started by developing or selecting five team-made common formative assessments. At my previous school, Westside Elementary, teachers started with five common assessments and then moved to common assessments for every essential learning concept. Each teacher on the team gives the assessments within the same week. The results are then brought to the weekly team collaboration meeting for analysis; teams plan how to provide nonproficient students more time and support to meet the standard.

Promote Confirmed Instructional Practices

When there is an unwavering focus on student learning, the effectiveness of any specific teaching strategy is judged in terms of assessment results. A particular instructional strategy is successful if it results in measurable student learning. Confirmed practice is that which produces results. Principals can guide teachers in examining their assessment results to determine the effectiveness of their instruction. I guided teachers at Santaquin Elementary by frequently attending weekly team collaboration meetings and participating in data discussions. I encouraged teachers to share instructional strategies that resulted in high levels of student learning. Precise academic standards, a common curriculum, team-made common formative assessments, and confirmed instructional practices are all tightly linked in effective assessment leadership. A weak link reduces the chain's strength and potential. When all links are strong, student learning is maximized.

Promote Systems of Prevention and Intervention

When teacher teams collaboratively examine the results of their team-made common formative assessments, they can identify struggling students who need more time and support along the way to meeting the standard. Principals can lead in the design of schoolwide systematic interventions to help all students become proficient through providing additional time and support (DuFour, DuFour, & Eaker, 2008). Assessment results indicate where instruction can be improved to prevent students from falling behind. Assessment results can also be used to target students for specific interventions.

Response to intervention (RTI) is federal legislation to help all students become successful through a system of additional support when a student experiences difficulty in learning.

Although RTI can be used as a replacement for the discrepancy model to identify students with disabilities for special education, its primary purpose is to provide timely, appropriate interventions for all students through a schoolwide response that is the responsibility of regular education. Special education should be considered only when students do not respond to increasingly focused, research-based interventions (Buffum, Mattos, & Weber, 2009). Assessment is the key to determining the effectiveness of any intervention. Assessment *leadership* is the key to the effectiveness of response to intervention.

At Westside Elementary, we developed a schoolwide tiered system of interventions based on our school's resources (our time, people, and money). We collaboratively used assessment data to identify students for interventions. Each school's needs and resources are unique; begin the process by having teachers brainstorm all of the school's resources. Discuss how those resources are currently used to support student learning. Make a list of those resources; categorize them into like groups. Make existing interventions explicit. Share the information with all teachers to spread practices from one class or grade level to another. Brainstorm how existing resources could be used in new ways or more effective ways to increase student learning. Measure the effectiveness of interventions with assessments.

Principals Guide Collaborative Teams

Assessment work is best accomplished by teams of teachers teaching the same content or grade level, rather than by teachers working in isolation. Principals as assessment leaders provide the necessary time, training, and system of support required of successful teaming (Turk, Wolff, Waterbury, & Zumalt, 2002). Assessment leaders guide the work of collaborative teams in developing, using, and refining assessments—especially team-made common formative assessments. Teachers in a collaborative culture use assessment data to discover ways to improve teaching and learning. Principals can help teachers in this process by meeting regularly with teams, by providing meaningful assessment data, and by modeling probing questions about the data. Which students need more time to master this concept? How can the team provide this additional time and support?

Guide Job-Embedded Staff Development

Principals can guide teachers in using assessment data to improve teaching and learning through job-embedded staff development. Among other issues, teachers often need training in breaking down assessment results to answer specific questions: What do these data tell us about what students know and can do? What do these data tell us is still missing? What misconceptions, if any, need correcting? Teachers need training to unlock the information within the assessment data.

Improving the educational experiences of all students and increasing the capacity of schools requires an investment in the knowledge and skills of educators through professional development (Elmore, 2004). In the traditional delivery method for professional development, teachers attend random workshops on a variety of topics in which they are interested. But as schools shift from teacher isolation to collaborative teaming, professional development must also shift to support collective learning. Job-embedded professional development moves a school staff from a workshop format to the school site (DuFour, 2001). Assessment leadership includes guiding teams in using their own student assessment data to improve teaching and learning.

Guide Collective Growth

Principals guide collective growth through job-embedded professional development. Rick DuFour (2001) states that principals must help identify the specific competencies needed by the staff to reach the goal of improved student achievement, and then principals must sustain commitment to those strategies and programs until the staff acquires and uses the intended knowledge and skills. The effectiveness of that staff development must be evaluated on the basis of improved assessment results. Collective capacity increases as principals guide collaborative teams in developing and selecting team-made common formative assessments and then using data from those assessments to improve teaching and learning. Principals guide collective growth when they provide staff development on quality assessments and help teachers examine the alignment of assessments and instruction to standards—not simply to textbooks. Principals guide collective growth when they coach teams to examine each test item for effectiveness, to revise and refine tests over time, and to analyze assessment results. Analyzing assessment data provides feedback to teachers and principals about the effectiveness of their improvement efforts.

Guide Inquiry

Principals guide inquiry as collective learning through data analysis. DuFour (2000/2001) describes collective inquiry as the engine of school improvement, growth, and renewal. Questioning the status quo, seeking new methods, testing those methods, and then reflecting on assessment results builds a school culture of continuous improvement in teaching and learning.

At Westside Elementary, for example, our kindergarten teachers wanted to know which intervention was most effective in helping students learn letters and sounds so that we could best use our additional Title I resources to make a difference. Because our state only provided half-day kindergarten, we hypothesized that perhaps extending the day for one hour with a certified teacher would make a difference—or we could take the same funding and provide ten minutes each day of individual or small-group tutoring on letters and sounds with teacher assistants. Teachers used their assessment data to identify students for additional time and support. Students were randomly assigned to each treatment group. At the end of a designated time, we assessed students and analyzed data from both groups. As we collaboratively examined the data, we determined which of our improvement efforts had the greatest impact on students and by how much. We found that with our available time, money, and people resources, in our school setting, ten minutes a day of individual or small-group tutoring produced the greatest student gains. We then chose to continue this intervention for our students and discontinue the extended-day class. As principals guide inquiry with teams, teachers learn the inquiry process and begin action research on their own.

Guide Shared Personal Practice

Assessment leaders guide teachers in sharing personal practice. When individual teachers achieve extraordinary assessment results, they can help other teachers improve by modeling their effective teaching practices. Sharing personal practice includes teachers discussing their own practice, observing each other teach, and then talking about what was modeled and what was observed. Teachers can refine their practices through feedback from their peers. Moving to this level of collaborative work demands a high level of relational trust among team members. Respect, personal regard, competence, and personal integrity (Bryk & Schneider, 2003)— the building blocks of relational trust—must be operational before shared personal practice can be fully implemented.

Assessment leaders identify teachers for others to observe because of their great assessment results. Joan Richardson (2003) described these teachers who demonstrate "positive deviance" as those who produce high levels of learning for students. They can spread their influence over a school by having teachers observe them, and then allowing those teachers to implement or refine those new practices with feedback through observations. Through shared personal practice, internal variation across classrooms is reduced, with more and more teachers gravitating toward best practices.

At Westside, teachers met weekly as collaborative grade-level teams to celebrate success, plan for instruction, review assessment results, and plan interventions. When assessments indicated that one particular teacher got exceptional results, others on the team wanted to observe that teacher teaching that particular content. The curriculum coach attended the observation with teachers to help them process specific instructional methods that were being used. I supported the work by making sure teachers' classes were covered so that they could watch each other. Sometimes I took the whole grade level for a short time to practice program songs or to play a physical education game. Teachers observing each other using confirmed instructional practice made a huge difference in spreading best practices throughout our school. Instructional leaders identify pockets of excellence in a school using assessment data and then spread that "positive deviance" by guiding teachers in sharing exemplary teaching practices.

Principals Provide and Manage Data

Assessment data represent facts or figures that must be changed to useful information to inform instruction and measure student progress. The process of transforming data to information "requires putting data in context, and this typically requires a basis of comparison" (DuFour et al., 2008, p. 465).

Teacher teams generate their own common team-made formative assessment data. They have a basis of comparison among the team. However, there are some data that principals need to provide to teachers: standardized test data, criterion-referenced year-end test data, statistical data, and schoolwide perception data obtained through surveys. In Nebo School District, principals have one staff development day near the end of September to analyze the previous year's data with our teachers. We provide teachers with data on this day and help teachers draw meaning from the data. Because technology makes it possible to provide reams of data, principals must select the data reports that will be most helpful for teachers. Year-end-test comparative data reports help teachers see how their students performed overall and on specific content standards in comparison to other students in the grade level at the school, district, and state level. Teachers receive feedback on the progress of individual students in their classes with progress scores that compare proficiency levels with last year's individual student performance. This provides teachers with specific information on how much students progressed during the year they were in that particular teacher's class. We have schoolwide data to compare how our students performed in relation to other similar schools in the district. We examine standardized test results, perception data, discipline data, and attendance. Teacher teams then set SMART goals for the year based on last year's data.

Principals can compile data from year to year to look for trends over time. Principals must be able to retrieve valuable data, help teachers draw meaning from it, manage that data, and store it for future use.

Principals Monitor Improvement Efforts

Schools can evaluate the effectiveness of their efforts in terms of results—not just "I think" or "I feel." What evidence do we have that student learning occurred? Which of our improvement efforts made the biggest difference and by how much? Teachers and school leaders assess students and use data to make instructional decisions to improve student learning.

Monitor Student Progress

Principals who are assessment leaders monitor the progress of individual students in their schools (Huff, 2007). This monitoring by principals increases teacher accountability and ensures a collective effort in meeting individual student needs. Some principals monitor student progress using spreadsheets, notes, lists of nonproficient students, and assessment walls or boards—all for the purpose of having discussions with teacher teams about individual student progress.

At Santaquin, teachers submitted the results of their common reading assessments to the principal three times each year—in September, January, and May. I entered the data in a spreadsheet so that we could sort the data by grade level with inverse ranking according to reading level. We then used this information to plan interventions for students who are reading below grade level. The same data were used to monitor student progress on our school assessment wall. In the faculty room, we had a large sixteen-foot-wide pocket chart on the wall. Reading levels were listed across the top, color-coded according to grade level. Within the plastic strips on the pocket chart, individual cards for each student were placed in the pocket chart underneath the student's corresponding reading level. Each grade level had a different color card; each teacher within the grade level had a different color dot on front of the card. The front of the card had the student number and a list of interventions the student was receiving. On the back of the card was the student's name, along with an assessment record that included the date of the assessment and reading level. As students improved in reading, as measured by the common assessment or by ongoing running records, their cards were moved up on the assessment wall. The wall made it easy to monitor struggling students according to their cards and view schoolwide reading progress.

Monitor Reflective Dialogue

Reflective dialogue about assessment results is essential in monitoring a school's improvement efforts. Principals monitor reflective dialogue by participating in data discussions with teams. When teachers have opportunities to reflect on their practices and dialogue with their collaborative team about their collective learning, they are able to make the connections they need to change practice for improved instruction, which in turn leads to improved student learning (Kruse, Louis, & Bryk, 1994; Newmann & Wehlage, 1995; Bryk, Camburn, & Louis, 1999). Personal reflection is good, but reflective *dialogue* helps teachers build on each other's ideas and expand their own learning in ways that they cannot do alone. Reflective dialogue "deprivatizes" teaching and holds practice, pedagogy, and student learning under scrutiny (Sebring, Bryk, Easton, Luppescu, Thum, Lopez, & Smith, 1995). This scrutiny challenges any current teaching practices that do not produce evidence of student learning. Reflective dialogue about assessments focuses teacher teams on results.

At both Westside and Santaquin Elementary, teachers begin weekly collaboration by celebrating student success. Teachers personally reflect on which of their students improved and why that improvement occurred. They then share that information, and the team then engages in reflective dialogue. What strategies were used to produce results? How was success measured? What can other teachers learn from this to apply in their own settings with their own students?

The next part of the collaboration agenda focuses on assessment results. Which students among the team are still struggling with a particular concept? What interventions can we use to help all students within the grade level reach proficiency?

When teacher teams appear to be stuck in analyzing data, and reflective dialogue is not happening during collaboration, one strategy that helps stimulate reflective dialogue is to pose probing questions to the team: "What does your assessment data tell you? Do you see any patterns or trends in the data? Where were you successful? Where are students still struggling? What ideas and strategies do you have for improvement? Did students score poorly because of instruction, or because of a poorly written test question?" Posing questions helps the team members reflect and draw meaning from the data on their own, which is much more empowering than having everything pointed out to them that perhaps they do not initially see.

Monitor Tangible Products

If schools are effectively using assessments to drive instruction and measure student progress, they produce tangible products (Huff, 2007; DuFour, DuFour, Eaker, & Many, 2006). Principals act as assessment leaders when they expect and monitor these products. Specific products or artifacts that schools produce as evidence when they are using assessments to monitor results may include:

- Newsletters to parents with school data results

- School data report cards

- Professional development agendas indicating staff training on assessments

- Grade-level common team-made formative assessments

- Reading Achievement Plans that include assessments to measure progress

- Assessment walls, charts, and spreadsheets

- Individual, class, grade level, and school assessment summaries

- Schoolwide reading assessments

- Grade-level data summary sheets

- Team learning logs with assessment summaries

Assessment leaders expect and inspect assessment products. These products hold teams accountable for their assessment work. They are evidence that a school is monitoring the effectiveness of their efforts through results.

Principal Leadership in Assessment

Principals become stronger instructional leaders in assessment by *doing assessment work*—by practicing the skills outlined in this chapter, and by reflecting on and evaluating their personal effectiveness. If principals delegate all assessment work to others, they will miss out on the growth and learning that come with doing the work. Without the involvement of the principal, the school is more likely to have pockets of excellence, where some teams become proficient in using assessment to improve teaching and learning and other teams lag behind. For schoolwide improvement, principals must step up as instructional leaders to build, promote, guide, provide, and monitor assessment work in their schools.

References

Bryk, A. S., Camburn, E., & Louis, K. S. (1999). Professional learning community in Chicago elementary schools: Facilitating factors and organizational consequences. *Educational Administration Quarterly, 35* (Supplemental), 751–781.

Bryk, A. S., & Schneider, B. (2003). Trust in schools: A core resource for school reform [Electronic version]. *Educational Leadership, 60*(6), 40–45.

Buffum, A., Mattos, M., & Weber, C. (2009). *Pyramid response to intervention: RTI, professional learning communities, and how to respond when kids don't learn.* Bloomington, IN: Solution Tree.

Cooper, H. (2007). *The battle over homework: Common ground for administrators, teachers, and parents.* Thousand Oaks, CA: Corwin.

Covey, S. R. (2004). *The 7 habits of highly effective people.* New York: Free Press.

DuFour, R. (2000/2001, Winter). Professional learning community. *Leadership Academy Developer.* Accessed at http://info.csd.org/staffdev/rpdc/darticle.html on April 14, 2004.

DuFour, R. (2001). In the right context: The effective leader concentrates on a foundation of programs, procedures, beliefs, expectations, and habits. *Journal of Staff Development, 22*(1). Accessed at www.nsdc.org/library/publications/jsd/dufour221.cfm on April 14, 2004.

DuFour, R., DuFour, R., & Eaker, R. (2008). *Revisiting professional learning communities at work: New insights for improving schools.* Bloomington, IN: Solution Tree.

DuFour, R., DuFour, R., Eaker, R., & Many, T. (2006). *Learning by doing: A handbook for professional learning communities at work.* Bloomington, IN: Solution Tree.

Elmore, R. F. (2004). *School reform from the inside out: Policy, practice, and performance.* Cambridge, MA: Harvard Education Press.

Fisher, D., Lapp, D., & Flood, J. (2005). Consensus scoring and peer planning: Meeting literacy accountability demands one school at a time. *Reading Teacher, 58*(7), 656–666.

Huff, S. B. (2007). *Professional learning community leadership: A collective case study of principals acquiring the skill and will to transform their schools by continuous improvement in teaching and learning.* Unpublished doctoral dissertation, Brigham Young University, Utah.

Kruse, S., Louis, K. S., & Bryk, A. (1994). Building professional community in schools. *Issues in Restructuring Schools, 6,* 3–6.

Lee, V. E., Smith., J. B., & Croninger, R. G. (1995). Another look at high school restructuring. *Issues in Restructuring Schools, 9,* 1–10.

McLaughlin, M. W., & Talbert, J. E. (2001). *Professional communities and the work of high school teaching.* Chicago: University of Chicago.

Morrissey, M. S. (2000). *Professional learning communities: An ongoing exploration.* Austin, TX: Southwest Educational Development Laboratory.

Newmann, F. M., & Wehlage, G. G. (1995). *Successful school restructuring: A report to the public and educators.* Madison: Center on Organization and Restructuring of Schools, School of Education, University of Wisconsin–Madison.

Reeves, D. (2005). Putting it all together: Standards, assessment, and accountability in successful professional learning communities. In R. DuFour, R. Eaker, & R. DuFour (Eds.), *On common ground: The power of professional learning communities* (pp. 45–63). Bloomington, IN: Solution Tree (formerly National Educational Service).

Richardson, J. (2003). *From the inside out: Learning from the positive deviance in your organization.* Oxford, OH: National Staff Development Council.

Scribner, J. P., Cockrell, K. S., Cockrell, D. H., & Valentine, J. W. (1999). Creating professional communities in schools through organizational learning: An evaluation of a school improvement process. *Educational Administration Quarterly, 35*(1), 130–160.

Scribner, J. D., & Reyes, P. (1999). Creating learning communities for high-performing Hispanic students: A conceptual framework. In P. Reyes, J. D. Scribner, & A. Paredes Scribner (Eds.), *Lessons from high-performing Hispanic schools: Creating learning communities* (pp. 188–210). New York: Teachers College.

Sebring, P. B., Bryk, A. S., Easton, J. Q., Luppescu, S., Thum, Y. M., Lopez, W. A., & Smith, B. (1995). *Chartering reform: Chicago teachers take stock.* Chicago: Consortium on Chicago School Research.

Turk, R. L., Wolff, K., Waterbury, C., & Zumalt, J. (2002). What principals should know about building and maintaining teams. *NASSP Bulletin, 86*(630), 15–23.

Wiggins, G., & McTighe, J. (2005). *Understanding by design.* Alexandria, VA: Association for Supervision and Curriculum Development.

CHRIS JAKICIC

Chris Jakicic, EdD, has worked as an adjunct instructor at National-Louis University as well as Loyola University Chicago, where she earned her doctorate of education. She is the former principal of Woodlawn Middle School in Long Grove, Illinois, where she guided the staff toward a collaborative culture focused on learning and assessment *for* learning practices. Teachers began collaborating to write common assessments, engaging students in self-assessment, and making grades more transparent. Dr. Jakicic then designed a one-day workshop for all middle school teachers in the district to train them about why writing and using common assessments is so essential. She has published articles in the *Journal of Staff Development* and *Illinois School Research and Development Journal* and is a contributor to *The Teacher as Assessment Leader* (Solution Tree, 2009) and *The Collaborative Teacher: Working Together as a Professional Learning Community* (Solution Tree, 2008).

THREE

A Principal's Guide to Assessment

Chris Jakicic

All educators are facing tough scrutiny about student achievement issues in this era of high-stakes testing. Principals often wish that someone would hand us a guidebook explaining how we can truly ensure that all of our students will learn. In the absence of such a guidebook, we must look at the research about what successful schools have done to improve their achievement levels and decide how we can apply these practices to our own schools. With this in mind, it would be hard to ignore the compelling research about the benefits of using assessments to guide our instructional practices as we work to help all students learn at high levels.

One of the most cited pieces of research about the effects of assessment is summarized in Paul Black and Dylan Wiliam's article "Inside the Black Box" (1998). The authors examined over 250 international research studies about schools successfully improving student learning and concluded that schools could expect a .4 to a .7 standard deviation increase in student achievement if teachers implement formative assessments in classrooms. This level of improvement is significant enough for any principal to want to duplicate those results.

This chapter explores what principals need to know to support teachers as they create and use an effective assessment system that includes formative assessment. I will also consider problems that might emerge as teachers use new assessment practices and suggest solutions.

What Is a Balanced Assessment System?

One of the first considerations when evaluating the effectiveness of your assessment practices is whether teachers and administrators get the information they need as a result of the assessments currently in use. Teachers want to know which of their students are learning and, if some are not, what they need to do to help those students. Principals want to know if there are curriculum, instruction, or pacing issues that must be changed to create a culture in which all students are able to learn. In order to obtain all the information they need, educators need a balanced assessment system that includes both formative and summative assessments.

The National Center for Fair and Open Testing (2007) defines *summative assessment* as "the attempt to summarize student learning at some point in time, say the end of a course" (p. 1). Teacher-created final exams, achievement tests, and state tests are all examples of summative assessments. Summative assessment data are used to give grades, to determine whether the curriculum and instructional practices being used are effective, and whether the pacing provided appropriate time for students to learn the material being taught.

James Popham (2008) defines *formative assessment* as "a planned process in which teachers or students use assessment-based evidence to adjust what they're currently doing" (p. 6). These assessments can include quizzes, worksheets, or other classroom activities that provide feedback to teachers about whether students have learned a particular learning target—while they are still teaching that unit. Formative assessments are written around learning targets that teachers have identified as the specific knowledge and skills their students need to understand a standard. For example, in science, students are taught how to use the scientific method to solve a problem. Teachers who are familiar with this unit know that the concept of control and variable is more abstract than other concepts in the unit, so they plan to do a short assessment after teaching the concept of control and variable to see whether the students understand it. With the results of their formative assessment, the teachers know which students need more help to attain this learning target.

Rick Stiggins, Judith Arter, Jan Chappuis, and Steve Chappuis (2004) use the term *assessment* of *learning* instead of *summative* assessment. Stiggins defines assessments *of* learning as "those assessments that happen after learning is supposed to have occurred to determine if it did" (Stiggins et al., 2004, p. 31). He explains that assessments *for* learning (formative assessments), by contrast, are intended to provide information to teachers and students *during* the learning process. No matter what terminology is used, researchers clearly acknowledge that teachers need access to both types of assessment data.

Even more recently, some researchers are writing about another type of assessment, what Kim Marshall (2008) is calling *interim* assessments, also known as *benchmark* assessments. These assessments are given every four to nine weeks to provide teachers with information about whether their students are making progress toward mastery of their grade-level standards. These assessments are often developed by a team of teachers and are used to discuss how to respond to students who are not learning, to ensure that students are retaining the information they have learned, and to predict which students will need more support to attain mastery of grade-level standards.

Assess Your Assessments

The first recommendation for any school evaluating their current assessment practices is to create a list of all the assessments currently being given to students and note who develops the assessment and who uses the information. Then, the teachers and principal together should examine the list to see what areas are not covered adequately by current assessments and what areas are overcovered through assessments that provide duplicate information. If there are areas of duplication, consider eliminating one or more tests. Alternately, use one of the duplicate assessments for progress monitoring of only those students who are experiencing difficulty so that teachers know if their supports are working.

In my own school, Woodlawn Middle School in Long Grove, Illinois, we learned that we had multiple summative assessments for our students in many areas, but few formative assessments. For example, we were using the Measures of Academic Progress (MAP) twice a year, as well as quarterly benchmark assessments in reading. In addition, of course, we had the results of the state assessment. Teachers believed we were doing too much testing; however, we also realized that we didn't have any formative assessments to tell teachers what they needed to do the next day in their classrooms. After examining our assessments, we decided to add formative assessments and to eliminate one of the times during the year that we administered the MAP test.

An important decision schools must make is whether teachers will establish "common" assessments designed and administered by teams, or whether each teacher will develop and use his or her own assessments. On one hand, developing assessments as teams creates discussion about what is important to teach and what mastery will look like; this helps to create the "guaranteed and viable curriculum" that Robert Marzano (2003) tells us is the most important factor for successful schools. Teams of teachers can then share effective instructional strategies and can respond to student needs collectively. On the other hand, teachers who work independently can accomplish the work more expeditiously because they don't need common planning time. They'll still need time to write good assessments, but teachers who teach the same subject or grade level won't all need time together.

Principals must facilitate the decision about whether teacher assessments will be common or individual early in the process so that teachers know the expectations upfront. Once teachers have moved forward with writing their own assessments, it may be much harder to backtrack and create team assessments. If the school decides that the assessments should be common, it will be important for the principal to create a schedule that allows for common planning time or consider how to use staff development time for assessment writing.

Support the Development of an Assessment System

Larry Ainsworth and Donald Viegut (2006) lay out the support teachers will need as they work through the process of developing assessments: professional development, time for writing assessments and analyzing results, clerical help, and opportunities for coaching and discussion around assessment. While all of these needs apply to either individual or common assessments, their application will be different depending on which process a school uses.

For example, initial staff development about how to write and use good assessments will be the same in either case, but follow-up coaching and support will be very different. If teachers use common assessments, they will be able to help each other analyze and respond to the data. If teachers are working individually, the principal will want to assure that all teachers are being coached about how to effectively use the data. When thinking about coaching individual teachers, consider whether the teacher has enough experience and background to effectively analyze the data. For example, Roberta Buhle and Camille Blachowicz (2008/2009) describe a coaching session with a kindergarten teacher who saw that a pre-assessment she had given indicated that most of her students knew the names of the letters, and yet still intended to follow the typical plan to teach a letter-of-the-week. The coach intervened to point out the flaw in this thinking. This example shows how important it is for the principal or the coach to be on the lookout for teachers who need more help understanding how to respond to their data.

How Frequent Is Frequent Enough?

Once teachers begin working on their assessment system, the next question that will likely emerge is, How frequently must we assess to collect the information we need to make a difference? At Woodlawn, we started by developing what we now call benchmark assessments, which were given at the end of each quarter. While these assessments helped us know whether students were learning, they didn't tell us soon enough to intervene and didn't provide specific enough information about what students hadn't learned. So we reviewed the research and started with Black and Wiliam's article (1998), which only had a brief mention of frequency: "It is better to have frequent short tests than infrequent long ones. Any new learning should first be testing within a week of a first encounter, but more frequent tests are counterproductive." Wiliam (2007) updates and clarifies the issue of frequency:

> The kinds of formative assessment practices that profoundly impact student achievement cannot wait until the end of a marking period, or even the end of an instructional unit. If students have left the classroom before teachers have made adjustment to their teaching on the basis of what they have learned about students' achievement, then they are already playing catch up. (p. 191)

He then refers to specific instructional practices described as "classroom assessment: minute by minute, day by day" (Leahy, Lyon, Thompson, & Wiliam, 2005); this suggests that classroom teachers will see benefits increase with daily formative practices.

Similarly, Marzano (2007) examines a meta-analysis of the research on how the frequency of formative assessment affects student achievement (Bangert-Drowns, Kulik, & Kulik, 1991), specifically what happens to student achievement in a fifteen-week course of study as the frequency of assessment during that time changes. He finds that if students are given five assessments during that time, they should expect an increase of 20 percentile points. The achievement increases as the number of assessments increases.

So, how frequent is really frequent enough? The final answer probably relies most on how teachers plan to *respond* to students who aren't learning and may change as teachers become more proficient at using the results of the assessment they give. At Woodlawn, frequency of assessment increased from four times a year to common formative assessments every few weeks and then to formative classroom assessments written by individual teachers as often as needed.

To facilitate decisions around frequency, principals should consider asking questions that help teachers clarify their own work: "Do you have the information you need to adjust your instruction? Do you know which students are struggling early enough to help them before the unit is completed? When students are struggling, do you know what is unclear to them? Do you have the information to determine whether students *already* know the information you are teaching?" These questions will help teachers decide if they need more frequent assessments.

Won't Additional Testing Take Time Away From Teaching?

During initial implementation, if this question isn't being asked publicly, principals should be aware that it is likely being asked privately. Until teachers see the benefit for their students in their classroom, they are reluctant to see the worth of *more* assessment. This question is most often asked when teachers have been focused on using summative tests; they see assessment as something that occurs *after* teaching or something that is used to identify students who haven't learned the material. Once teachers become more familiar with formative assessment practices and how to involve students in their own learning, they see these practices as part of their instruction rather than as a separate activity.

Buhle & Blachowicz (2008/2009) suggest coaching can be an effective staff development practice during this transition to a system that uses more formative assessment. Coaches help teachers realize that formative assessment can become a part of their instructional practices.

How Do We Make Sure We Can Write Good Assessments?

Woodlawn teachers were also concerned about whether the assessments they were writing would provide usable information. With the myriad of test banks stocked with items already written and often linked to state standards, would it be more expeditious to use these test banks rather than write our own assessments from scratch?

In an effort to get things started, principals may be inclined to look for outside resources to help their teachers, but there are other matters to consider. For example, writing and designing assessments creates embedded opportunities for *teacher* learning. When a teacher designs an assessment to provide feedback about student learning, she must determine what she wants to assess, what proficiency will be for each target, and how she will respond when students didn't learn the essential concepts. Teachers who work together in collaborative teams discuss exactly what they believe a standard means, exactly what they think students should be able to do as a result of their learning, and exactly how it will "look" when students have learned. Choosing items from a test bank eliminates all of these rich discussions.

As Carol Tomlinson (2007/2008, p. 11) tells us, "Informative assessment isn't separate from the curriculum." No matter how closely linked to the curriculum any external set of assessments is, it will never match the taught curriculum. This doesn't mean that teachers can't or shouldn't look at the assessment materials that are part of their adopted curriculum for ideas or even sample items. But it is critical that teachers choose and edit items with care to give them information to identify students' strengths and weaknesses. For example, elementary teachers might use the assessment materials from their reading series to find grade-level appropriate texts to use to write their common assessment. They might even use some of the questions that came with the series, but they should supplement those with their own questions to create a well-designed assessment of whether students can use the specific reading strategy taught that week.

As a principal who faced this question, I needed to consider why teachers were concerned about developing their own assessments. Generally, two areas concern teachers. Some teachers feel they don't know how to write good test items, and many teachers are overwhelmed at the thought of all the assessments they will have to create to get the data they want. Thus, the first step for the principal is to help design a plan for implementation so that teachers aren't overwhelmed. Teachers should start with one subject area. For example, in elementary schools, teachers start with either reading or math and get more comfortable with the process. Once they've had some experience working as grade-level teams in discussing learning targets and proficiency standards, they could work more independently to finish the final assessments. At middle school and high school levels, teachers who teach more than one level of a subject or more than one subject may find that completing one subject area first gives them enough experience so that when they start the second area, they complete the task more quickly.

For teachers who are concerned about how to write qual-ity items, a review of the research should help them feel more comfortable. *Classroom Assessment* for *Student Learning* (Stiggins et al., 2004) provides a thorough discussion on the variety of assess-ment methods and what quality assessments look like. Sometimes teachers worry that they don't know as much about statistics as the authors of their achievement tests and state tests. Douglas Reeves (2007) addresses the issue of "psychometric perfection" when he suggests that short, teacher-created assessments have a clear advantage for teachers who want to respond immediately to the students who need more time and support. Though short tests or quizzes administered to get immediate feedback might not be statistically perfect, the advantage of immediate feed-back to teachers and students is worth the possible downside. In the worst case, Reeves suggests, a student may get additional instruction he might not need, but this situation is better than the possibility that a needy student might not get help in a timely fashion if teachers wait to design perfect tests. Teachers *can* design effective assessments once they understand the basics of assessment design. Principals should then facilitate discussion around assessment results and whether those results are helping teachers know how to respond in their classrooms.

Trusting Each Other With Assessment Results

No matter what kind of assessment system a school designs, there will be some assessments that all teachers who teach the same grade level or subject area give together. If teachers are designing common formative assessments, this will occur on a regular basis. If each teacher designs his own assessments, teach-ers will still have common test data from state tests. Principals who want to use data effectively must develop a culture that supports sharing of both data and instructional strategies. At my school, teachers were initially reluctant to compare their results, but over time, this issue seemed to disappear as teachers began to trust each other and to believe that sharing results made them better able to help students.

Focus on Finding Solutions

Principals should understand that when one teacher's results are worse than others, two things can happen. That teacher might become concerned that she will be judged as a poor teacher—or she might ask her colleagues to share teaching strategies so that everyone's results improve. Principals are responsible for helping develop and support a culture that encourages the second scenario.

I used specific strategies to develop this culture. The first was to model an acceptance of data as factual information that doesn't have to lead to making excuses. In the past, if some scores were lower than we hoped, I would have given a list of "possibilities" for why we had failed. After learning more about assessment practices, however, I guided our team to list our hypotheses for how we could *improve* what we were doing. We talked about the things we could control and put aside excuses based on what we couldn't control. Sure, we wished that all of our students were ready to learn and had parents who were following through at home, but we really couldn't control those things. Rather, we brainstormed ways to help students who weren't supervised after school and weren't getting their homework done.

If the only tool teachers have to respond to students who aren't learning is to help those students in their own classrooms or keep them after school, teachers will have a more difficult time embracing frequent assessments as the solution to students not learning. If, on the other hand, the entire staff works to build a schedule and system that provides support, teachers will see assessments as a means to identifying students who will get extra help from the entire team.

Avoid Comparisons

Principals must be especially careful never to compare one teacher to another. While it is natural to want to use data to evaluate teachers, it is important to use this information cautiously. Encourage teacher teams to analyze their own data and create their own understanding of the strengths and weaknesses that emerge. For some teachers, this may be the first time they see their results compared to their colleagues. At my school, in the beginning, we went out of our way to make the data anonymous. Each teacher got back his or her results and the total group's results for comparison. However, it wasn't long before teachers asked to receive data back by teacher. Today, teachers receive reports that identify each teacher's scores and the total team's results. Once teachers trust each other, the information they can get this way becomes much more important than anonymity.

While state and achievement test data have been available to teachers for years, they aren't always provided in a timely way or disaggregated by teacher. Teachers need a chance to look at their individual results, compare their results with others, and come to their own conclusions—without consequence. At Woodlawn, they certainly got better at doing so with some practice. Many teachers were surprised to discover that their colleagues used different instructional strategies than they did and that sometimes the instructional strategies changed the results.

My most important role during this time was to model how to analyze and use the data we were getting. I attended data meetings, participated in finding solutions to problems, and encouraged teachers to take risks for improvement, hoping that doing so would support a culture that valued results. Principals should ensure that teachers are comfortable understanding their results and how to use them in their classrooms to help students.

Managing Data

If teachers don't get their results back in a format that allows them to understand the information or quickly enough to respond the next day in their classroom, they are unlikely to effectively use the assessment data to benefit their students. Thus, principals will want to consider what type of data management system they will need to accelerate data analysis for teachers.

Data management most likely will require technological support. In my own school, this meant that I had to be willing to pilot a new computerized system of data analysis. Even though I had more tasks already on my "to do" list than I really felt I could accomplish, in the long run, putting in the time to learn and modify the program was well worth it. I learned so much about how the programs worked and what they could do that I was able to help teachers through the initial "growing pains" of implementation. It is important for principals to familiarize themselves with the technology their teachers are using, to make it as user-friendly as possible. No matter what your own comfort level with technology is, you should be willing to "feel the teacher's pain"!

So, what did the data management system do that was helpful? First of all, teachers need to be able to use selected-response (multiple choice, matching, and true/false) questions as well as rubric data. The data management system should be able to accommodate both data types. The data system must also be able to aggregate data from students to compile classroom, team, and school results; that is, teachers should be able to look at an individual student's results, the total results for a whole class, and (for middle school and high school teachers) all of their classes together. If teachers are writing common assessments, they need to see their data compared to the other teachers on their team. Equally important, the system should allow teachers to disaggregate their data in various ways, such as by learning target or standard and by individual students. My teachers particularly liked the reports that listed which students hadn't mastered specific learning targets.

Teachers will also benefit from item analysis data. This allows a teacher to examine specific questions to find out what students knew and didn't know. For example, in a multiple-choice question, a teacher might add certain distractors to see which ones students pick when they don't know the correct answer. Then the teacher has a better understanding about how to respond to students who didn't master the material. Teachers will also want to be able to link specific questions to state or local learning standards so that they can monitor progress around each standard.

Most of all, the system should allow teachers to administer a selected-response assessment and receive the data back in very little time. If the purpose of the assessment is to know how to respond immediately to a student who hasn't learned a concept, the teacher really needs to know by the next day which students need help. Principals can work out ways to simplify the process of gathering and analyzing data. For example, in my school, we were able to train a very capable instructional assistant to run the computer system and print the reports. Teachers could anticipate getting their results the next day, in plenty of time to react to student needs. For extended response and performance assessments, of course, the time it takes for the teacher to evaluate student work and provide feedback will necessarily delay having the results immediately. However, teachers can use these systems to analyze results to see patterns related to learning for their students and the students on their team.

Is there a point at which too much information gets in the way? The system we used provided teachers with some statistical information that was more than they needed or wanted to have. Rather than trying to make all teachers relearn the dreaded statistics course they had to take in college, we agreed that we would leave the information on the reports in case they became useful in the future, but that teachers would only use the data they found helpful.

Using Data to Improve Student Achievement

The real power of assessment data lies in how teachers respond to it in their classrooms. If teachers fail to respond or just reteach using the same methods they used the first time, there is little likelihood that needy students will benefit. If, on the other hand, teachers use the results to identify which students need more help, and more specifically, exactly what kind of help they need, there is a strong expectation that needy students will benefit.

Thomas Guskey (2007/2008) calls these responses "corrective activities" and suggests that teachers must use different strategies that meet the specific learning needs of each student. He recommends that teachers share their instructional practices so that they each have multiple ways to teach a concept. If teachers spend time early in a unit making sure that students understand initial content, Guskey argues, they will be able to make up that time once students are confident learners.

Principals must be explicit about the need to respond to the data. Facilitate discussions about how to respond, both individually in classrooms and collectively through team and school intervention programs. As teachers become comfortable with the fact that *something* will happen for students as a result of assessment data, they become more comfortable with developing and using additional assessments.

Looking Forward

Once teachers become familiar with writing and using assessments, a new concern will likely emerge: teachers who are using formative assessments in their classrooms or on their teams to guide their instructional practices will want to rethink how they are using these assessments in determining student grades. Stiggins et al. (2004) suggest that when using assessment *for* learning "the grading function is laid aside. This is not about accountability—those are assessments OF learning. This is about getting better" (p. 31).

Traditional grading and reporting systems are based on an average of all of the student's work during the reporting period. Using formative assessments as feedback about what has been learned and what is still unclear assumes that learning isn't static, but that students will continue to learn more as time goes on (O'Connor, 2002). In fact, Jacqueline Clymer and Dylan Wiliam (2006/2007) state, "The second requirement of an assessment system that supports learning is that it should by dynamic rather than static. Grades based on the accumulation of points over time are counter-productive." They suggest that a grade should represent learning at the end of the grading period. Thomas Guskey and Jane Bailey (2001) address some teachers' concern that students might not take formative assessments seriously by suggesting that counting these assessments for grades will limit students' creativity and willingness to take risks as they learn new material. Rather, they advise teachers to make sure students understand the purpose of these assessments.

These questions are also likely to cause teachers to address other issues around grading practices: what to do with late work, should zeroes be permitted, should each teacher use his or her own grading system, or should all teachers use a schoolwide system, and so on. Principals must be prepared to address these questions by reading widely about reporting and grading practices and encouraging teachers to do the same.

Student Learning Is Our Goal!

If student learning is our goal, we must also be willing to continuously learn ourselves. When my teachers began addressing the issue of assessment, I didn't feel prepared to answer their questions and concerns. I wanted that one guidebook that had all the answers. What I discovered was that as a profession, we are still learning about good assessment practices. As educators, we must be open to changing our thinking as we learn more through professional learning and feedback in our own classrooms and schools.

References

Ainsworth, L., & Viegut, D. (2006). *Common formative assessments: How to connect standards-based instruction and assessment.* Thousand Oaks, CA: Corwin.

Bangert-Drowns, R. L., Kulik, J. A., & Kulik, C. C. (1991). Effects of classroom testing. *Journal of Educational Research, 85*(2), 89–99.

Black, P., & Wiliam, D. (1998). Inside the black box: Raising standards through common assessment. *Phi Delta Kappan.* Accessed at www.pdkint/org/kappan on January 10, 2007.

Buhle, R., & Blachowicz, C. L. Z. (2008/2009). The assessment double play. *Educational Leadership, 66*(4), 42–46.

Clymer, J. B., & Wiliam, D. (2006/2007). *Improving the way we grade science.* Accessed at www.ascd.org/publications/ecuational_leadership/dec06/vol64/num04/Improving_the_Way_We_Garde_Science.aspx on December 23, 2008.

Guskey, T. (2007/2008). The rest of the story. *Educational Leadership, 65*(4), 28–34.

Guskey, T. R., & Bailey, J. M. (2001). *Developing grading and reporting systems for student learning.* Thousand Oaks, CA: Corwin.

Leahy, S., Lyon, C., Thompson, M., & Wiliam, D. (2005). Classroom assessment: Minute by minute, day by day. *Educational Leadership, 63*(3), 19–24.

Marshall, K. (2008). Interim assessments: A user's guide. *Phi Delta Kappan.* Accessed at www.pdkintl.org/kappan/k_v90/k0809ma1.htm on October 5, 2008.

Marzano, R. (2003). *What works in schools: Translating research into action.* Alexandria, VA: Association for Supervision and Curriculum Development.

Marzano, R. (2007). *The art and science of teaching: A comprehensive framework for effective instruction.* Alexandria, VA: Association for Supervision and Curriculum Development.

National Center for Fair and Open Testing. (2007). *The value of formative assessment.* Accessed at www.fairtest.org/files/FormativeAssessment_0.pdf on December 12, 2008.

O'Connor, K. (2002). *How to grade for learning: Linking grades to standards.* Thousand Oaks, CA: Corwin.

Popham, W. (2008). *Transformative assessment.* Alexandria, VA: Association for Supervision and Curriculum Development.

Reeves, D. (2007). Challenges and choices. In D. Reeves (Ed.), *Ahead of the curve: The power of assessment to transform teaching and learning* (pp.183–204). Bloomington, IN: Solution Tree.

Stiggins, R., Arter, J., Chappuis, J., & Chappuis, S. (2004). *Classroom assessment* for *student learning: Doing it right—Using it well.* Portland, OR: ETS Assessment Training Institute.

Tomlinson, C. A. (2007/2008). Learning to love assessment. *Educational Leadership, 65*(4), 8–13.

Wiliam, D. (2007). Content *then* process: Teacher learning communities in the service of formative assessment. In D. Reeves (Ed.), *Ahead of the curve: The power of assessment to transform teaching and learning* (pp.183–204). Bloomington, IN: Solution Tree.

DENNIS KING

 Dennis King, EdD, is a consultant and assistant professor of education at Baker University. He is the former district assistant superintendent of school improvement for the Blue Valley School District in Overland Park, Kansas, which was selected as a best-practice district by the American Productivity and Quality Center and the Data Quality Campaign. Dr. King earned his doctorate from St. Louis University and has devoted eighteen years of his twenty-four-year career to administrative positions, including assistant principal, principal, and executive director of school improvement. In addition to his work in the Blue Valley School District, he has consulted with teachers and administrators throughout the United States on assessment and professional learning communities. He is a contributor to *The Collaborative Teacher: Working Together as a Professional Learning Community* (Solution Tree, 2008).

FOUR

Building Assessment Expertise Through Twenty-First-Century Professional Development

Dennis King

In recent years, principals and administrators have lined their shelves with books and articles focused on assessment. Companies have raced to develop the next best "formative" assessment to offset the summative No Child Left Behind mindset of many educators. However, as Rick Stiggins and Jan Chappuis (2006) note, we cannot circumvent the point that teachers need not just better assessments, but better assessment *expertise*. The emerging drawback of "off-the-shelf" assessments is that they lack real tools to help teachers understand the proven strategies that help students learn more. The standards-based movement has enabled teachers to become clearer about what students should learn. As a consequence, high-quality professional development to create clarity and to build coherence in assessment has never been more critical. Leaders face the challenge of helping teachers understand and apply the essential practices of student assessment that improve individual and collective student achievement.

To help our teachers arrive at a deeper understanding of the assessment process, we cannot use a typical workshop format (Stiggins & Chappuis, 2006). Developing critical twenty-first-century assessment expertise goes beyond teaching people how to create a test. It goes beyond showing how to convert rubric scores to grades or how to develop a standards-based report card. "True assessment leadership," Stiggins and Chappuis argue, "examines long-established assessment practices that are harmful to students and their learning, such as factoring practice work (such as homework) into the final grade, giving tests without further understanding what specific learning each item addresses, and keeping students in the dark about the learning for which they are responsible" (2006, p. 13). As we begin to build assessment expertise, we must consider two issues: how the assessment itself is used as a tool to gather information about student learning, and how grading is used to evaluate the evidence of student learning and communicate the results to teachers, students, and parents to guide the learning process.

If our desire is for students to learn more and at higher levels of achievement, we must shift from twentieth-century assessment practices of testing, scoring, and reporting to twenty-first-century practices of establishing clear learning targets—for both our students and teachers—monitoring learning, intervening, and standards-based reporting. This chapter will explore effective strategies and guiding principles for professional development that supports that transition.

Setting Goals for Professional Development

Our future and the future of our organizations are determined by the fundamental choices we make and the values and purposes we select. Clearly defined fundamental choices, values, and purposes organize activities, maintain focus, and sustain efforts. They are also filters through which we can consider the desirability of our intentions and beliefs (Sparks, 2006). The process of clearly defining goals allows both schools and districts to create a common vocabulary and design meaningful professional development.

Unfortunately, many processes and activities often included under the label of "professional development" lie beyond the scope of *effective* professional development. To clarify just what professional development means, consider this definition: "Professional development is a process that is (a) intentional, (b) ongoing, and (c) systemic" (Guskey, 2000, p. 16). Intentional, ongoing, and systemic processes allow schools and districts to create a focused support system to build capacity for teachers and principals.

Intentional Learning Outcomes

When establishing professional development goals, administrators must look beyond what presenters or trainers are expected to do while they are on site. Effective results-based professional development should be evident from a change in teacher practice and therefore increased student achievement *after* the professional development. Accordingly, Thomas Guskey suggests, a meaningful professional development goal might be "to provide participants with the knowledge of cooperative learning and the skills necessary for classroom applications that will result in more positive student interactions and improved student learning" (2000, p. 18).

Ongoing Learning

From an administrative standpoint, it is most desirable to have an effective assessment program that not only promotes learning for all students but also provides critical information to guide the selection of research-based interventions when a student is not learning a particular standard. If increasing numbers of schools adopt the response to intervention (RTI) process, as seems likely, ongoing professional development in assessment will become crucial to support proper implementation of assessment systems that both monitor *and* promote student achievement. In the coming years, educators will become more aware of student achievement gaps in general education classrooms. Faculty members will have to learn to analyze common assessment data and to develop monitoring systems to make sure all students are learning at high levels in all of our classrooms. The ongoing, cyclical nature of the RTI process will broaden the need for refined professional development that supports current best practice and introduces new research-based strategies.

Systemic Implementation

As Jeff Archer (2005) argues, it is too much to presume that every school has the capacity to bring its students to the levels of achievement demanded of them. The ability to identify and support *key* concepts—those that shift the school's culture toward student learning—is critical. As leaders, we must not be afraid to maintain a focus on those initiatives that will truly drive student achievement. Rick DuFour frequently discusses the need for a balanced, "loose and tight" approach to leadership (DuFour, DuFour, & Eaker, 2008). If our purpose is to create higher levels of student learning through assessment, then the professional development we offer should be "tight": focused, with a centralized purpose to build schoolwide assessment literacy for teachers, students, administrators, and community members. If the learning outcomes of the professional development sessions are too loose—if we offer a general menu with multiple options for teachers to choose from—we risk "fly by night" professional development that lacks the clarity required for successful and sustainable implementation.

Building Assessment Literacy

The wide range of testing in this age puts increased pressure on educational leaders throughout North America—pressure from both educators and noneducators. The current assessment conversation, though broad in scope, lacks a strong understanding of the basic principles that support the creation of accurate and powerful assessments. Moreover, the lack of assessment literacy leaves many educators unclear about the purpose of assessment and confused about the various types of assessment available. All too often, when the term *assessment* is used, the choral response from educators is "test." Leaders must create a twenty-first-century, assessment-literate culture that provides teachers with a stronger understanding of standards-based curriculum, of power standards, and of assessment skills and strategies.

A Curricular Foundation

Larry Ainsworth and Donald Viegut (2006, p. 53) define *assessment literacy* as "the ability to understand the different purposes and types of assessments in order to select the most appropriate type of assessment to meet a specific purpose." In the rush to develop an assessment-literate culture in which assessment is used not only to measure student achievement but also to engage students in a deep understanding of the curriculum, we risk taking a myopic view toward assessment. Curriculum conversations can become overshadowed by the demand for common assessments, for example, or common assessments may simply collect the five favorite test questions of each member of a math team. Our challenge is to create *connections* between assessment and curriculum through an assessment process that will not only measure proficiency but also support learning for all students. We cannot implement essential assessment best practices if the taught and assessed curricula are not aligned. To develop a deeper understanding of assessment, teachers and leaders must first become clear about what they want students to learn.

The introduction of response to intervention makes teaching a guaranteed and viable curriculum more imperative than ever. According to RTI principles, schools must have a research-based common core curriculum before they can begin to offer increasing levels of support to those students who struggle to learn the essential power standards (Buffum, Mattos, & Weber, 2009). Assessment linked to curriculum standards allows educators to closely examine data to make decisions about student learning and provide support and extra time on specific content topics.

Response to Intervention Tiers
Tier 1: Common Curriculum
Tier 2: Supplemental Support
Tier 3: Intensive Support

The development and use of research-based Tier 1, Tier 2, and Tier 3 interventions may appear to be a method to identify or serve students with learning disabilities. However, in RTI, best instructional practice and research-based interventions merge to improve learning for all students as soon as they demonstrate that they are having difficulty learning. The needs of the response to intervention process map out a path for professional development that supports curriculum and assessment strategies in the classroom.

Mapping Critical Concepts and Power Standards

Creating curriculum clarity through the mapping of the power standards or essential learnings is crucial to developing a deeper understanding of assessment. By using power standards to drive the curriculum, educators can reach a strong understanding of what skills and knowledge to assess for each standard (Ainsworth & Viegut, 2006). Without clearly defined power standards or essential learnings, teachers cannot develop a shared understanding of what to assess or how. Power standards allow teachers to focus on the essential concepts necessary for students to comprehend the content, rather than the entire list of standards. Without this essential step in creating a systemic assessment process, teachers will not have enough time to further develop their assessment skills, and the assessment literacy conversation will become moot.

Therefore, as we provide professional development, we must consider how to create a culture that will allow teachers to connect power standards to our assessment framework. Heidi Hayes

Jacobs (1997) discusses the need for teachers of the same grade level or course to work in horizontal teams to map what they are actually teaching in their classrooms. A clear understanding of taught curriculum not only enhances classroom instruction and assessment, but also lays the foundation for a sound RTI model; a curriculum map documenting the taught or implemented curriculum and its relation to the power standards builds the necessary framework for creating common assessments. After strong horizontal teams have been developed, vertical teams can evaluate both curriculum and assessment data to ensure that students are learning key concepts from grade to grade or course to course. Understanding how the curriculum spirals or has endurance from one grade level or course to the next will guarantee a strong curriculum throughout the K–12 experience.

Assessment Knowledge, Skill, and Capacity

Rick Stiggins states, "Teachers need to be far more assessment literate in the future than they are today or have been in the past" (as cited in Sparks, 1999, p. 17). Once teachers become clear about what students should learn in our standards-based culture, they must build a deep understanding of best methods to assess student work. Administrators need to evaluate whether their faculty and community can identify the difference between sound and unsound assessment practices, and whether they understand the full range of uses—and users—of assessment. The assessment conversation has permeated the landscape, but educators often fall short of understanding the purpose of assessment and the best type of assessment to measure what students should learn. Moreover, as schools and communities struggle to implement the sound progress-monitoring necessary to fuel the RTI process in general education classrooms, effective, nonbiased assessment practices are necessary to effectively gauge if students have closed the achievement gap.

Classroom Assessment

Accordingly, the next step toward building an assessment-literate culture is to expand the knowledge, skills, and capacity of both teachers and administrators on assessment itself. All too often, in our rush to implement change, we fail to create a deep understanding of the new content or concept. Stiggins (2002) suggests that only a few teachers are prepared to face the challenges of assessment because teachers have not been given the opportunity to learn about assessment. Unfortunately, licensure programs for both teaching and administration often lack the necessary instruction in specific school improvement strategies, let alone assessment.

As Stiggins points out, "Teachers have not been given the tools they need to help students succeed, and classroom assessment tools are the head of the list of what teachers need" (Sparks, 1999, p. 18). Teachers must be crystal clear on the types of learning targets and the most appropriate measures of those targets (Stiggins, Arter, Chappuis, & Chappuis, 2004). Ainsworth and Viegut (2006) advocate for providing teachers with opportunities to enhance the "tools" in their "toolkit" as they learn about the specific attributes of each type of assessment.

Collaborative Assessment

Professional development for assessment must create a common understanding and eliminate multiple interpretations within schools and school systems. As teachers begin to discuss various topics associated with assessment—such as common assessments, formative assessments, summative assessments, balanced assessment, assessment bias, assessment construction, and data analysis—administrators must establish a professional development process that allows collaborative grade-level or departmental teams to learn about, develop, and implement new assessment strategies consistently and sustainably. This means creating a process to merge critical new work into the essential routine of every teacher:

Every educator must understand the principles of sound assessment and must be able to apply those principles as a matter of routine in doing their work. Accurate assessment is not possible unless and until educators are given the opportunity to become assessment literate. [They] must understand student achievement expectations and how to transform those expectations into accurate assessment exercises and scoring procedures. (National Education Association, 2003, p. 4)

Moreover, Ainsworth and Viegut (2006) discuss the need for teacher teams to score assessments and to develop shared learning based upon the assessment results. As faculty members review their individual data on a common assessment and compare them to the team data, deep instructional questions can arise. Rick Stiggins, Judith Arter, Steve Chappuis, and Jan Chappuis (2004) note that professional conversations within a learning team enable the team members to anchor their new assessments and align them to the appropriate learning targets. The collaborative process creates the conduit for daily job-embedded professional development through the collective wisdom of a learning team (Ainsworth & Viegut, 2006). Without a strong collaborative environment *and* focused professional development, we risk teachers relying upon previous individual knowledge of assessment—which may be incorrect or inadequate.

Large-Scale Assessment

Finally, educators must become clear about the major types of assessment and what each assessment attempts to measure. For example, when discussing norm-referenced assessments or national assessments, it is essential to recognize that these standardized achievement tests have been passed from generation to generation to allow schools to compare students to other students across the nation. A state or provincial assessment compares students within the state or province on a specific standard; district assessments compare students throughout a district; common subject-area assessments compare students within a grade level or course. In many cases, these tests are designed to compare students within a local or external system and have not been changed to reflect the standards-based era; they do nothing to measure instructional quality or, consequently, student achievement (Popham, 2008b).

These large-scale assessments are often the sole source of data for teachers to consider when determining program efficacy and student achievement. However, we must understand the type of data these assessments represent and how administrators use the data to guide learning in the classroom. Therefore, our professional development should focus on the information found within these large-scale assessments and, once again, the purpose of large-scale assessments. All too often we distribute the assessment information and ask individual teachers to make decisions without providing a clear framework about the assessment and if the data can be used to guide the learning process for our students.

Administrative leaders constantly review student performance data and make student learning decisions based upon these summative data. Schools have become data rich and information poor. Assessment measures yield traditional data points buried in a multipage data summary. In many cases, school districts have invested in data-warehouse programs to better analyze student growth within the district. But assessment literacy is more than generating a pile of statistics that many educators don't understand and are often intimidated to learn. Educational leaders must build the capacity to move beyond the data-warehouse assessment analysis to a position that impacts instruction to help students learn more. Until leaders make the commitment to shift the assessment paradigm—from simply submitting the traditional data summaries required by communities and boards of education to helping teachers understand the *information* found within the data—educators will struggle to attain the depth of understanding necessary to advance student achievement.

Creating Assessment Literacy in the Community

As previously discussed, a focused professional development plan is critical to allow schools and school systems to develop an effective assessment program. However, the assessment cultural shift is dramatic enough that we must consider its effects on not just our internal community, but our external community as well. School board members, parents, and local universities also need "professional development" to become assessment literate. The development of an assessment-literate culture for the twenty-first century within our external community will pave the path for implementation of large-scale assessments that are diagnostic rather than comparative. It will allow schools and districts to openly discuss the controversial topic of grading as a method to evaluate the evidence produced through effective assessment strategies. Therefore, classroom practice may shift toward the use of standards-based grading instead of traditional report cards. These changes alone will start the journey toward a renewed assessment policy but will require the understanding and knowledge of our external communities for sustained implementation.

Creating sustainable assessment practice within our internal community requires partnerships with education programs in our postsecondary institutions. Bridging the gap between K–12 systems and teacher preparation programs is critical to strengthen our collective understanding of effective assessment strategies as opposed to a traditional testing practice. If these topics are not addressed at the university level, professional development will be stuck on a continuous cycle of teaching and reteaching practicing educators.

Establishing an assessment-literate culture within our entire school community provides the support for teachers to create a balanced assessment program, utilize standards-based report cards, plan next steps for instruction, provide detailed and descriptive feedback to students, and correctly identify what students know and don't know and their levels of achievement. More importantly, an assessment-literate community encourages students to take ownership of their own learning. Students will become more engaged as they recognize that assessment moves beyond the test and assessments are far more than a grade or proficiency measure. Parents and students will experience how assessment reinforces the nonnegotiables of learning instead of serving solely as a source of comparing, sorting, and reporting.

The time has come for policymakers to consider how best to influence the assessment conversation within their communities. As assessment polices become more refined, supporting balanced assessment programs, assessment will begin to extend beyond the traditional reporting and recording of national normed comparisons of schools and school districts. Policies will unify both our internal and external communities, creating the desired cultural implications for a sustained student achievement.

Advocating for Policy Changes

A critical element in the establishment of an assessment-literate culture is effective leadership that influences and changes policy. Policy changes are often necessary to allow the development of new assessment practices to evaluate educational effectiveness. As James Popham clearly states:

> The sad reality is that almost all of today's educational accountability tests are instructionally insensitive, incapable of detecting the difference between effective and ineffective instruction. When an instructionally insensitive test is used as an accountability test, the bulk of learning benefits from classroom formative assessment simply won't show up in the test results. (2008a, p. 123)

In order to create the necessary shift in assessment practice, leaders must evaluate their current assessment programs and make important decisions required to inform instructional practice within their schools and districts. Administrators must constantly monitor the relationship between assessment type and assessment purpose. If the purpose is to monitor student performance from a large-scale or "30,000-foot" perspective, then the traditional twentieth-century assessment models will work. However, the twenty-first-century model of assessment literacy requires promoting student learning by investigating assessment information at the one-foot level—closest to the student and teacher. In this model, instruction and assessment practice conversations within a collaborative team are necessary.

Administrators must look in the mirror and evaluate what they can do to influence practice. As Jim Collins (2001) argues in *Good to Great*, leaders should be forced to evaluate in particular what we should *stop* doing to allow us to maintain a focus on the desired outcome. If traditional assessment systems have no valid measure to help students learn more, we must develop a "start doing" list of practices that will both inform and enhance student achievement within our schools.

The opportunity to influence the external culture is essential to create a sustainable plan that gains the support of both school leaders and parents outside the schoolhouse doors. If the traditional standardized modes of assessment are inappropriate for evaluating educational effectiveness and do not leverage higher levels of student learning, administrators must advocate for an assessment system more aligned to the twenty-first century. However, as we develop a twenty-first-century assessment model, we must remember that parents and possibly school board members are accustomed to the standardized comparison model from the twentieth century. Ainsworth and Viegut (2006) identify four successful strategies to influence the external culture to gain support for an initiative that the internal organization wants to launch. These are:

1. Including influential leaders in the meetings of planning teams

2. Visiting the leaders' offices and places of employment in order to discuss the initiative in person

3. Sharing information relative to the initiative with other area schools and districts in hopes of developing a partnership agreement to promote the practice

4. Establishing regional councils to collectively share in the development of this important work

These four strategies are essential to build the knowledge base of the external leadership such as teacher association officers and board of education members.

Winning Parent Support

In addition to establishing support from community leaders, it is imperative to strategize a professional development plan to inform parents. As assessment programs are shifted to match system requirements of the twenty-first century, community members will have questions. Without their support, change is very difficult to sustain.

Consider this story of a middle school whose steady assessment practices transformed it into one of the highest-performing middle schools in Kansas, and indeed in the United States. Prairie Star Middle School in Leawood, Kansas, is one of eight middle schools in the suburban Blue Valley School District and serves over six hundred students in grades 6 through 8. The school's principal, Dr. Lyn Rantz, launched an initiative to develop an assessment-literate culture within the professional learning community (PLC) model for school improvement. At the outset, Dr. Rantz assembled a team of teacher leaders to create a student-learning focus throughout the school. This leadership team began to study assessment and investigate strategies to move beyond more traditional large-scale assessment concepts, as previously discussed. Dr. Rantz and the school's leadership team created an assessment cadre of five certified core teachers whose charge was to provide leadership and professional development for each of their interdisciplinary collaborative teams. An initial obstacle to this cadre's work became apparent as each teacher's assessment literacy and understanding were challenged by his or her previous training and practice. Through active research and study, however, the teachers in teams soon became very aware of the weaknesses of traditional assessment and the potential of the new assessment research paradigms. Conversations and professional practice within the school began to shift as teachers started discussing learning targets, student involvement, assessment methods, grading, and monitoring of student progress. Teachers soon discovered the vast array of possibilities in using more formative and diagnostic classroom assessment and relied less on the traditional summative, large-scale assessments. The analysis of assessment data became a more powerful tool as the teachers integrated their new assessment literacy into their daily collective practice.

The assessment initiative was one critical vehicle for Prairie Star's success, as teachers remained committed to the four corollary questions of a PLC: What do we want students to learn? How will we know they have learned it? What will we do if they don't learn it? What will we do if they have already learned it? (DuFour et al., 2008) The use of the collaborative team model created assessment literacy throughout the internal school community. As the cadre worked alongside the leadership team, teachers were collaborating and implementing balanced assessment practices for the twenty-first century. The school's student achievement soared as the percentage of students below standard on the state math assessment went from 34.2 percent in 2002 to 2.8 percent in 2008 to .7 percent in 2009. (Note: all data for

2009 are preliminary as of press time.) Similarly, the percentage of students placing below the standard on the state reading assessment went from 25.4 percent in 2002 to 3.3 percent in 2008 to .6 percent in 2009. Teachers soon realized that implementing a systemic and solid balanced assessment program not only benefited the low-achieving student population but also gave boosts to the mid-level and high-performing students. This was demonstrated as the percentage of students scoring in the "exemplary" category rose from 15.6 percent in 2002 to 45.4 percent in 2008 to 59 percent in 2009 in math, and from 9.1. percent in 2002 to 55.2 percent in 2008 to 62 percent in 2009 in reading.

In this example, the principal created assessment literacy by developing an assessment cadre to offer staff members ongoing professional development work sessions. Teachers were able to transfer their work from these general professional development sessions to job-embedded professional development through ongoing discussions in their collaborative team. In one short year, teachers began to develop common formative assessments. They worked extremely hard to unpack the standards into learning targets, developed strategies to involve students in the assessment process, and created a standards-based electronic report card for students and parents. Additionally, teachers met in large-group settings and analyzed their student performance data based upon the curriculum learning targets. The school then offered research-based interventions for students who required additional time and support within the learning target. The faculty of this school became truly assessment literate! Not only were teachers viewed as valuable resources within the district, student achievement soared to an all-time high in all subgroup populations.

However, as successful as this school became over a three-year period, the external community still struggled to understand the twenty-first-century model of assessment. Most parents and district administration only know the standardized twentieth-century model based upon reporting, points, and grades. In our efforts to develop strong assessment programs, our goal should be to create systemic leadership, support, and assessment literacy in all levels of administration and in our community—to build a united, assessment-literate community of internal and external stakeholders who support the assessment policies that increase student learning. Accordingly, this school developed a web-based gradebook organized by learning target (rather than by assignment), created flyers to effectively communicate the assessment practices of the school, and most importantly, engaged in crucial conversations with students to ensure they understood how learning targets form the path toward understanding the entire curricular standard.

Supporting Job-Embedded Learning

Paul Black and Dylan Wiliam (1998, p. 146) state, "There is a need now to move further to focus on the inside of the 'black box' and to explore the potential of assessment to raise standards directly as an integral part of each student's learning work." As we build the learning culture within our schools, we must investigate our process to create sustained professional development that will shift the school's culture. James Popham notes:

> These days we know much more about how to make professional development endeavors successful than we knew just a few decades ago. For instance, there is a near-universal agreement about the ineffectiveness of visiting luminaries giving one-shot professional development and leaving teachers to their own devices. The reason for this is simple: Human behavior is tough to change, and one-shot workshops, even extremely illuminating and extremely motivating ones, rarely bring about change in teachers' conduct. (2008a, p. 111)

In a twenty-first-century learning community, the essential knowledge and skills already within the school walls should further our learning; professional development should be embedded in action research. Creating a collaborative learning culture is the necessary condition for teachers to engage in the crucial assessment conversations and to experience job-embedded professional development. In addition, principals and leaders of grade-level or course teams must become crystal clear about the expected outcomes from those teams.

Ideally, "professional development . . . not only informs and motivates administrators and faculty but also [advances] the important work taking place [to] produce optimal results" (Ainsworth & Viegut, 2006, p. 113). As Kent Peterson and Terry Deal point out, "Leaders must shape and nourish cultures where every teacher can make a difference and every child can learn, and where there are passion and a commitment to designing and promoting the absolutely best that is possible" (2003, p. 8).

References

Ainsworth, L., & Viegut, D. (2006). *Common formative assessments: How to connect standards-based instruction and assessment.* Thousand Oaks, CA: Corwin.

Archer, J. (2005, September 14). Theory of action. *Education Week* [supplement], S3–S5.

Black, P., & Wiliam, D. (1998). Inside the black box: Raising standards through classroom achievement. *Phi Delta Kappan, 80*(2), 139–148.

Buffum, A., Mattos, M., & Weber, C. (2009). *Pyramid response to intervention: RTI, professional learning communities, and how to respond when kids don't learn.* Bloomington, IN: Solution Tree.

Collins, J. (2001). *Good to great.* New York: HarperCollins.

DuFour, R., DuFour, R., & Eaker, R. (2008). *Revisiting professional learning communities at work: New insights for improving schools.* Bloomington, IN: Solution Tree.

Guskey, T. (2000). *Evaluating professional development.* Thousand Oaks, CA: Corwin.

Jacobs, H. H. (1997). *Mapping the big picture: Integrating curriculum and assessment K–12.* Alexandria, VA: Association for Supervision and Curriculum Development.

National Education Association. (2003). *Balanced assessment: The key to accountability and improved student learning.* Washington, DC: Author.

Peterson, K. D., & Deal, T. E. (2003). *Shaping school culture: The heart of leadership.* San Francisco: Jossey-Bass.

Popham, J. (2008a). The assessment-savvy student. *Educational Leadership, 66*(3), 80–81.

Popham, J. (2008b). *Transformative assessment.* Alexandria, VA: Association for Supervision and Curriculum Development.

Sparks, D. (1999). Assessment without victims: An interview with Rick Stiggins. *Journal of Staff Development, 20*(2), 17–21.

Sparks, D. (2006). *Leading for results.* Thousand Oaks, CA: Corwin.

Stiggins, R. (2002). Assessment crisis: The absence of assessment FOR learning. *Phi Delta Kappan, 83*(10), 758–765.

Stiggins, R., Arter, J., Chappuis, J., & Chappuis, S. (2004). *Classroom assessment* for *student learning: Doing it right—using it well.* Portland, OR: ETS Assessment Training Institute.

Stiggins, R., & Chappuis, J. (2006). What a difference a word makes: Assessment "for" learning rather than assessment "of" learning helps students succeed. *Journal of Staff Development, 27*(1), 10–14.

TAMMY HEFLEBOWER

 As director of curriculum, instruction, and interim assessment for Douglas County Public Schools near Denver, Colorado, Dr. Tammy Heflebower ensures that every student in every classroom receives a quality education. Dr. Heflebower is a seasoned practitioner and public speaker with experience at the classroom and administrative levels. She earned her doctorate of education in educational administration from the University of Nebraska–Lincoln, and completed the Cooperative Urban Teacher Education Program in Kansas City, Missouri. As a fourth-grade teacher in Columbus, Nebraska, she received the District Distinguished Elementary Teacher Award. Dr. Heflebower has also worked as a middle school administrator; director of professional development; National Educational Trainer for the National Resource and Training Center at Girls and Boys Town in Nebraska; and adjunct professor of curriculum, instruction, and assessment courses at several universities. A prominent member of numerous educational organizations, Dr. Heflebower has served as president of the Nebraska Association for Supervision and Curriculum Development and as legislative liaison and board member for the Colorado Association of Educational Specialists. Her articles have been featured in the monthly newsletter *Nebraska Council of School Administrators Today* and other publications. She is a contributor to *The Teacher as Assessment Leader* (Solution Tree, 2009).

FIVE

A Seven-Module Plan to Build Teacher Knowledge of Balanced Assessment

Tammy Heflebower

Ensuring a balanced assessment system is imperative to student achievement. Assessment is an essential, systematic element of the learning process; it is used to make inferences about student learning based upon multiple sources of evidence—a process involving stakeholders such as students, parents, teachers, administrators, and policymakers. This global process of collecting, analyzing, and synthesizing information about students allows us to understand and describe them and their achievement more effectively (Brown, 1983; McTighe & Ferrara, 1998). As Kenneth Wolf (1993) maintains, in *informed* assessment, teachers engage in the process of systematically reviewing student work using multiple methods, across diverse contexts, and over time. Teachers must possess baseline knowledge about a variety of topics such as curriculum, instruction, physical and psychological development, and diversity: indeed, "a knowledgeable teacher is the foundation of informed assessment" (Wolf, 1993, p. 519). In addition, teachers need extensive knowledge of quality assessment methods that meet the standards for reliability and validity (Stiggins, 1995). Wolf (1993) suggests that the next steps in assessment literacy for teachers are greater pre-service and in-service preparation in classroom assessment. Teachers need administrative support, Wolf argues, because "extending the work of teachers who are practicing informed assessment will require greater respect and commitment from those outside the classroom" (p. 522). This chapter will explain a seven-module plan that principals and district administration can follow to support the creation of a balanced assessment system within the school or district.

Components of a Balanced Assessment System

The word *assessment* is derived from the Latin root *assidere*, which means to "sit beside" (McTighe & Ferrara, 1998). Although this may be a historically accurate definition of assessment, contemporary educators often reduce the assessment process to a grade, quartile, percentile, or raw score. Terms such as *assessment, testing,* and *evaluation* are also often reduced or conflated. *Assessment* is gathering and interpreting information in order to construe knowledge, skills, and characteristics of people; *testing* is a form of assessment often found in a pencil-and-paper format and frequently involves time limits, restricted access to resources, and a limited range of acceptable responses. *Evaluation* refers to the process of judging quality, value, or worth correlated to a set of criteria (McTighe & Ferrara, 1998). *Summative* assessments describe the degree of knowledge or proficiency attained at the culmination of a program of study. Conversely, *formative* assessment provides an ongoing diagnosis to assist educators when adjusting instruction and enhancing student achievement (McTighe & Ferrara, 1998; Stiggins, 2002).

The world of education continues searching for the best way to accurately assess student achievement. A comprehensive, balanced assessment system must include long-cycle assessments (such as statewide and nationally norm-referenced assessments), mid-cycle assessments (such as district benchmark and interim classroom assessments), and short-cycle assessments (such as quality questioning and daily formative assessment processes in the classroom) (Wiliam, 2007). Accountability systems cannot be based on a single measure of performance (Sirotnik & Kimball,

1999). In fact, Susan Fuhrman (2003) criticizes the national accountability system for often tying consequences to the performance on a single measure, and Robert Linn (2000) agrees that it is more appropriate to use multiple measures of student achievement. Multiple assessment methods provide an array of lenses through which to view student work. Student interviews, collections of student work, performance assessments, and pencil-and-paper tests are all valuable strategies in evaluation of student achievement (McTighe & Ferrara, 1998; Wolf, 1993).

Long-Cycle Assessments

One key component of a balanced assessment system is the use and analysis of the data obtained from long-cycle assessment measurement tools. Many would suggest that long-cycle tools such as norm-referenced assessments (NRAs) and criterion-referenced assessments (CRAs) are created with different purposes in mind. NRAs are designed to compare students to other students within the same normed group. This student-to-student comparison, along with often-limited alignment to local curricula and a design that spreads scores across a bell curve, makes it impossible for all students taking a NRA to be successful. CRAs, on the other hand, are designed to measure students against a set of criteria. They are often directly aligned to the local curricula, and it *is* possible for all students to be successful on such assessments. As J. Richard Harsh (2000) points out, these NRAs and CRAs "direct attention to different uses and references for information and decision-making. Their combined contributions allow a more detailed and comprehensive means of assessing the outcomes of an educational program" (p. 1). It would not be appropriate to consider large-scale assessments as the only part of an assessment system.

James Popham (2003a, 2003b) and Rick Stiggins (1991) describe norm-referenced tests as *national exams* and criterion-referenced assessments as *state-specific* or *local* assessments. State assessments are usually criterion-referenced, yet they are often used in ways not originally intended, such as to make comparisons against other students or among districts and schools—a typical function of NRAs. Although both types of assessments can be used to make comparisons, the primary purpose of a NRA is to make comparisons among student groups. The primary purpose for a CRA, on the other hand, is to show specific competency levels on state or local criteria. (Note: comparisons can be made with CRAs to the NCLB index of the percentage of students at the "proficient" level, but as each state determines its own proficiency levels, one would likely have more confidence in comparisons made between results from the same exam.) Five national standardized tests are used extensively in U.S. public schools. Three major measurement companies construct state-specific tests, often along the lines of the national standardized tests (Popham, 2003b; Stiggins, 1991); in fact, "state-specific tests often perform measurement tasks that are essentially identical to those performed by national tests [norm-referenced tests]" (Popham, 2002, p. 19). In order to provide comparative interpretations, there must be sufficient score spread and few enough items for the assessment to occur within available time frames.

Most educators would characterize large-scale assessments as summative—occurring after a segment of instruction and period of time. Large-scale assessments often catch a "bad rap," as teachers feel they lie at the crux of the accountability movement. Yet these assessments are essential for informing us about how students are performing comparatively with others in similar normed groups across the state and country. This assists schools and districts with some comparative information useful for school improvement. Summative large-scale assessment provides useful data that can be used formatively, to some degree, to make large-scale comparisons—for example, to examine subgroups of student performance and trends over time. Such data should not be used *solely* to draw conclusions about individual performance. Large-scale data help us note subgroups and normed comparisons, yet aren't as effective for individual performances on criteria due to the limited item sufficiency about most content areas.

Additionally, it is important to note that some large-scale assessments do not measure achievement, but rather *aptitude*. Achievement tests are intended to measure students' knowledge and skills, whereas aptitude tests like the Scholastic Aptitude Test (SAT Reasoning Test™) and ACT® serve to predict how well a student will perform in subsequent academic settings (Popham, 2002). Both aptitude and achievement tests provide us with important information. However, many educators and parents alike are not fully aware of their intended purposes and appropriate uses. Some states use or are considering all-aptitude tests such as EXPLORE®, PLAN®, and ACT as their statewide assessment systems for middle and high schools. Unless students have had the opportunity to learn all of the content prior to these assessments, we cannot accurately use them to obtain achievement information. Using data obtained from achievement *and* aptitude assessments informs teachers as to how students are progressing based upon cognitive abilities. For example, one would expect a student who performs well on an aptitude test to also have strong achievement test results. If discrepancies between aptitude and achievement occur, delving deeper into data analysis may be warranted.

Discrepancies can have many causes. We have all heard stories of capable students who find it humorous to create artistic designs on the bubble sheet, in which case their aptitude test scores might be much higher than their achievement test scores, as aptitude tests have independent performance portions. Students who do not take large-scale assessments seriously might have more capability than shown by their performance on annual statewide assessments. Or consider the student with an extremely high aptitude whose daily achievement or performance on annual testing suggests placement in multiple study halls; this student might classify herself as a hands-on learner who does not perform well on large-scale assessments. Some students are better at performance types of assessments included in the aptitude-testing format, which may provide opportunities to demonstrate what they know and can do verbally or in a more creative format. That same student may struggle with the tediousness of a "fill in the bubble" exam. For example, a thirteen-year-old boy may be completely engaged and may demonstrate quite elevated levels of understanding when asked to show his knowledge and understanding of key elements in a novel by locating songs that depict similar story elements and putting the songs in the order with a written description of the correlation to the assigned story. This student may be unmotivated to show similar comprehension, however, if asked to simply read a passage and respond to a list of multiple-choice comprehension questions on a large-scale assessment.

Mid- and Short-Cycle Assessments

Those charged with the incredible task of teaching must clearly understand the various perspectives and uses of assessment information. Increasing teachers' assessment literacy enables them to merge technical quality into the mid- and short-cycle (daily) assessments that are administered in classrooms at the local level. Mid-cycle assessments such as a unit or chapter exam are more summative in nature and are used periodically after a segment of learning. Short-cycle assessments provide teachers with very regular information about student performance; they include quizzes, in-class work, and even daily questioning. When quality conditions are met, these teacher-based assessments become very powerful (Neill, 2003; Popham, 2003a; Roschewski, 2002; Stiggins, 2002). When teachers trust the results of mid-cycle and short-cycle assessments, they are armed with relevant and reliable findings to assist with important ongoing instructional decisions. Teacher training to develop assessment literacy is paramount for informed evaluation and is one of the first steps in the development of common and interim assessments. It is important to create common interim assessments so teachers have valid information during conversations about student work. When results on common assessments are disclosed, more meaningful applications regarding intervention responses can be shared, suggested, and observed. Interim assessments provide teachers with information at the point of instruction, rather than waiting for results typically obtained one time per year, often after the assessed students have advanced into a successive year.

In creating teacher training programs to improve local assessment skills, consider the criteria developed by the Nebraska Department of Education, in collaboration with the Buros Assessment Institute. Nebraska attempted to keep federal and statewide accountability closer to the classroom, and its groundbreaking School-based Teacher-led Assessment and Reporting System (STARS) did just that. STARS was designed to accurately reflect student achievement while maintaining the control for learning at the classroom level. This objective aligns with Jay McTighe and Steven Ferrara's (1998) suggestion that "the primary purpose of classroom assessment is to inform teaching and improve learning, not to sort and select students or to justify a grade" (p. 1).

The common thread for the STARS balanced assessment system in design and review of local systems was known as the Six Quality Criteria. These criteria include the following:

1. Local assessments reflect state standards—standards and assessments are aligned, and there is sufficiency of coverage to determine adequacy.

2. Students have the opportunity to learn the content before the assessment—there is correlation among curriculum, instruction, and assessment.

3. Assessments are free from bias—the assessments are valid.

4. Assessments are at the appropriate level—readability and expectations are congruent to the level of the learner.

5. Evidence of reliability is demonstrated—objective and subjective measures are used as appropriate to glean trustworthy evidence.

6. Mastery levels are appropriate—cut scores are statistically determined, not arbitrarily identified (Nebraska Department of Education, 2002).

These criteria represent sound characteristics of quality assessments as defined by the *Standards for Educational and Psychological Testing* (American Educational Research Association, American Psychological Association, & National Council on Measurement in Education, 1999). They were specifically designed for classroom-based or district interim assessments and infused into existing processes.

Facilitating Training Modules With Teachers

The teacher training modules described in the following seven sections cover some of the relevant topics and processes essential to a balanced assessment system that have been discussed earlier in this chapter. Those leading these modules should be well versed in technical assessment design. You might want to have an outside expert begin the modules, allowing you as a building or district leader to follow up with your own staff afterward, depending on your own and your staff's assessment knowledge and abilities, and your comfort in proceeding alone without an outside expert. Ensure that the facilitator knows the learning outcomes expected for each module. The number of attendees can vary, as long as there are groups of teachers with available work time. The principal *and* staff should attend the trainings to build a culture of collective assessment literacy.

The timeline for implementing the modules is dependent upon the assessment literacy and application levels of your staff.

One way to begin facilitating these training modules is to conduct an assessment-literacy needs assessment to determine whether staff understand the types and purposes of assessment. Consider posing some assessment-related statements and asking teachers to rate their confidence about each item on a Likert scale such as the following:

1. I know the difference between large-scale, mid-cycle, and short-cycle assessments, and I could give examples of each.

2. I understand the difference between achievement and aptitude, and I can explain the purposes and appropriate uses of assessing each to a noneducator.

3. I can clearly articulate differences between summative and formative assessment. Some sample definitions and examples of differences include:

4. I have a strong sense of data analysis and can make sense of assessment information for instructional implications.

Using a scale allows teachers to self-select their understanding and application of assessment concepts. An open-ended portion after each question that asks for rationale and examples might better reveal common understandings and misunderstandings. These can then be specifically addressed in the formal modules.

Module One: Understanding Assessment Types and Purposes

Module One can be a sixty- to ninety-minute segment. Often the facilitator will lead direct instruction about various types of assessments, their purposes, and appropriate uses of results. Throughout this session, ensure foundational understandings, but use various instructional strategies to enhance participant engagement, such as mixing and matching assessment types with purposes and uses or role playing the varied users of assessment.

Using a jigsaw process will accelerate the reading portion and allow the group to focus on the highlights of quality assessment-item construction. Module One should include topics such as:

- The differences between criterion-referenced and norm-referenced assessments and their corresponding appropriate uses

- Summative and formative assessment research and practices, including the research dialogue regarding long-, mid-, and short-cycle assessment

- Perspectives on assessment from various users

- Item-quality development or refinement

Regarding the last point, it is helpful in this first module if teachers leave with an item revision strategy they can use immediately to enhance existing assessment items; this will increase their "buy in" to the process.

Module Two: Ensuring Assessments Align With the Essential Learnings or Standards

Module Two is critical, as many of the other modules are dependent upon the quality of work completed here. The facilitator should take about thirty minutes to describe the Module Two objectives, and leave the remainder as work time for staff. Ensure that teachers complete at least one or two solid sample rubrics that define the specific knowledge and skills for each level of proficiency. These are called *proficiency level descriptions*, and the rubric created and used in assessment development prior to item writing (see table 5.1). Typically, that will take one or two hours. It may require follow-up time in other sessions for teachers to share and compare their work. The collaboration and conversations that occur during these discussions about varied levels of proficiency for an essential concept and/or skill are so valuable. Provide enough time to get the clarity needed, as it will expedite the processes used later.

Table 5.1: Sample Rubric for Proficiency Level Descriptions

Second Grade Essential Learning #1: Develops an understanding of the base-ten numeration system and place value concepts.			
Beginning	Progressing	Proficient	Advanced
Student determines the total of a group of counters (divided into groups of ten) by counting all or counting on.	Student counts by tens and then counts the ones to determine the total.	Student knows the number of tens and ones in a group of counters and automatically knows the total without needing to count.	Student can reorganize tens and ones to know the total (that is, 7 tens and 12 ones).
Student needs to count to confirm or figure out 10 plus a number (–teen numbers) or a –teen number minus 10.	Student knows 10 plus a number (–teen numbers) and knows a –teen number minus 10.	Student knows 10 more or less and 20 more or less than a number without counting.	Student knows 100 more or less and 10 more or less than a three-digit number.
Student may or may not rote count in units (2, 5, 10) but does not understand what it means to count in units.	Student understands what it means to count in units (2, 5, 10) but does not know the rote counting sequence.	Student counts in units (2, 5, 10) and in multiples of hundreds, tens, and ones with ease and accuracy.	

Source: Douglas County Public Schools, 2007; used with permission.

Before beginning this module, the facilitator of the module should ask teachers to bring two assessments to the training: (1) an assessment they use and think is high quality and (2) one for which they would like more feedback. The facilitator leads conversations of validity for one of the assessments by asking teachers to create proficiency level descriptions for the essential learning or standard(s) the assessment is measuring. These descriptions resemble rubric design, as they require teachers to consider the knowledge and skills necessary for demonstration at varied levels of proficiency. This is also a time to discuss the need to include enough high-quality items (that is, to achieve *sufficiency*) for each level of proficiency to ensure not only that students have the opportunity to express such knowledge and skill, but also that they have done so thoroughly enough to deem accurate assessment. Teachers should work together to write proficiency level descriptions; these will guide all of their alignment efforts and peer review. A technical manual can guide further efforts on site.

Module Three: Ensuring Opportunity to Learn and Developmentally Appropriate and Bias-Free Assessment

Module Three can be completed in a ninety-minute segment. This module should emphasize the importance of providing students with the opportunity to learn the content *prior* to the assessment. Although this seems obvious, facilitators and teachers in most middle and high schools have not engaged in a thorough analysis to determine whether students are afforded the opportunity to learn the content deemed essential by the district, regardless of the pathway they take through their educational experience. This is also the time to encourage teachers to peer review the assessments they are referencing, so as to validate or invalidate as a team the appropriateness of the content, format, and readability of the assessment items. Additionally, teachers should be trained on the importance of *bias awareness*: that is, teachers must be aware of how assessments that include offensive content, stereotyping, unfair representations, unfamiliar situations, or poorly written items can cause a student to perform poorly. Such assessments will not allow the instructor to accurately make valid inferences about student performances. Providing training, guided practice, and independent reviews of assessment items regarding bias is a means for further validating assessments.

Module Four: Setting Appropriate Cut Scores

Module Four will take approximately sixty minutes for the facilitator to share the key ideas and have teachers apply them to an existing assessment. During this module, teachers will usually raise questions about grading practices, a natural connection to the topic.

The module should begin with the facilitator sharing the concept and need for appropriate "cut score" development; these are not the same as the arbitrary grading scale levels used by most teachers. *Cut scores* reference the lines that separate varied levels of achievement—often mastery from nonmastery. Many methods are available, depending upon the nature of the assessment and number of students taking the assessment. However, modified Angoff or modified contrasting group methods often feel more applicable to classroom-based assessments and are user-friendly to most teachers. The *modified Angoff method* takes into account the difficulty of the items or testing opportunities and uses such information to deem a total of correct items or opportunities for each level of proficiency—that is, the range of score points or items that students must achieve to reach a specific level of achievement. A *modified contrasting group method* uses actual student performances on the assessment items; teachers use a mean or median calculation to find the points or number of items separating the varied proficiency levels.

Using the proficiency level descriptions they designed in Module Two, in this module, teachers develop cut scores using an appropriate method. Validating the scores through teacher dialogue—trying to fit their thoughtfully developed cut scores into typically illogical grading scales—often provides the most stimulating of conversations about classroom practice. It also provides a rationale for addressing evaluation practices as a team, school, and district.

Module Five: Ensuring Reliability

Module Five takes approximately thirty to sixty minutes for the direct instruction and application—less if the facilitator decides to teach about reliability more conceptually or if he or she selects only one form of reliability to emphasize and apply. Either way, it is best treated as a separate session since it can be easily confused with Module Four content. Selecting and concentrating instruction on a few appropriate methods is helpful. For immediate application and deeper understanding, provide time for teachers to apply reliability operations directly to an assessment they are currently using.

Teachers realize the complexity and the importance of designing or purchasing quality assessments. They know that reliability is a critical factor of assessment quality. They often confuse reliability with validity, however, and so Module Five focuses on defining reliability.

A *reliable* assessment interpretation measures the consistency or dependability of the assessment results. Controlling for error within an assessment is an important part of reliability, and it means that teachers are conscious about elements that may not distinguish between a student who has mastered the content and performs well from one who has not mastered the content and performs similarly (Gareis & Grant, 2008). A *valid* assessment interpretation, in turn, accurately measures the intended learning targets—a topic addressed in Module Two. In Module Five, the facilitator explains appropriate reliability methods for the type and nature of the assessment.

One way to think about the difference between validity and reliability is to imagine a target with a bullseye that represents the learning goal. If an assessment is neither valid nor reliable, student learning "arrows" will be distributed at random all over the target. If it is reliable but not valid, the student learning arrows will cluster in one spot—but the wrong spot! Student performance will be consistent (that is, reliable), but it will not have met the learning goal, because the assessment was not a valid test of the learning goal. When the assessment is both reliable and consistent, all the student arrows will cluster at the bullseye, showing that students consistently demonstrate learning of the selected goal.

We have already addressed the importance of making class-room-based assessments free from bias, developmentally appropriate, and with sufficient items for making a judgment about a student's performance. Therefore, we have already worked very hard to ensure a more reliable assessment. Decision consistency and split half are two additional reliability methods that work well for classroom-based or district interim assessments. *Decision consistency* requires teachers to compare two equivalent assessment events to see if they have achieved consistency in student performance (Cunningham, 1998). For example, a teacher might administer two forms of a test that he believes are virtually identical in nature of items and content; if so, students should perform consistently on the two forms, making the same "decisions" on the correct answers. Alternately, the teacher could "decide" (predict) how students will perform on each item on the assessment, and then compare his predictions to students' actual performance (Buckendahl, Impara, & Plake, 2004; Green, Camilli, & Elmore, 2006). In this example, it is imperative that teachers know their students and the content well in order to use a prediction of performance prior to the actual administration, as the prediction and the performance each count as one "decision." To evaluate whether consistency has been achieved, teachers calculate the percentage of correct matches between the two events. If their predictions match the actual student responses, that is deemed a match. For example, if seven of ten student responses match between the two versions of the test or match to the teacher's prediction, the assessment's reliability would be 70 percent. Seventy percent might be the minimum acceptance of reliability.

In the *split half* method of ensuring reliability, the teacher splits the testing items in half on the assessment. For example, items 1 and 2 might be classified as virtually identical items in difficulty and format. If a student gets item 1 correct, she would be expected to get item 2 correct. Use this procedure throughout the assessment (aligning item 1 with item 2, item 3 with item 4, item 5 with item 6, and so on). The percentage of correct matches is calculated as in the decision consistency method; be sure to include enough items to create a meaningful data pool.

As a building or district leader, you may decide to calculate reliability "behind the scenes" without requiring teachers to have firsthand knowledge of various reliability types and methods and without involving students directly. You have this option if enough students are available (over fifty) and you use more student-based methods such as Kuder Richardson 20 or 21, or coefficient alpha. This is important, as these reliability methods require statistical calculations that may cause fear and anxiety for teachers concerned with the mathematical calculations. There are also inherent understandings about dichotomous (right/wrong) and polychotomous (variations) correct responses when determining appropriate uses of reliability methods. This is a complicated section that takes technical knowledge.

Module Five is also a time to discuss dependent and independent items. *Dependent* items require students to have proficiency of one portion of a question in order to be proficient on another section. Once teachers understand this complicating factor, they either write more independent items or vary points for the reliant parts of dependent items.

The last step in reliability to teach in this module is the creation of a table of specifications and the use of field-testing. A table of specifications provides specific information about the assessment, such as how much time students typically need for a certain segment, what kinds of accommodations or modifications can be appropriately made without diluting the validity of the assessment, and other pertinent information to ensure administration with fidelity.

Although this thorough process seems labor-intensive, it is really workable with teachers after they get through one assessment (particularly if they start with a common assessment).

Module Six: Using Short-Cycle Assessments

Module Six can usually be completed in forty-five to sixty minutes. Short-cycle assessments, such as daily formative assessments—quizzes, peer feedback, and classroom questioning—are the most relevant and provide the most immediate information to instructors. This module should ensure that teachers know effective questioning techniques and quality criteria for classroom-based assessments; these will produce the reliable and valid information sought.

Teachers use questioning techniques regularly. However, the importance of using higher levels of questioning is a critical assessment conversation (Wiliam, 2007). Higher levels of questioning encourage deeper critical and creative thinking during direct instruction and classroom discussions. Teachers can push their questioning to higher levels of taxonomies by offering fewer "right or wrong" responses and offering more open-ended options. Other quality questioning techniques include using proper wait time, using students' names after posing the question (rather than before), and asking students to substantiate their responses with relevant data sources.

Sharing the research about the importance of feedback for students as well as questioning effectiveness and noneffectiveness is a great opening to this module. There are many quality resources on this topic to guide learning and provide teachers with opportunities to evaluate their own questioning tendencies. Relevant authors include James Dillon (1988, 1990), Francis Hunkins (1976), Jackie Walsh and Beth Sattes (2004), and Edwin Susskind (1972).

Module Seven: Implementing Effective Evaluation

Module Seven will likely begin the first of many conversations about evaluation and can be overviewed in 90 to 120 minutes. After teachers obtain strategies for increasing the quality of mid-cycle and short-cycle assessment modes, it is appropriate to further engage in the topic of effective evaluation. Much has been written on this topic, so many resources will provide assistance, including the works of Thomas Guskey and Jane Bailey (2000), Robert Marzano (2000), Ken O'Connor (2002), and Douglas Reeves (2000, 2002).

The facilitator can begin the session by asking teachers to share existing grading practices. Next, teachers can discuss rationale and action steps for using standards-based evaluation and systems that support consistency and coherence throughout the building and the district. Provide teachers with other examples of standards-based report cards or gradebooks, and connect their grading expectations to the proficiency level descriptions discussed in Module Two to further these important conversations.

Structures for Effective Assessment Conversations

The work of the assessment leader is not done after the modules are complete. Effective assessment demands a setting in which teachers have opportunities to work collaboratively—to establish sound and shared visions of curricula and clear instructional goals, and a setting with comprehensive schoolwide systems for evaluating and reporting student performance (Wolf, 1993). Teachers should be directly involved in assessment activities— embedding assessments in their instruction, scoring the assessments, evaluating inter-rater reliability, and discussing standards for good student work with colleagues, parents, and students (Lewis, 1996). Teachers are not automatically good writers or evaluators of tests, however, so support structures—planned opportunities for professional discourse—are essential (Lewis, 1996). Otherwise, poorly developed and implemented standards and assessments will likely become a distraction and source of frustration (Gandal & Vranek, 2001).

As educators collaborate, they often realize that a few multiple-choice items are only one of many ways to assess student achievement, and as a result, performance assessments are gaining momentum in many states: "open-ended alternative assessment formats, such as performance-based assessment and portfolio assessment, evaluate students more equitably and ultimately improve student learning in the classroom" (Mills, 1996, p. 2344). Popham (2002) concurs and contends that incompatible missions exist when norm-referenced tests are used to evaluate schools: "Our chief concern should be determining the quantity and quality of what students have learned" (p. 19). When decision makers rely too heavily upon tests with the purpose of providing relative scores, objective data on what students have actually learned takes a backseat to comparative data. According to Popham (2003b), the reason for this problem is the necessary score spread in a norm-referenced test (the bell curve), which "leads to the creation of standardized achievement tests that do a dismal job of measuring how much students have learned in school" (p. 19). Without effective classroom assessment, it is virtually impossible for teachers to know whether or not students are learning what is important for them to learn. McTighe and Ferrara (1998) explain classroom assessment purposes well: "Fairness in classroom assessment refers to giving all students an equal chance to show what they know and can do" (p. 8).

Reculturing for Quality Assessment

The seven modules in this chapter are based on a thorough literature review on the topics of assessment, accountability, and change. Writer Michael Fullan (1991) discusses the role of the individual within a system undergoing reform in his book *The New Meaning of Educational Change*. Fullan points to two types of reform: restructuring and reculturing. *Restructuring* is the sort of reform that provokes a change of the administrative process, but does not affect the foundation of classroom teaching and learning in the schools where it has been introduced. *Reculturing*, on the other hand, is a change in the total environment of the organization that creates a different way for people to perform their job. Therefore, reculturing massages the unique traits of individual teachers in such a manner that it impacts the teaching and learning core of the school. John Flett and John Wallace (2002) surmise from this research that "mandated curriculum reform at the classroom level is difficult to effect due to the considerable autonomy afforded teachers" (p. 330).

Classroom teachers' level of autonomy, their growth in professional development, and their everyday instructional decisions in the classroom are important dynamics in today's world of high-stakes mandated testing. The individual teacher's decision to develop as a professional or not, to understand assessment or not, to follow the curriculum or not, to teach to the test or not, or simply follow his or her own path plays a major role in the assessment and accountability movement. In the end, Sandra Cimbricz (2002) summarizes the impact of teachers on the assessment movement when she writes that the "influence of state mandated testing depends on how teachers interpret the testing and use it to guide their actions" (p. 1).

The idea that accountability alone can improve student achievement has been challenged; moreover, accountability systems provide no prescription for improvement (Hanushek & Raymond, 2001). No Child Left Behind puts a premium on testing but may not have any real effect on student learning. James Harvey (2003) asserts that it is "easier to talk about test scores than to talk about learning" (p. 20). A criticism of large-scale assessment driven reform is that schools are held accountable in areas they cannot control (Ramirez, 1999). Assessments take into account factors not associated with the specific school being measured for accountability. Betty Steffy and Fenwick English (1997) state that 89 percent of the variance on the National Assessment of Educational Progress could be attributed to number of parents living in the home, education of the parents, community type, and the state poverty rate. Fuhrman (2003) refers to holding students to a common level of performance as a status score that "reflects the students' background as much as it does any learning that took place in the year of testing" (p. 3). Harvey (2003) is also critical of the requirements of NCLB and concludes that the federal accountability model will "run up against the universal challenges of race, class and poverty" (p. 18).

Knowing that national normed scores are flawed or only a piece of the picture, principals must focus on developing teacher capacity to improve local assessments and teacher understanding of national assessments. Building leaders must understand the value of all types of assessments, when used according to their intended purposes. It is even more important to put our time and energy into those types of assessments that show the greatest gains for student achievement, namely those classroom-based common assessments. A thorough blending of long-cycle, mid-cycle, and daily assessments creates the comprehensive portfolio teachers need to make instructional decisions that lead to successful learning environments.

References and Resources

American Educational Research Association, American Psychological Association, & National Council on Measurement in Education. (1999). *Standards for educational and psychological testing.* Washington, DC: American Psychological Association.

Bandalos, D. L. (2004). Can a teacher-led state assessment system work? *Educational Measurement, 23*(2), 33–40.

Brown, F. G. (1983). *Principles of educational and psychological testing* (3rd ed.). New York: Holt, Rinehart & Winston.

Brown, S. M., & Walberg, H. J. (1993). Motivational effects on test scores of elementary students. *Educational Researcher, 86*(3), 133–136.

Buckendahl, C. W., Impara, J. C., & Plake, B. S. (2004). A strategy for evaluating district developed assessments for state accountability. *Educational Measurement, 23*(2), 15–23.

Cimbricz, S. (2002). State-mandated testing and teachers' beliefs and practice. *Educational Policy Analysis Archives, (10)*2, 1–14. Accessed at http://epaa.asu.edu/epaa/v10n2.html on November 18, 2008.

Commission on Instructionally Supportive Assessment. (2001, October). *Building tests to support instruction and accountability: A guide for policymakers.* Los Angeles: Author.

Cunningham, G. K. (1998). *Assessment in the classroom: Constructing and interpreting texts.* London: Routledge.

Dillon, J. T. (1984). Research on questioning and discussion. *Educational Leadership, 42*(3), 50–56.

Dillon, J. T. (1988). *Questioning and teaching: A manual of practice.* London: Routledge.

Dillon, J. T. (1990). *The practice of questioning.* London: Routledge.

Douglas County Public Schools. (2007). *CIA guide.* Accessed at https://its-csnap01.dcsdk12.org/stdWeb/cia_browser/cia_browser.aspx on May 18, 2009.

Flett, J., & Wallace, J. (2002). Change dilemmas for classroom teachers: Curricular reform at the classroom level. *International Journal for Educational Reform, 11*(4), 309–333.

Fuhrman, S. (2003, September). Redesigning accountability systems for education. *CPRE Policy Briefs,* 1–9.

Fullan, M. (1991). *The new meaning of educational change.* New York: Teachers College.

Gandal, M., & Vranek, J. (2001, September). Standards: Here today, here tomorrow. *Educational Leadership,* 7–13.

Gareis, C., & Grant, L. (2008). *Teacher-made assessments: How to connect curriculum, instruction, and student learning.* Larchmont, NY: Eye on Education.

Green, J. L., Camilli, G., & Elmore, P. B. (Eds.). (2006). *Handbook of complementary methods in education research* (3rd ed.). Mahwah, NJ: Lawrence Erlbaum Associates.

Guskey, T. R., & Bailey, J. M. (2000). *Developing grading and reporting systems for student learning.* Thousand Oaks, CA: Corwin.

Hanushek, E., & Raymond, M. (2001). The confusing world of educational accountability. *National Tax Journal, 54*(2), 365–384.

Harsh, J. R. (2000). The forest, trees, branches and leaves, revisited—norm, domain, objective and criterion-referenced assessments for educational assessment and evaluation. *Association for Measurement and Evaluation in Guidance, 43,* 1–16.

Harvey, J. (2003). The matrix reloaded. *Educational Leadership, 61*(3), 18–21.

Hunkins, F. P. (1976). *Involving students in questioning.* Boston: Allyn & Bacon.

Hunkins, F. P. (1995). *Teaching thinking through effective questioning* (2nd ed.). Norwood, MA: Christopher-Gordon.

Klingner, J. K., Vaughn, S., & Boardman, A. (2007). *Teaching reading comprehension to students with learning disabilities.* New York: Guilford.

Lewis, A. C. (1996). Making sense of assessment. *School Administrator, 53*(11), 8–12.

Linn, R. (2000). Assessments and accountability. *Educational Researcher, 29*(2), 4–16.

Linn, R. (2003, September 19). Task force seeks early end to exam. *Salt Lake Tribune,* p. B3.

Linn, R., Baker, E., & Betebenner, D. (2002). Accountability systems: Implications of requirements of the No Child Left Behind Act of 2001. *Educational Researcher, 31*(6), 3–16.

Marzano, R. J. (2000). *Transforming classroom grading.* Alexandria, VA: Association for Supervision and Curriculum Development.

McTighe, J., & Ferrara, S. (1998). *Assessing learning in the classroom* (2nd ed.). Washington, DC: National Education Association.

Mills, S. S. (1996). Classroom assessment format and its potential impact on student learning: Implications for school reform and equal educational opportunity (Doctoral dissertation, University of California, Los Angeles, 1996). *Dissertation Abstracts International, 57(06A),* 2344.

Nebraska Department of Education. (2002). *School-based teacher-led assessment and reporting system: A summary.* Lincoln, NE: Author.

Neill, M. (2003). High stakes, high risk. *American School Board Journal, 190*(2), 18–21.

O'Connor, K. (2002). *How to grade for learning: Linking grades to standards* (2nd ed.). Glenview, IL: Pearson Education.

Plake, B. S., & Impara, J. C. (2000). *Technical quality rubric for Nebraska's district performance ratings.* Lincoln, NE: Buros Center for Testing.

Plake, B. S., Impara, J. C., & Buckendahl, C.W. (2004). Technical quality criteria for evaluating district assessment portfolios used in the Nebraska STARS. *Educational Measurement, 23*(2), 10–14.

Popham, W. J. (2002). Right task, wrong tool. *American School Board Journal, 189*(2), 18–22.

Popham, W. J. (2003a). *Test better, teach better: The instructional role of assessment.* Alexandria, VA: Association for Supervision and Curriculum Development.

Popham, W. J. (2003b). Trouble with testing: Why standards-based assessment doesn't measure up. *American School Board Journal, 190*(2), 14–17.

Ramirez, A. (1999). Assessment driven reform: The emperor still has no clothes. *Phi Delta Kappan, 81*(3), 204–208.

Reeves, D. B. (2000). *101 questions and answers about standards, assessment, and accountability.* Englewood, CO: Advanced Learning.

Reeves, D. B. (2002). *The daily disciplines of leadership: How to improve student achievement, staff motivation, and personal organization.* San Francisco: Jossey-Bass.

Roschewski, P. (2002). *Promising practices, processes, and leadership strategies: Building quality local assessment—An executive summary.* Lincoln: Nebraska Department of Education.

Roschewski, P. (2004). History and background of Nebraska's School-based Teacher-led Assessment and Reporting System (STARS). *Educational Measurement, 23*(2), 7–9.

Steffy, B., & English, F. (1997). *Curriculum and assessment for world-class schools.* Lancaster, PA: Rowman & Littlefield.

Sirotnik, K. A., & Kimball, K. (1999). Standards for standards-based accountability systems. *Phi Delta Kappan, 81*(3), 209–214.

Stiggins, R. J. (1991). Facing the challenges of a new era of educational assessment. *Applied Measurement in Education, 4*(4), 263–273.

Stiggins, R. J. (1995). Professional development: The key to a total quality assessment environment. *NASSP Bulletin, 79*(573), 11–19.

Stiggins, R. J. (2002). Assessment crisis: The absence of assessment for learning. *Phi Delta Kappan, 83*(10), 758–765.

Susskind, E. C. (1972). *Questioning and curiosity in the elementary school classroom.* Ann Arbor, MI: University Microfilms. (ERIC Document Reproduction Service No. ED049030)

Susskind, E. (1979). Encouraging teachers to encourage children's curiosity: A pivotal competence. *Journal of Clinical Child Psychology, 8,* 101–106.

Walsh, J., & Sattes, B. (2004). *Quality questioning: Research-based practice to engage every learner.* Thousand Oaks, CA: Corwin.

Wiliam, D. (2007). Content *then* process: Teacher learning communities in the service of formative assessment. In D. Reeves (Ed.), *Ahead of the curve: The power of assessment to transform teaching and learning* (pp. 183–204). Bloomington, IN: Solution Tree.

Wolf, K. P. (1993). From informal to informed assessment: Recognizing the role of the classroom teacher. *Journal of Reading, 36*(7), 518–523.

PART TWO

Collecting, Interpreting, and Reporting Data

WILLIAM M. FERRITER

 A National Board Certified Teacher, Bill Ferriter has been honored as a North Carolina Regional Teacher of the Year. Bill has worked as a contractor for Pearson Education Solutions, designing professional development courses that empower educators with twenty-first-century skills. His trainings include the creative use of blogs, wikis, and podcasts in the classroom; the role of iTunes in teaching and learning; and the power of digital moviemaking for learning and expression. Bill has also developed schoolwide technology rubrics and surveys that identify student and staff digital proficiency at the building level. Bill has published articles in the *Journal of Staff Development, Educational Leadership,* and *Threshold.* Starting in September, 2009, he will write a column on technology in the classroom for *Educational Leadership.* His blog, the Tempered Radical, earned Best Teacher Blog of 2008 from Edublogs. He is a contributor to *The Teacher as Assessment Leader* (Solution Tree, 2009).

SIX

Plug Us In, Please: Using Digital Tools for Data Collection

William M. Ferriter

Teaching has long been an isolated profession in which individual practitioners made decisions about the direction of their lessons based on intuition rather than evidence. Relying on nothing more than hard-won experience—and cultural norms that leave professional actions unquestioned—many classroom teachers inadvertently fell into comfortable patterns where data played almost no role in selecting instructional practices or in identifying students in need of differentiated instruction.

Pushed by new principals and policies, however, most educators have jumped feet-first in recent years into data-driven decision making—but even the most motivated and capable often fail miserably and walk away frustrated. So what goes wrong? And more importantly, how can school leaders find a way to make sure that the same unfortunate circumstance doesn't befall the professionals working in their buildings?

Data collapse, the complete failure of data-driven practices to take hold in a school despite the honest efforts of administrators and educators alike, is influenced by many factors. First, experienced teachers have been allowed to work for years without having to focus on results. They may have well-established norms defining the scope of their professional responsibilities, but those norms often have little to do with outcomes. Teachers spend their time and attention focused on teaching rather than learning, a practice only reinforced by leaders who haven't established or enforced clear expectations that data should be used to drive school-based decisions.

Second, teachers and teams often try to tackle data with almost no training. Even educators who are successful by conventional definitions have rarely been formally prepared to analyze learning results; what's more, pre-service education and in-service professional development programs have only recently started offering meaningful coursework in data-driven decision making.

Most importantly, though, data collapse occurs when schools fail to provide their teachers with the time and the tools to collect, manipulate, and analyze data effectively. With good intentions and limited budgets, leaders try to introduce straightforward and affordable tools such as data notebooks and data walls to faculty decision-making processes. While data notebooks and walls have been embraced as an accomplished practice by many experts interested in seeing the work of schools become more systematic and targeted (Halverson, Prichett, & Watson, 2007), there is a simple flaw in this plan: it is impossible to overestimate just how much energy data notebooks and walls can require of teachers in order to be effective. Equipped with nothing more than three-ring binders, colored dividers, and an endless supply of poster board, pencils, and sticky notes, faculties begin disaggregating the results of common assessments given to groups ranging from fifty to four hundred students. Increasing complexity is added as teachers attempt to track performance by student, subgroup, and skill—three logical steps taken by any educator seeking actionable information to shape instruction. Eventually, the process of collecting and recording data becomes too time-consuming to be seen as valuable by teachers who are already overwhelmed by the new demands of their work.

Digital Tools for Formative Assessment

The good news for any school working to ensure that outcomes play a more important role in day-to-day decision making is that a wide range of efficient digital data solutions can be adopted tomorrow. This chapter will explore how four different schools and systems are using districtwide formative assessments, student responders, handheld computers, and spreadsheet applications like Microsoft Excel to make the critical steps of data collection and manipulation easier. Then, we'll connect the research done by Bob Marzano about the impact that monitoring and feedback have on student achievement to digital data solutions. Finally, we'll review the steps school leaders must take in order to ensure that new electronic tools can facilitate meaningful work in their buildings.

Districtwide Formative Assessment Software

When they first learned that their district (the Wake County Public School System in Raleigh, North Carolina) had invested in an online software application known as Blue Diamond that was designed to deliver regular common formative assessments to students in math and reading, sixth-grade language arts and social studies teachers Mike Hutchinson and Emily Swanson were skeptical. "Something just didn't seem right about promoting multiple-choice tests as a responsible form of assessment in a content area like ours that isn't black and white," explains Swanson. "Can you really tell if a child understands an author's point of view from nothing more than a bubble sheet?" (E. Swanson, personal communication, December 10, 2008)

The Blue Diamond assessments were designed to be given every three weeks and included short reading selections followed by seven to ten multiple-choice questions tied to the skills covered in North Carolina's Standard Course of Study. To Hutchinson, these were just another excuse to push social studies further to the side. "I'm a social studies guy," he says, "so I like to protect the time that our students spend studying the world. . . . What's worse, the original plan had us delivering the assessments to students on the computers in our lab. There was no way that was going to work—our network was bound to crash more than once!" (J. M. Hutchinson, personal communication, December 10, 2008)

Swanson and Hutchinson's worst fears were realized as their school began administering the district's common reading assessments in the spring of 2005. Unaccustomed to the demands of up to a hundred new users working simultaneously online, the school's network failed miserably, freezing students out of the required assessments. Answers were lost, teachers grew frustrated, and students sat bored. "It couldn't have been any worse," says Swanson. "We didn't believe in multiple-choice tests to begin with, we couldn't get the computers to work when we went to the lab, and we found the reading selections and questions to be almost impossible for our students. Nothing seemed easy!"

Understanding that common formative assessments were essential to the highly functioning learning teams that their building was trying to create, though, Hutchinson and Swanson refused to give up on Blue Diamond. "It wasn't perfect," explains Hutchinson, "but it was at least one common assessment that we didn't have to create or grade—and it certainly helped to target our teaching. By looking at the questions on each of the upcoming exams, we knew which reading skills we were supposed to be emphasizing in class."

Better yet, these districtwide common formative assessments allowed Swanson and Hutchinson's learning team to collect and analyze student learning data quickly. After scanning pencil-and-paper responses into a central computer (to avoid overwhelming the network), teachers could generate any number of charts and graphs showing the performance of entire classes or individual students. "I've been using Blue Diamond for the past four years now, and I'm not even sure I've figured out all of the different ways that you can disaggregate student performance!" says Swanson.

"You can set benchmarks and sort your classes into three different categories: above, at, or below standard. You can compare the performance of your students against the performance of other teachers in your school or district. You can track mastery by individual objective, get item analyses to see which skills posed students the most trouble as a group, and see the progress of a student or a class over time. It's really pretty amazing to get that much information without being crushed by paperwork. I use it all the time to figure out which of my students need extra help." Teachers can often intuitively identify which students need extra help in general, but often only the most accomplished and experienced have a sophisticated understanding of exactly which skills have been mastered by which students at any given time. Technology makes fine-grained actions and decisions possible for every teacher.

"And our team has started to use it to figure out which teachers are doing great work around individual skills," adds Hutchinson. "We really are all about figuring out what works with our kids, and by looking at our Blue Diamond numbers, we can spot trends in our teaching that we wouldn't have noticed before. In fact, we started showing our students how to annotate text while reading this year because we noticed that the teacher whose students always seemed to outperform the rest of the kids was an annotation junkie. If it was working with her classes, it's likely to work with ours too."

While they both believe that the common formative assessment tool provided by their district has benefited their work immensely—guiding their instruction, providing quick common evidence of individual students in need of extra help, spotlighting mastery of specific objectives and skills—Swanson and Hutchinson are adamant that assessment *can't end* with three prepackaged digital quizzes a month. "The best assessments that we use are the ones we write ourselves," says Swanson, "because when we write our own assessments, we have these really amazing conversations about what we expect our students to learn—and those conversations are incredibly valuable for our own growth as a team. If we only used Blue Diamond for common assessments, we'd never learn more about teaching and learning—and learning about teaching and learning is exciting."

"But if it hadn't been for Blue Diamond, I don't know if we'd ever have gotten around to taking action for individual students," adds Hutchinson. "While I love the assessments that we write ourselves, I also love knowing that every three weeks I'm going to get immediate feedback on the skills that my kids have mastered combined with lists of students that need some extra help. Our district's common formative assessment tool helps me to make informed decisions and saves me time all at once. It's definitely not as bad as I thought it would be!"

Student Response Systems

Located in Richmond, Virginia, the Henrico County Public School System (HCPS) has long been a leader in the use of technology for teaching and learning. Most recently, HCPS has been studying the impact that interactive whiteboards paired with student response systems have on the teaching/learning process. Specifically interested in determining whether "the use of the interactive whiteboards with responder software would allow for more frequent monitoring of student learning and allow for quick adjustments to the teaching process based on this monitoring," district leaders paired teachers in twenty classrooms—ranging from first-grade reading to high school chemistry—with whiteboards and sets of student responders and then "matched" each interactive classroom with a similar classroom that did not have access to new technologies (Henrico County Schools, 2007, p. 1).

All participants were surveyed and teachers in interactive classrooms were observed at the beginning of Henrico's study, measuring their ability to monitor student learning and to make adjustments to instruction based on evidence. This early work with teachers in both types of classrooms provided a baseline for comparisons that researchers later used to document changes in assessment practices as new technologies were incorporated into instruction. Next, every participating teacher was observed on six different occasions, with researchers collecting data on the number of times that teachers used questioning to assess student learning and changed course based on monitoring (Henrico County Schools, 2007).

What researchers found in Henrico County was interesting: HCPS teachers paired with interactive whiteboards and class sets of student responders asked more questions—to monitor the learning of one student, to monitor the learning of several students, and to monitor learning of entire classes—than their colleagues working without new technologies. More importantly, teachers in interactive classrooms asked more questions at the application, analysis, synthesis, and evaluation levels of Bloom's taxonomy than their peers (Henrico County Schools, 2007).

Demonstrating higher levels of confidence in their ability to monitor student learning than co-participants in classrooms without student responders, teachers in Henrico's interactive classrooms also reported that ongoing formative measures of performance were easier than they'd ever imagined (Henrico County Schools, 2007). No longer was assessment a cumbersome process consuming inordinate amounts of time. Instead, it could be done quickly—which seemed to increase a teacher's willingness to ask questions in class. With immediate evidence of levels of student mastery, teachers could make more effective decisions about whether classes were ready to move forward or were in need of reteaching.

Finally, HCPS researchers found that responder technologies had a positive impact on student efforts at self-monitoring and assessment. Rather than having to wait days—or even weeks—to receive feedback about their mastery of classroom content, students were able to immediately see which questions they'd answered correctly as individuals and as an entire class. They were also able to make private comparisons between their own performance and the performance of their peers, creating a sense of transparency, excitement, and urgency often absent in more traditional classroom learning environments (Henrico County Schools, 2007).

What lessons can we learn about digital assessment tools from Henrico? First, ongoing monitoring of learning in traditional classrooms can be informal and fleeting. Teachers ask questions, give answers, and make observations hundreds of times each day without a systematic way to collect ongoing evidence about the performance of their entire class—let alone the performance of the individual students that they serve. Knowing that frequent progress monitoring is a logistical nightmare, teachers in traditional classrooms appear to ask fewer questions and tend to avoid higher-order questions requiring complex answers.

In classrooms with student responders, ongoing monitoring of learning is instant and "doable." Teachers and students alike have immediate feedback about levels of individual and collective mastery that they can use to make fluid adjustments during the course of instruction—an essential characteristic of assessment *for* learning. Teams can return to spreadsheets generated automatically by responder software to spot trends in their data and to identify students in need of remediation or enrichment—and all of this work can be done without spending hours needlessly recording results. Teacher confidence levels in their ability to monitor learning rise, resulting in regular assessment of the kinds of higher-level thinking skills that are often avoided in more traditional classrooms (Henrico County Schools, 2007).

Handheld Computers, Netbooks, and Convergence Devices

One of the most highly regarded predictive measures of reading ability in the primary grades is the DIBELS screening developed by Roland Good at the University of Oregon. At its core, the DIBELS screening is a performance assessment built around a series of one-minute student readings that teachers monitor for mastery of a number of specific reading skills—initial sound fluency, letter naming fluency, phoneme segmentation fluency, nonsense word fluency, and word use fluency. DIBELS requires teachers to test individual students at least three times a year, depending on the identified strengths and weaknesses of each child. The results of every assessment are then recorded, suggesting a future plan of action to classroom teachers (Hupert, Heinze, Gunn, Stewart, & Honey, 2007).

While schools in forty-nine states use DIBELS because of its accuracy, it can be nothing short of an intimidating data challenge for anyone administering the assessment in its pencil-and-paper form. At any given time, a teacher has to know which reading skills students are struggling with in order to select the proper subtest to deliver. Then, extensive sets of leveled reading materials are needed to ensure that students see new texts each time assessments are given. While a child is reading, mispronounced words must be carefully noted and time must be carefully kept. Finally, teachers must design a recording system that highlights progress over time. Any breakdown in this process—losing track of reading selections, failing to note progress correctly, misinterpreting results, allowing tests to run long—can limit the overall effectiveness of the DIBELS assessment.

Which is why New Mexico became one of the first states to purchase Wireless Generation's mCLASS:DIBELS software, developed in collaboration with the DIBELS authors for use on handheld computers. Over the 2003–2004 school year, almost five hundred K–3 teachers working in thirty-two Reading First schools began delivering the DIBELS test digitally (Hupert & Heinze, 2006). Assessment changed almost immediately for these teachers. Each could access class rosters directly from their hand-held devices. The Wireless Generation software then indicated the appropriate subtests and reading selections for individual students based on previous performance.

As students worked their way through reading selections, teachers used their handheld computers to note missed words. When time expired for each one-minute assessment, the number of words read correctly was automatically calculated, and a student's risk category—defining the amount of support needed to meet grade-level expectations—was automatically identified. Teachers could instantly navigate to graphs showing assessment results plotted over time against a benchmark line, indicating the likelihood that a student would reach required reading targets given current levels of performance. Once teachers synced their handhelds with school computers, results became available to other school professionals supporting the reading program (Hupert et al., 2007).

The benefits of introducing the digital version of the DIBELS in New Mexico's Reading First classrooms have been undeniable. Assessments can be administered quickly and with more consistency because teachers don't have to struggle to identify exactly which subtests students need to take or which reading selections to use. Time spent on data entry—a task that consumes teachers giving the paper-and-pencil versions of the DIBELS assessment—is eliminated, giving everyone from the classroom to the district boardroom instant access to results. Attractive charts and graphs are generated easily, making progress visual and approachable to teachers, parents, and students (Hupert et al., 2007). Teams are using the time that they save and the information that they generate to make immediate adjustments to their instructional program, to identify areas for professional development, to help parents better understand the progress of their children, and to engage students in self-assessment (Hupert & Heinze, 2006).

While New Mexico's work with handheld computers targets reading teachers in primary grades, there are broad lessons to be learned for teachers working in all subject areas and grade levels. Handhelds, including convergence devices like BlackBerries and iPhones—as well as small, portable netbook computers that offer the convenience and comfort of a nearly full keyboard and computer screen—paired with the right software applications can make formative assessment based on observations of individual students manageable. Teachers working in science classrooms with handheld devices can note student actions during lab activities. Math teachers can record successes demonstrated as students work out problems in small groups. Social studies teachers can document contributions to classroom conversations, art teachers can indicate mastery of new techniques, and physical education teachers—who observe performances every day—can identify trends in motor development.

Perhaps most importantly, however, observations collected digitally become instantly available, allowing teachers and teams to spend planning time manipulating information—looking for patterns, identifying trends, tracking progress, planning future actions—rather than trying to organize the data that they've collected. As researchers Kristin Bennett and Ann Cunningham (2007) write, "The most efficient way to capture, document, and analyze formative data on individual student performance over time requires technology, and handheld computing devices provide the most productive way to capture this data in the classroom without wasting full instructional time" (p. 2).

Spreadsheets and Pivot Tables

Parry Graham, principal at Lufkin Road Middle School in the Wake County Public School System, understands the importance of automating data streams and believes that digital tools like districtwide formative assessment systems, class sets of student responders, netbooks, and handheld computers can all play a vital role in driving the work of today's practitioner. But he's also got a budget to manage. "I'd love to give every one of my teachers a set of student responders and a handheld computer," he explains. "Those are the kinds of tools that—when used properly—can have an incredible impact on the instructional decisions of teachers and teams. I just don't have enough extra money to make that happen" (F. P. Graham, personal communication, December 3, 2008).

For Graham, then, tools that are universally available or provided by the district have become key players in the data efforts of his building. "It's not like we can just give up on data because we can't afford new equipment," he writes, "We've got to find ways to use what we have in order to do the same kinds of work that the tools we don't have can do. The best 'free' tool that we've got is Microsoft Excel, which is loaded on every machine in our entire system."

While some might argue that Excel is a program without a place in conversations about using twenty-first-century tools to collect, manipulate, and analyze student learning data, Graham disagrees. In fact, rarely a week goes by where he doesn't find a new way to use this often overlooked application to crunch a few numbers. "I'll give you a specific example," he writes. "In my school (as in many schools), minority students (particularly African American and Hispanic students) are underenrolled in advanced-level math classes. I asked my data manager to put together a spreadsheet of all the students in the building, the scores that they had received on the previous year's standardized math test, and the math course level they had been placed into, along with demographic information.

"Once I had that spreadsheet, I was able to—with just a couple clicks of the mouse—create a pivot table that broke down that aggregated data into specific subgroups. For example, if I wanted to see a list of all the sixth-grade African American students who scored at the advanced level on their fifth-grade math standardized test but were placed into basic sixth-grade math, BOOM—there it was. Now, neither my spreadsheet nor my pivot table tell me whether or not those students were placed appropriately—it's entirely possible that they were—but I was quickly able to turn a high-level trend into individual names.

"And, after I pass along my spreadsheet to the math teachers, they can use it to zero in on specific students. If the department develops a goal to increase minority representation in higher-level math classes, they can (in no more than a couple of seconds) generate a list of promising students based on standardized test scores. That's what pivot tables allow you to do—move quickly and seamlessly between the aggregated, high-level trends and the individual, disaggregated names and faces."

Introducing Excel and pivot tables to his learning teams hasn't been without its challenges for Graham. Most importantly, Excel is far less intuitive than Microsoft Word or PowerPoint—two tools that teachers have grown comfortable with—and pivot tables require a certain level of expertise to create and manipulate. Time also remains a barrier because unlike data collected by districtwide common assessments, student response systems, and handheld computers, results have to be entered into Excel by hand. For Graham, however, the alternative is even more time consuming: trying to record, manage, and analyze data in sophisticated ways using simple tools.

The bottom line is that digital tools can make data collection and management more approachable for classroom teachers. Schools that work to incorporate districtwide formative assessments, student responders, handheld computers, netbooks, and/

or spreadsheets into their feedback and monitoring systems are tapping into a powerful source for school improvement.

Relevant Theory and Research

Working as a senior scholar at McREL, an associate professor at Cardinal Stritch University in Milwaukee, and the president of Marzano Research Laboratory, Bob Marzano has spent the better part of his career attempting to identify a handful of high-impact, research-based practices for driving change in education. While K–12 practitioners and school leaders can find meaningful support in any of Marzano's many books, *What Works in Schools: Translating Research Into Action* (2003) might just be his most important title.

Effectively serving as a meta-analysis of every significant research study on achievement in the past three decades, *What Works in Schools* details the essential factors at the school, teacher, and student levels that influence the success or failure of the children in our classrooms. As Marzano writes, "My basic position is quite simple: Schools can have a tremendous impact on student achievement if they follow the direction provided by the research" (2003, pp. 4–5).

One of the most interesting findings of Marzano's research is perhaps one of the least surprising: achievement increases in environments where students receive ongoing and effective feedback about their learning. The idea that success hinges on something as simple as classrooms where teachers monitor mastery of essential outcomes and students are intimately aware of their own progress would seem obvious to most parents, principals, and practitioners. Less obvious, however, is the *degree* to which achievement is influenced by feedback. According to Marzano, when paired with individualized, challenging, and developmentally appropriate goals, effective feedback is the *second most important* school-level factor for improving student achievement.

To drive meaningful change, then, school leaders must only ask one relatively straightforward question: What does *effective* feedback look like? Does it include the interim and end-of-quarter report cards sent home by teachers? What about the dozens of tests, quizzes, homework assignments, and projects that teachers review and grade each day? Are corrections made during the course of classroom conversations, comments added to completed tasks, or words of praise offered for a job well done forms of effective feedback?

Marzano asserts that effective feedback is defined by two key characteristics: it must be (1) timely and (2) specific to the content being learned. Timely feedback is gathered and reviewed by teachers and students *during* the course of a learning experience or a period of study. Unlike summative assessments designed to serve as a *summary* of content mastery, timely feedback is formative, *informing* both teachers and students and allowing for the *formation* of new learning plans.

Feedback specific to the content being learned is tailored to the instruction actually delivered in a teacher's classroom. Schools providing feedback specific to the content being learned articulate performance measures aligned with the full range of knowledge and skills to which students are exposed. Children in schools offering feedback specific to the content being learned have a more complete understanding of their own academic strengths and weaknesses than their counterparts in traditional buildings that rely on the standardized testing of a small subset of skills defined in state or district curriculum guides as indicators of progress.

Today's teachers approach the challenge of providing effective feedback by creating quarterly assessments with their colleagues, complete with pre- and post-tests that can be used to highlight student knowledge gains. A handful of essential outcomes are identified—eliminating overwhelming curricular expectations—and rubrics are used for assessing growth over time. Report cards are redesigned—deconstructing standards and tracking student progress towards a collection of clearly defined skills and dispositions. No longer is student achievement reported in terms of ambiguous number or letter grades. Instead, student progress is measured against specific, measurable, and attainable learning targets (Marzano, 2003).

The challenge is that providing this level of feedback can be nothing short of overwhelming. While most teachers theoretically agree with Marzano that skill-level feedback is a best practice worth pursuing, the time spent collecting and manipulating results multiplies exponentially. New assessments must be written to break learning outcomes into their component parts, new data recording systems must be developed to highlight students who have mastered individual skills, and new reporting systems must be designed to make growth over time transparent.

Tomorrow's teachers will use digital tools to make this complex work manageable. Performance indicators will be stored on handheld computers, netbooks, or convergence devices used to record classroom observations of content and/or skill mastery, taking advantage of a source of sophisticated evidence long overlooked due to a lack of an efficient system of record-keeping. Teachers will flex instructional plans and assessments, using student responders to gain instant feedback on questions connected directly to *each day's learning.*

Results entered from both tools will be automatically uploaded to widely available spreadsheet or database applications—eliminating time wasted on data entry—where pivot tables will be used to spotlight patterns in mastery across grade levels, classrooms, and student subgroups. Targeted information generated from districtwide formative assessment systems will be used by teachers, teams, and/or instructional support professionals working beyond the classroom to quickly sort students in need of remediation or enrichment—and parents and students will have instant access to results, empowered as achievement allies for perhaps the first time.

To put it simply, automating data collection, recording, and reporting will allow tomorrow's teachers to spend more time doing the high-yield, knowledge-based work that they are capable of: identifying and immediately responding to learning trends in their student populations. Twenty-first-century teachers will become what Thomas Friedman (2006) calls "The Great Synthesizers, The Great Explainers, and The Great Leveragers," bringing together disparate bits of information from a range of digital sources to make new discoveries and taking action based on their findings. Their work, like the work of the best leveragers in the business world described by EDS futurist Jeff Wacker in *The World Is Flat*, will center on using automated data and information to "not only catch a problem, but quickly come up with a solution that will fix the problem for good, so it will never happen again" (Friedman, 2006, p. 288).

Feedback to both practitioners and students in schools embracing digital tools for data collection and analysis will finally meet essential expectations for timeliness and specificity because the barriers posed by traditional assessment and reporting practices will be removed. No longer will motivated teachers walk away from professional behaviors that they believe in because of the labor-intensive demands of data. Instead, their assessment efforts will be defined by fluid responses to existing performance.

Recommendations

So, what will this transition take? Nothing more than a foundational belief on the part of school leaders that the human capacity of classroom teachers is wasted when teams spend inordinate amounts of time recording and manipulating student learning results, and a commitment to the kinds of tools and training that can make inefficient practices obsolete.

Effective feedback systems are essential to the success of high-performing schools. An effective feedback system targets the collective efforts of teachers, provides insights into the strengths and weaknesses of individual students, and highlights instructional strategies that are working. Investing in and mastering the use of tools like districtwide formative assessments, student responders, handheld computers, netbooks, and spreadsheets can make the process of collecting, analyzing, and reporting learning results efficient and nonthreatening for learning teams.

Following are several suggestions to guide school leaders interested in seeing digital tools become a part of the assessment practices of their buildings.

Don't Forget That Digital Tools Are Not Guaranteed Tickets to Data Confidence

One of the biggest mistakes made by school leaders considering digital options for data collection and reporting is holding on to the flawed belief that *tools alone* will improve the assessment practices in their buildings. "If we provide every teacher with a handheld or set of student responders," the thinking goes, "then they'll be data whiz kids in no time."

The reality is that most teachers—including those with handhelds and student responders in their classrooms—are far from being data whiz kids! While they often have a deep and meaningful understanding of the strengths and weaknesses of the students that they serve, they struggle to align assessments with the skills and concepts being measured. They lack formalized processes for deconstructing learning targets and for identifying essential outcomes worth measuring. They're not sure how to make sense of the stream of information that they collect, and focusing attention on schoolwide priorities can be overwhelming.

Even worse, many teachers—particularly those working in schools serving high percentages of students living in poverty—have become intimidated by data. Assessment means evaluation. Numbers are used as cudgels to publicly shame schools (Perlstein, 2007). Confusing terms like *regression to the mean, p-value,* and *standard deviation* fill documents littered with *raw scores, cut scores,* and *scale scores* that are used to single out schools for celebration and ridicule. Statisticians, economists, and university professors offer findings after conducting extensive studies involving thousands of students in hundreds of districts, sending the message that data are best left to those with extensive time, training, and education.

As a result, becoming a data-driven organization requires more than an investment in new tools. It also requires an investment in teachers. Rebuild confidence by redefining data. Set aside complicated reports, and show teams practical examples of action steps that can be taken from evidence collected at the classroom level. Train teacher leaders in each grade level and department to serve as conversation starters and data workhorses. Remind teachers that data doesn't have to mean multiple-choice testing by reintroducing—and supporting the use of—alternative sources of information about student learning.

Several simple successes are going to need to come quickly before your teachers will buy in to the idea that data are worth embracing, and these successes depend on far more than nifty sets of new tools.

Select Tools That Reflect Your Core Beliefs on Instruction and Assessment

High-functioning learning communities are always driven by the core beliefs detailed in their mission, vision, values, and goals statements. Working together, parents, principals, and teachers define priorities that carry great implications for instruction and assessment. Decisions in buildings where students are well schooled in a core curriculum that emphasizes basic skills are likely to be significantly different from those in student-centered buildings encouraging children to pursue areas of deep personal interest (DuFour & Eaker, 1998).

Be sure to reflect on your building's core beliefs when selecting digital tools to introduce to teachers. Start by imagining what you'd most like to see happening in your classrooms. Do you want teachers engaged in ongoing conversations with students, collecting information from informal observations and interactions? If so, handheld computers with survey applications would enhance the feedback systems in your buildings. Are you asking teams to make fluid and ongoing instructional adjustments based on daily evidence of understanding? Then student response systems would provide immediate, actionable feedback to your teachers. Is consistency of assessment across entire grade levels important to you? Then schoolwide formative assessment software might be worth pursuing.

Consider writing a detailed scenario describing the feedback systems and assessment decisions of a fictional teacher or team, effectively translating your vision into action. Then, use your scenario as a guide when reviewing the features of new digital tools, speaking with sales representatives, or selecting specific products and programs to pursue. Stories help to make complex ideas concrete—and will keep you focused on the core beliefs of your learning community when making decisions about the kinds of digital tools that can best influence feedback and assessment in your classrooms. (Visit **go.solution-tree.com/assessment** to download a story for staff discussion.)

Prepare For and Provide Ongoing Technical Support

Building leaders interested in introducing new digital tools to their teachers need to face an uncomfortable reality: despite investing millions into technology upgrades, instruction in today's classrooms remains largely unchanged. In many schools, textbooks still drive curricular decisions, whole-class instruction continues to be the norm, and the line for the photocopier is as long as ever. As technology changes the face of fields ranging from economics to the environment, education remains resistant to digital innovation (Rhode Island Department of Elementary and Secondary Education, 2006).

Ask any classroom teacher why new technologies fail to gain a foothold, and she'll give you a decidedly straightforward answer: it's hard to believe in digital tools when they're always broken. In conversations with teachers in dozens of districts across the United States, it has become apparent that unlike businesses, which systematically invest significant resources into developing the infrastructure and human capacity necessary to support emergent uses of digital tools, schools struggle to find the resources to ensure that technology can be used without fail. Often, setup and repair duties at the school level fall to classroom teachers with a personal interest in electronics or to an educational professional working beyond the classroom—regardless of aptitude or experience—who has flexible hours during the school day to troubleshoot digital dilemmas. Budget constraints paired with limited time and expertise mean that applications are rarely updated and broken devices are rarely replaced, resulting in mismatched sets of poorly maintained equipment running out-of-date software.

For teachers, this means that technology is unpredictable at best—and completely unreliable at worst. Carefully planned lessons are ruined when the Internet crashes. Multiple students are forced to share the same machine after half the desktops in the computer lab refuse to start. Firewalls block access to unexpected sites. Batteries die on laptops as groups collaborate around shared assignments. Applications freeze on machines with insufficient memory. Usage demands on the school's network slow browsing to a crawl—and each time technology fails, the digital confidence of teachers wavers. "I'm not going to bother using new tools," they argue. "They're always more hassle than they're worth."

Building digital resilience requires careful planning before making digital purchases. Be sure to budget for professional development designed to introduce teachers to the features and flaws of any device, program, or software that you select. Effective training should prepare teachers to troubleshoot common problems and highlight a handful of high-value applications that teams can master immediately. Consider using free communication and collaboration tools like blogs or wikis as forums for sharing implementation successes across your entire organization. Incorporate "tech success" minutes in faculty meetings, spotlighting teams with innovative ideas. By providing teachers with multiple opportunities to see how new digital tools are changing instruction and assessment in your building, you will increase the likelihood that effective practices spread and confidence grows.

Confidence depends on much more than training, however. It also depends on a reasonable guarantee that new software and tools will be maintained and updated properly, be repaired as needed, and remain useful throughout their life cycle. Understanding the total cost of ownership of the digital solutions that you are exploring includes planning for future scalability, recognizing the impact that chosen products will have on your existing server and storage capacity, and finding tools compatible with current applications being used by your teachers (Rust & Stegman, 2003). Ask yourself if new devices have the potential to grow with your organization. How will you replace units over time? Will extra equipment or add-ons be needed—or desired—to take full advantage of the potential in your purchases? Are there hidden costs—licensing fees, software requirements, ongoing upgrades—that you need to consider?

By earmarking 30 percent of your technology budget for training, repair, and support—even if it requires scaling back on initial plans for implementation—you'll increase the chances that your technology-enhanced assessment efforts are a success.

Remember That Time Is Another Powerful Tool

Building data literacy in your faculty, investing in solutions that align with your community's core values, and ensuring that technical glitches don't cripple your attempts to change assessment are essential first steps toward improving the quality of feedback offered in your school, but none of these steps can have a significant impact on learning alone. Once you've provided teams with the training, tools, and tech support necessary to collect and manipulate data, you need to begin finding time for teachers to take action. Results, after all, are meaningless if they aren't used as catalysts for meaningful change.

Teachers need two specific time commitments in order to take advantage of data collected by digital tools. First, they need time built into the school calendar to analyze learning. No matter how easy new investments make it to collect and report data, heavy lifting is required to answer the question, What does this all mean? Teachers focused on results will have powerful conversations with one another about the characteristics of effective instruction, redesign the work that they are doing together, and polish their understandings of the teaching-learning transaction. New questions will be asked, new answers will be sought, and new discoveries will be made (Graham & Ferriter, 2008).

Enabling this work requires school leaders to redefine professional development. Principals must believe that the shared thinking generated by their teachers and teams is a valuable form of meaningful learning. To overlook the importance of time for collective reflection is to overlook the most important "product" of data-driven decision making.

Once teachers have answered the question, What does this all mean? they'll naturally begin to ask, "So, what do we do next?" Using new tools to identify learning trends and students in need of remediation and enrichment enables systematic follow up—and systematic follow up requires school leaders to rethink the typical school day. Accomplished principals encourage teams of teachers to regroup students across grade levels and classrooms, allowing some teachers to work with small clusters of students while others offer whole-class lessons to larger numbers of students who have mastered essential content. They eliminate traditional morning, lunch, and afternoon duties for practitioners by using noninstructional personnel to supervise students, thus creating opportunities for short remediation or enrichment sessions throughout the school day. They prioritize academics for struggling students, rethinking the menu of electives offered by their buildings and services offered by support staff (Graham & Ferriter, 2008).

When accomplished principals encourage innovative approaches to training, scheduling, instructional delivery, and staffing, they ensure that investments in digital tools for data collection and reporting are not wasted.

Conclusions

Conversations around assessment and feedback have changed in dramatic ways as schools scramble to respond to the expectations of the federal government's No Child Left Behind legislation. Understanding that teachers have the greatest impact on student achievement, decision-makers are pushing for real change in the classroom. No longer is it enough for intuition to drive action. Instead, concrete evidence collected on an ongoing basis and shared with parents and students must form the foundation of any plan for improvement.

There is no question that efforts to systematically identify and intervene on behalf of struggling students are forcing teams and teachers to work in new and exciting ways. In many places, however, these efforts haven't resulted in significant change because teachers and teams continue to struggle to master data analysis.

Relying on simple practices to do complicated work, their actions are simultaneously well intentioned yet ineffective.

To Richard Elmore, these frustrations are evidence of a failure on the part of decision-makers working beyond the classroom. He writes:

> Accountability must be a reciprocal process. For every increment of performance I demand from you, I have an equal responsibility to provide you with the capacity to meet that expectation. Likewise, for every investment you make in my skill and knowledge, I have a reciprocal responsibility to demonstrate some new increment in performance. . . . At the moment, schools and school systems are not designed to provide support or capacity in response to demands for accountability. (Elmore, 2002, p. 5)

The first step that you can take to ensure that the teachers in your school are prepared to meet new demands for accountability is to invest in the kinds of tools, time, and training that can make meaningful feedback and ongoing, targeted assessment possible. To do otherwise is to limit the overall success of your organization—and to shortchange the students sitting in your classrooms.

For a detailed examination of specific digital tools and what to look for when selecting digital tools for your school, visit **go.solution-tree.com/assessment** and download the document, "Digital Assessment Tools for Twenty-First-Century Learning Teams."

References

Bennett, K. R., & Cunningham, A. C. (2007). *Handhelds for formative assessment in the elementary school.* Winston-Salem, NC: Wake Forest University.

DuFour, R., & Eaker, R. (1998). *Professional learning communities at work: Best practices for enhancing student achievement*. Bloomington, IN: Solution Tree (formerly National Educational Service).

Elmore, R. (2002). *Bridging the gap between standards and achievement: The imperative for professional development in education*. Washington, DC: The Albert Shanker Institute.

Friedman, T. L. (2006). *The world is flat: A brief history of the twenty-first century*. New York: Farrar, Straus, and Giroux.

Graham, P., & Ferriter, B. (2008). One step at a time. *Journal of Staff Development, 29*(3), 38–42.

Halverson, R., Prichett, R. B., & Watson, J. G. (2007). *Formative feedback systems and the new instructional leadership*. Madison: Wisconsin Center for Education Research.

Henrico County Schools. (2007). *Study of Promethean interactive whiteboards in classrooms: Report of findings*. Richmond, VA: Henrico County Schools.

Hupert, N., & Heinze, J. (2006). Results in the palms of their hands: Using handheld computers for data driven decision making in the classroom. In M. Van't Hooft and K. Swan (Eds.), *Ubiquitous computing in education: Invisible technology, visible impact* (pp. 211–229). Mahwah, NJ: Lawrence Erlbaum Associates.

Hupert, N., Heinze, J., Gunn, G., Stewart, J., & Honey, M. (2007). *An analysis of technology-assisted progress monitoring to drive improved student outcomes*. Brooklyn, NY: Wireless Generation.

Marzano, R. J. (2003). *What works in schools: Translating research into action*. Alexandria, VA: Association for Supervision and Curriculum Development.

Perlstein, L. (2007). *Tested: One American school struggles to make the grade*. New York: Henry Holt and Company.

Rhode Island Department of Elementary and Secondary Education. (2006). *Instructional technology vision, goals and assumptions*. Accessed at www.ride.ri.gov/instruction/intech/default.aspx on April 25, 2009.

Rust, B., & Stegman, E. (2003). *K–12 school districts: Why total cost of ownership (TCO) matters*. Stamford, CT: Gartner Research.

NICOLE M. VAGLE

 Nicole Vagle is an independent consultant and president of Lighthouse Learning Community, Inc. Nicole was formerly a high school reform specialist for Minneapolis Public Schools, where she worked closely with school and district staff to support the implementation of small learning communities. This high school reform work also included coaching individuals and teams of secondary administrators and teachers in examining data and promoting high expectations for all students. Nicole was also the training coordinator for the Osseo (Minnesota) Area Schools' Data Program Templates Project in collaboration with the University of Minnesota. As training coordinator, she helped elementary and secondary educators design templates to track and analyze data. Intrigued by the powerful impact teacher leaders have in schools and districts, she later became a program evaluator and trainer at the Princeton Center for Leadership Training in New Jersey. Nicole produced a training DVD that illustrates a protocol for examining the effectiveness of assessments and improving student learning. She continues to work with schools and districts nationwide to increase understanding of developing and using assessments to promote student learning. She is a contributor to *The Teacher as Assessment Leader* (Solution Tree, 2009).

SEVEN

Finding Meaning in the Numbers

Nicole M. Vagle

Every year, countless educators, schools, jurisdictions, and districts embark on the venture of examining data with high expectations of improving student learning. We often begin this endeavor by deepening our understanding of formative assessment. Frequently, our first realization is that we need to use assessment data to change our instruction. So we start collecting the data, and then displaying the data. Our software programs produce professional-looking graphs and provide countless options for reports organized by teacher, demographics, program, reading level, and more. This technology is a powerful tool and an important resource for our work in promoting learning; however, in too many cases, the charts and the graphs become the end product. When we check data analysis off our list once the table is complete, when we score assessments weeks after administering them, when we fail to implement the responses we planned after analyzing our data, we have stopped short of capitalizing on the power of data to promote learning. The end goal is to *use* the data to help students understand what they need to do next and to help us understand what we, as educators, need to do next to help students learn more.

The research shows that effectively examining data and student work increases student learning (Love, 2003; Schmoker, 2006). In one study, Nancy Love, Katherine Stiles, Susan Mundry, and Kathryn DiRanna (2008) describe findings from the Using Data

Project, conducted in collaboration with the nonprofit research and development organizations WestEd and the Technical Education Research Center. The idea behind the project was to "develop, field-test, and pilot a program to provide educators with the skills, knowledge, and dispositions to put school data to work to improve teaching and learning" (p. 12). In this project, data coaches from participating schools were trained to facilitate collaborative inquiry conversations with the intent of helping teachers analyze data and subsequently make instructional decisions that promote learning. In an unpublished report, John Zuman (2005) finds significant gains in achievement, a narrowing of the achievement gap, and increased collaboration as a result of participating in this project (cited in Love et al., 2008). From the extensive work of Love et al. (2008) emerges a focus for schools "moving toward high-capacity uses of data . . . [that includes] a strong foundation in data literacy and collaborative inquiry knowledge, skills, and dispositions as well as spiritual and moral commitment to serve each and every student" (p. 11).

If school leaders are to provide this type of vision and practice, they must be armed with a solid understanding of the role data play in student learning and teachers' professional practice. Administrators also need to know *how* to support teachers in shifting to a more collaborative culture, to learning-focused work, and to a results- and action-oriented environment (DuFour, DuFour, & Eaker, 2008; Schmoker, 2006).

In this chapter, I will use the research on examining assessment data and student work to describe characteristics and challenges of finding meaning in our data. Then I will explore two leadership charges based on Love et al.'s study of the Using Data Project (2008): (1) creating a culture of collaborative inquiry and (2) building data literacy. Finally, I will identify practical strategies and protocols to lead these efforts in school settings.

Characteristics and Challenges of Finding Meaning in Data

Love et al. (2008) articulate six assumptions that further contribute to a deeper understanding of sound data work.[1] Three of these assumptions are addressed throughout this chapter to inform strategies for finding meaning in and using data collaboratively to improve student achievement:

Assumption 1. Making significant progress in improving student learning and closing achievement gaps is a moral responsibility and a real possibility in a relatively short amount of time—two to five years. It is not children's poverty or race or ethnic background that stand in the way of achievement; it is school practices and policies and the beliefs that underlie them that pose the biggest obstacles.

Assumption 2. Data have no meaning. Meaning is imposed through interpretation. Frames of reference—the way we see the world—influence the meaning we derive from data. Effective data users become aware of and critically examine their frames of reference and assumptions (Wellman & Lipton, 2004, pp. ix–xi). Conversely, data can also be a catalyst to questioning assumptions and changing practices based on new ways of thinking.

Assumption 3. Collaborative Inquiry—a process where teachers construct their understanding of student learning problems and invent and test solutions together through rigorous and frequent use of data and reflective dialogue—unleashes the resourcefulness and creativity to continuously improve instruction and student learning. (Love et al., 2008, pp. 10–12)

[1] For the purpose of this chapter, the term *data work* refers to any time when students' work, scores, actions, or words are analyzed to gain insight into their learning needs before action is taken (such as instructional response, curriculum modification, or assessment revision).

Fostering these assumptions in our culture and practice is a challenge facing all educators. In essence, if we are to be data savvy, we need to believe our students can achieve. Dalton Sherman, a fifth-grade student from Dallas, Texas, was the keynote speaker for the Dallas Independent School District's launch of the 2008–2009 school year. He confidently took the stage and proclaimed:

> I believe in me. Do you believe in me? Do you believe that I can stand up here, fearless, and talk to over 20,000 of you? Hey, Charles Rice Learning Center, do you believe in me? That's right, they do! Because here's the deal: I can do anything . . . be anything . . . create anything . . . dream anything . . . become anything . . . because you believe in me. (Sherman, 2008)

For eight minutes, this young man mesmerized educators as he spoke of the power of believing in students, believing in our colleagues, and believing in ourselves. His passionate challenge captures the essence of Assumption 1.

Assumption 2 highlights the importance of the meaning we make from the numbers. Finding meaning in the numbers requires that we ask effective questions about our own assumptions, bias, and the context in which the data were collected so that the actions we take as a result of the data really help students learn. Marnie Thompson and Dylan Wiliam (2007) describe this view of learning:

> Teachers cannot create learning—only learners can do that. What teachers can do is to create the situations in which students learn. The teacher's task, therefore, moves away from "delivering" learning to the student and towards the creation of situations in which students learn. (pp. 5–6)

In the same fashion, administrators and teacher leaders create situations in which the stakeholders in our school communities (teachers, leaders, families, community members, and students) make meaning out of the data we collect.

The way we support and facilitate finding meaning in data builds a culture that promotes collaborative inquiry—Assumption 3. Finding meaning in the data also requires that we remember the faces behind the numbers: our students. The implications of data work reach far beyond success on standardized assessments; our use of data can change the course of students' lives. As Love et al. (2008) note, "School improvement without will and moral purpose—without a genuine commitment to all students—is an empty exercise in compliance that, in our experience, can do more harm than good" (p. 11).

Leading Effective Data Use

Administrators can lead teachers and teams toward finding meaning in the numbers by (1) fostering collaborative inquiry and (2) building assessment literacy. The following sections outline strategies and specific tools and protocols (that is, a series of steps that help focus conversation) that will embed practices and create the culture and context for high-capacity data work.

Fostering Collaborative Inquiry

Administrators, teachers, and other educators play a critical leadership role in creating a culture of possibility in which all those in the school believe that they can and do impact student learning in significant ways. This confidence has proven to be a key ingredient in the actual achievement of our students (Dweck, 2006; Reeves, 2007).

Strategy A: Promote Efficacy

In order to create a culture of high achievement, leaders must help the members of the school community believe that they have the capacity to overcome challenges such as students who are reading below grade level, who don't hand in homework, or who appear to lack motivation. Jim Collins (2001) draws on the notion of efficacy in his compelling study of companies that moved from good to great. He attributed this transformation to what he calls "Level 5 Leadership." Robert Marzano, Timothy Waters, and Bryan McNulty (2005, p. 20) quote Collins' description of Level 5 leaders in great companies as those who "blend personal humility with intense personal will. They exhibit intense commitment to doing what matters most in their companies regardless of the difficulties. When things go wrong, they tend to look inward for the reasons as opposed to ascribing blame to external factors." Doug Reeves (2007) also identifies this idea of efficacy in schools in his description of a review of data that explored the gain scores in schools during the 2005–2006 school year:

> In schools where teachers examined the evidence of the impact of teaching effectiveness on student achievement and regarded their professional practices as the primary causes of student achievement, the gains in student achievement were three times higher than in those schools where the faculty and leaders attributed the causes to factors beyond their control. (p. 246)

Principals can open this discussion by asking the school leadership team this question: What are the causes of student achievement? Together, divide the responses into two categories: "factors within our control" and "factors outside our control." If most responses fit into the category "factors outside our control," your work must focus on helping staff members understand how they might support learning differently. They need to see concrete examples of how they might impact the learning of struggling students. If responses are focused on "factors within our control," then staff members are ready to explore implementation ideas that go beyond the status quo.

Strategy B: Set Norms for Relationships

Setting norms for relationships and logistics lays the foundation for sound data work; it establishes boundaries and trust so that team members can celebrate their strengths and strategize through their struggles.

Robert Garmston and Bruce Wellman (1999) articulate seven norms of collaboration during team discussion; while all are important and interdependent, the last three stand out as common norms that help move a group forward:

1. Pausing

2. Paraphrasing

3. Probing for specificity

4. Putting ideas on the table

5. Paying attention to self and others

6. Presuming positive intentions

7. Pursuing a balance between advocacy and inquiry

Identifying these relationship norms is only the beginning; team members must then hold one another accountable to those norms. In guiding and supporting team meetings, principals can model and describe the last three items in the following ways:

- Be aware of your verbal space in the conversation. Those who speak often in the group can hold back and encourage or invite those who do not speak as often to contribute their ideas.

- Understand that people's ideas, actions, and words most often come from the best intentions.

- Seek to understand those ideas with which you do not agree, and be strident in your support of your position.

Strategy C: Set Norms for Logistics

Next, the team must set logistic norms for how members will work together. For example, the team might decide how the group will handle moments when the norms are not being followed, how formal decisions will be made, and how conflict will be handled. All members of the team must understand and articulate these norms and understand and articulate their rationale and purpose. For a deeper look at collaboration in theory and action, consult Garmston and Wellman (1999).

Figure 7.1 describes a protocol some teams use to lay a foundation for this culture of collaborative inquiry. It shows a sample facilitator's agenda for the first meeting of a team that has been formed to regularly examine samples of student work in order to align assessments to standards and respond to gaps in student understanding.

Figure 7.2 (page 158) shows another approach that can contribute to a culture of collaborative inquiry. When we ask staff to think about the worst and best possible outcomes of analyzing and responding to data, we eliminate "parking lot conversations" by providing a venue first to share and discuss the feelings and fears of those who are uncertain of what examining data actually means, and then to imagine the great possibility in this work and how it could authentically support teaching and learning. (This protocol draws on the work of Bob Chadwick [1999]. Consult the website Looking at Student Work [www.lasw.org] for an additional list of protocols, research, and resources for focusing these conversations. Although this protocol identifies common assessments as a focus, the questions may be easily applied to other data work.)

STEP 1: Set the context, clarify relationship norms, and build trust.

Discuss the following questions:

1. What are you hoping to get out of this process?
2. What do you hope will change as a result of this process?
3. What norms will our team establish in order to get the best results out of this process?
    *   How will our team handle conflict? (For example, if a team member is upset about a comment made or a discussion that occurred)
    *   How will our team make decisions?
4. When and how will we assess the process? How will we measure success?
    *   What student achievement indicators will we examine?
    *   What kind of recordkeeping will we use?
5. What kinds of professional development experiences have we experienced that were particularly useful? How could we integrate some of those experiences into this process?

STEP 2: Identify logistical tasks for examining samples of student work.

Set a calendar of dates and times for the meetings. Indicate on the schedule which teacher will bring assignments and student work for team discussion, and who will help facilitate and record.

Outline the meeting process:

1. The teacher bringing the student work gathers copies of the assessment for each member of the team and copies of the student work samples (six to fifteen pieces, depending on the size of the group).
2. The facilitator (team members may rotate this role if there is not an outside facilitator) will bring:
    *   Recording sheets for the protocol
    *   Sticky notes to label student work
    *   Copies of standards or other documents to help guide work

Figure 7.1 Sample first meeting agenda.

STEP 1: Identify and record worst- and best-case scenarios.

Discuss the following questions:

1. What is the worst possible outcome of analyzing and responding to common assessment data?

2. What is the best possible outcome of analyzing and responding to common assessment data?

STEP 2: Plan to make the best-case scenario the outcome.

Ask the following questions:

1. Why are we doing this?

2. What will we commonly assess?

3. When will we meet together to focus on common assessment work such as the following?

   - To establish a learning target goal for the assessment

   - To create or revise a common assessment that measures the learning goal

   - To administer a common assessment

   - To analyze and plan a response

   - To implement the response

4. How will we make decisions?

5. What will our norms of being together look like?

Figure 7.2 Setting the context for examining common assessment data.

Building Data Literacy

Marzano et al. (2005) reviewed thirty-five years of research on leadership and school effectiveness to identify specific behaviors of educational leadership that impact student learning. These include:

- Monitoring student progress on specific learning goals

- Supervising teachers

- Promoting high expectations for student achievement and teacher performance

- Focusing on basic skills

- Monitoring the curriculum (p. 23)

The strategies described in this section help define some of the actions leaders can take to demonstrate some of these behaviors. Strategy D addresses how to identify the capacity of various types of data to support a school culture in effectively monitoring learning goals and promoting high expectations for students. Strategy E provides tools for administrators to structure opportunities for educators to pose quality questions and facilitate dialogue. These data conversations provide opportunity to support teachers in holding students to high expectations while monitoring learning goals and the curriculum. This dialogue also holds teachers to high expectations as it sends a message that we believe teachers can and do influence student learning. Finally, Strategy F describes the types of tools helpful in gathering and organizing data. These resources can make data work much more efficiently. Let's look at each of these strategies in more detail.

Strategy D: Define the Data's Purpose, Role, and Use

By being intentional about the data we analyze—by understanding the capacity of the data, both the advantages and the limitations—we begin to create the *data literacy* essential to improving student learning. In seeking to define the data's purpose, role, and use, ask questions such as:

- What data do we collect?

- How much of our data inform instruction?

- How much provide evidence of curriculum or program effectiveness?

- How much indicate our students' learning needs and strengths?

(Visit **go.solution-tree.com/assessment** to download "Types of Data," a detailed table that describes the different types of data available to many school communities, the potential the data have to inform work, and specific questions to guide data analysis.)

Being data literate means that we understand the purpose and use of various types of data. For example, when we analyze results from an end-of-unit exam, we expect that students have already learned what we are assessing. If we discover significant gaps in student understanding, however, addressing these learning needs becomes more complicated. If closing the gaps is essential to future success, we may spend a few extra days addressing the misconceptions. If the learning is essential, yet we know it will reappear as a focus in a future unit, we may plan to address the misconceptions later. If the learning is not as essential, we may decide to adjust our curriculum and instruction for the following year. The primary intent of this end-of-unit data analysis is to monitor the effectiveness of the curriculum and the assessment itself. Data analysis thus becomes a natural part of our instructional planning.

Strategy E: Pose Quality Questions and Facilitate Dialogue

Marzano et al. (2005) identify Peter Block among a group of prominent leadership theorists. They note that

Block (2003) frames leadership as the act of effective questioning. . . . For Block, critical leadership skills include convening critical discussions, naming the question, focusing discussion on learning as opposed to premature closure on solutions, and using strategies for participative design of solutions. (pp. 19–20)

Asking good questions and drawing teachers, support staff, counselors, community members, and even students in as partners on the journey of increasing student learning contribute to a culture where collaborative inquiry is ingrained. When we ask good questions, we create opportunities to examine our beliefs and our practices. When we question our practices and use evidence to determine the next best course of action, we are problem solving at a deeper level. In the best scenario, our preconceived notions will be affirmed or dispelled with evidence and focused dialogue (Love et al., 2008).

Protocols are tools containing questions that keep our conversations focused on learning. The protocol in figure 7.3 (pages 162–163) is designed for teams analyzing data from common assessments (whether the assessment was created by the team or the district, or included with a curriculum or textbook). With minor revisions, any individual teacher could use these questions to act on assessment information.

High-quality, productive conversations about student learning are the goal, so occasionally examining the process ensures that the protocol is still helping the conversation stay on track and support student learning and teacher practice. Ask, "What's working? What's challenging? Where are we getting bogged down? How might we revise our process to keep us focused on our ultimate purpose?"

STEP 1: Prepare to analyze and respond to common assessment data to ensure accurate and reliable scoring.

Step 1 is used only if the common assessment is of a type—such as a written explanation, a presentation, or an essay—that requires a scoring rubric. Otherwise, begin the protocol at Step 2.

1. Each team member brings two or three random samples of student work from the common assessment.

2. The team labels each piece of student work with a number (with names removed or hidden).

3. Individually, team members use the rubric to score each piece. (The team sketches out a 4-point rubric if one has not been created: 3 and 4 describe levels of proficiency, and 1 and 2 describe levels below proficient.)

4. Team members share individual scores and come to consensus on each piece of work, discussing discrepancies by using evidence from the student work itself.

5. Individual teachers score the rest of their own students' work from the common assessment.

STEP 2: Gather and organize common assessment data.

1. Gather and organize classroom common assessment data by learning target or standard, by individual student, and by teacher.

1. Create a visual representation of the data (on chart paper, with stacks of actual student work, in Excel templates, or with software data reports, if available). Again, ensure the visual is organized by learning target or standard, by individual student, and by teacher.

STEP 3: Examine the data and identify areas for team discussion. (Adapted from Erkens, 2009)

Ask individual teachers to reflect on the following critical questions:

1. Overall, which learning target was my students' strongest?

2. Which was my students' weakest?

3. How can I improve in that area?

Ask the team to reflect on the following critical questions:

1. Which learning targets from the assessment require more of our attention?

Figure 7.3: Common assessment analysis and response protocol.

2. Which classrooms or teachers need additional support?

3. Which of our students did not master which learning targets? (If one learning target is identified, students are sorted by their needs for enrichment, more practice, or intervention. If multiple learning targets are identified, students are sorted by the learning target on which they most need to work.)

4. Are there parts of the assessment that need to be modified or revised?

STEP 4: Plan a response based on the data analysis.

Ask the team the following questions:

1. Given their learning needs, how could we support the students who do not understand and need intervention?

   - How could we support the students who have some understanding, but need a little more practice?

   - How could we support the students who understand and need enrichment?

1. How will we implement the response ideas?

   - A classroom response means that individual teachers implement the response in their own classrooms. In this scenario, the team may collectively plan and design the response, or each teacher may plan one part of the response and then share it with the rest of the team.

   - A team response means that each teacher on the team takes one group of students, based on their learning needs, and works with that group of students during a designated time frame. For example, Teacher A takes the students who need intervention; Teacher B works with the students who need a little more practice, and Teacher C works with the students who need enrichment.

   - In some cases, students who need intervention have more intensive learning needs. If this is the case, the team may identify possible structures or resources in the school designed to support students who need significantly more time to master these essential learning goals.

1. When and how will we check in regarding the effectiveness of our response?

Table 7.1 is a template for organizing the learning targets that need work, planning the responses by learning target, organizing the individual students who need work on each target, and identifying the adults who will work with each group of students.

Table 7.1: Plan a Team Response to the Data

Learning Target (Area of Focus Based on Analysis of Common Assessment Data)	Adults Who Will Facilitate or Teach	Students Who Will Be Involved	The Plan of Action

Strategy F: Provide Tools to Gather and Organize Data

If we are going to analyze data effectively, we must pay attention to certain characteristics so we can more efficiently understand our data, identify individual student learning needs, and plan our responses. First, organize data by learning outcome. For example, in the subject of writing, we may score individual pieces of writing for organization, support, and conventions. Then we can organize the data by learning outcome on charts such as those shown in tables 7.2 (teacher data template) and 7.3 (team data template, page 166). If the assessment is scored by item (for example, a twenty-question multiple-choice assessment), record the number of items measuring each learning target in the second row, and record each student's scores accordingly. In this case, students receive a score for each learning target represented on the assessment.

The template in table 7.2 is designed for teachers to record individual student data from an assessment by learning target. If the assessment is common, then each teacher on the team records data on a separate sheet. Adjust the number of columns to accommodate the number of learning targets or standards measured, and adjust the number of rows to accommodate the number of students.

Table 7.2: Sample Teacher Data Template for a Writing Assessment

Learning Target or Standard	Organization	Support	Conventions
Number of Points or Description of Possible Rubric Scores for Each Learning Target or Standard	( )	( )	( )
Student 1			
Student 2			
Student 3			
Student 4			
Percentage Proficient			
Number Proficient			

Table 7.3 (page 166) is a template for the team to record data by learning target and teacher.

Table 7.3: Sample Team Data Template for a Writing Assessment

Learning Target or Standard	Organization	Support	Conventions	Overall Percentage Proficient
Number of Points or Description of Possible Rubric Scores	( )	( )	( )	( )
Percentage of Students Proficient on Each Learning Target or Standard				
Teacher A				
Teacher B				
Teacher C				
Overall Team				
Raw Numbers of Students Proficient on Each Learning Target or Standard				
Teacher A				
Teacher B				
Teacher C				
Overall Team				

Both of these templates are important for data analysis as they allow the team to effectively identify strengths and weaknesses by learning target of individual students as well as by teacher or classroom in order to identify strong instructional practices that produced achievement. These insights support data analysis in planning an appropriate response.

If the data from the assessment are organized by individual item (problem or question) and learning target, then create a table in which one column represents each item (see table 7.4). If the assessment is multiple choice, insert the actual student

Table 7.4: Sample Data Report by Item for Mathematics Assessment

| | | | | Learning Targets | | | |
| | | | Fractions | Fractions | Problem Solving | Problem Solving | Money and Problem Solving |
	ELL Status	Reading Level	Item 1	Item 2	Item 3a	Item 3b	Item 4
Student 1	Teacher A						
Student 2	Teacher A						
Student 3	Teacher A						
Student 4	Teacher A						
Student 5	Teacher A						
Student 6	Teacher B						
Student 7	Teacher B						
Student 8	Teacher B						
Student 9	Teacher B						
Student 10	Teacher B						
Student 11	Teacher C						
Student 12	Teacher C						
Student 13	Teacher C						
Student 14	Teacher C						
Student 15	Teacher C						

response (A, B, C, and so on) to gather more information about students' level of understanding. For constructed-response items, include a column for the response (item 3a) and a column for a rubric-scored student explanation of the response (item 3b). It's better to choose these templates on smaller assessments where you are going to use results to adjust instruction. Entering item data without technology tools is time consuming and most often associated with larger end-of-course or unit exams when item analysis is more about analyzing the test than adjusting current instruction.

Table 7.5 shows the rubric used to score item 3b, a constructed-response math problem included in the test data displayed in table 7.4.

Table 7.5: Rubric for Scoring Constructed-Response Items in Math Assessment

4	Written explanation gives a well-developed description of the process and demonstrated sophisticated mathematical understanding.
3	Explanation clearly describes the process and demonstrates mathematical understanding.
2	The explanation is somewhat clear. A few details are left out and/or mathematical vocabulary is limited.
1	The explanation is unclear or contains little or no description of the process or mathematical concepts.

It is very important to start small by finding efficient ways in which the data analysis and response can impact learning. For example, a biology teacher began analyzing data from one class to construct a picture of his students' proficiency on particular learning targets. Table 7.6 shows how he organized the data by learning target and by individual students (for illustration purposes, data for only seven of seventeen students are included). Organizing the data in this manner allows a teacher to group students together who need to work on the same learning objectives. If the data indicate that many students are struggling with one learning target, the teacher may group students according to levels of proficiency on that target and design differentiated responses based on which students need enrichment (mastered the learning target), more practice (proficient on the learning target), or intervention (not yet proficient on the learning target).

Table 7.6: Student Proficiency on Learning Targets for High School Biology

Student	Knows How the Age of a Fossil Is Determined	Understands How Fossils Are Used to Learn About the Earth's Past	Understands the Difference Between Biogenesis and Spontaneous Generation	Understands Where Fossils Are Found
Student 1	Yes	Yes	Yes	Yes
Student 2	Yes	Yes	No	Yes
Student 3	Yes	Yes	Yes	Yes
Student 4	No	Yes	Yes	Yes
Student 5	No	Yes	Yes	Yes
Student 6	Yes	Yes	No	Yes
Student 7	Yes	No	Yes	Yes
Number of Students Proficient	13 (76.5%)	14 (88.2%)	10 (70.6%)	17 (100%)

In grade-level or content teams, data should be organized first by classroom or teacher (see tables 7.3 and 7.4, pages 166–167), then by individual student. Removing student names on the data lessens the potential of any preconceived notions of achievement clouding the analysis; reveal names later, when planning responses, to ensure that the learning needs of individual students are met.

Students' levels of proficiency should be based on their progress toward learning targets and not on their overall average. Thus, the scoring mechanism must indicate a level of proficiency by each learning objective rather than an overall percentage or mark. Without this level of specificity, collective scores tell us very little about what students understand and what they need to do next.

A Note on Tools

Technology tools can help teams collect, organize, and analyze data efficiently. These tools are beneficial, but not having them does not stop us from doing quality data work. Consider the pile-and-plan method, in which teachers bring their assessments to the table (individually or as a team) and make three piles of student work: (1) students who understand and need enrichment, (2) students who mostly understand the concept but need a little more practice, and (3) students who need improvement. The team then designs activities or lessons for each group of students, and individual teachers or teams of teachers implement these responses. Other teams have taken this same concept and instead created tables and graphs on chart paper. There are many options for collecting and using data. The purpose remains the same regardless of how your staff choose to organize data: meeting the learning needs of all students through rich conversations about current realities, action plans, and implementation.

Moving Beyond Accountability

During a recent assessment training I facilitated, a social studies teacher waved me over and made this remark:

> When we started this a few years ago, I thought that common assessments and examining data were about teacher accountability. After this morning, I'm thinking they are more about helping students learn and helping us, the teachers, help students learn.

This is the "aha!" moment that we seek in the work of planning, administering, analyzing, and responding to assessment data in collaborative teams. While teacher accountability is often a byproduct of this work, it is not the central focus. If this work were only about teacher accountability, then collecting graphs would be acceptable. A culture of collaboration focused on learning and results means that administrators create structures and opportunities for this dialogue while continually promoting a vision grounded in student learning. While accountability is clearly an important characteristic of effective leadership focused on learning, leaders do not just establish high expectations and then allow teachers—and thus students—to sink or swim. Leaders look at their expectations, figure out the pathways to meeting those expectations, and scaffold support. In striving for this level of data literacy and collaborative inquiry, we embark on a journey toward schools that believe in the capacity of all students, teachers, and leaders to learn and achieve in profound ways.

References and Resources

Ainsworth, L., & Viegut, D. (2006). *Common formative assessments: How to connect standards-based instruction and assessment.* Thousand Oaks, CA: Corwin.

Block, P. (2003). *The answer to how is yes: Acting on what matters.* San Francisco: Berrett-Koehler.

Chadwick, B. (1999, July). Consensus Building Institute at Eden Prairie Schools, Minnesota.

Collins, J. (2001). *Good to great: Why some companies make the leap . . . and others don't.* New York: Collins Business.

Davies, A. (2007). *Making classroom assessment work* (3rd ed.). Courtenay, British Columbia: Connections Publishing.

DuFour, R., DuFour, R., & Eaker, R. (2008). *Revisiting professional learning communities at work: New insights for improving schools.* Bloomington, IN: Solution Tree.

Dweck, C. (2006). *Mindset: The new psychology of success.* New York: Random House.

Erkens, C. (2009). *Building common assessments* [training materials]. Bloomington, IN: Solution Tree.

Garmston, R., & Wellman, B. (1999). *The adaptive school: A sourcebook for developing collaborative groups.* Norwood, MA: Christopher-Gordon.

Guskey, T. (2007). Using assessments to improve teaching and learning. In D. Reeves (Ed.), *Ahead of the curve: The power of assessment to transform teaching and learning* (pp. 15–29). Bloomington, IN: Solution Tree.

Love, N. (2003, January). Uses and abuses of data. *ENC Focus: Data-Driven Decision Making, 10*(1), 14–17.

Love, N. (2005, Fall). Bringing data literacy to districts. *Hands!, 28*(1), 10–13.

Love, N., Stiles, K., Mundry, S., & DiRanna, K. (2008, Fall). Passion and principle ground effective data use. *Journal of the National Staff Development Council: Examining Evidence, 29*(4), 10–19.

Marzano, R. J., Waters, T., & McNulty, B. A. (2005). *School leadership that works: From research to results.* Alexandria, VA: Association for Supervision and Curriculum Development.

Reeves, D. (2007). Challenges and choices: The role of educational leaders in effective assessment. In D. Reeves (Ed.), *Ahead of the curve: The power of assessment to transform teaching and learning* (pp. 227–251). Bloomington, IN: Solution Tree.

Sadler, D. R. (1989). Formative assessment: Revisiting the territory. *Assessment in Education: Principles, Policy & Practice, 5*(1), 77–85.

Schmoker, M. (2006). *Results now: How we can achieve unprecedented results in teaching and learning.* Alexandria, VA: Association for Supervision and Curriculum Development.

Sherman, D. (2008). *Keynote speech for the Dallas Independent School District's launch of the 2008 school year.* Accessed at www.youtube.com/watch?v=yZm0BfXYvFg on November 26, 2008.

Thompson, M., & Wiliam, D. (2007). *Tight but loose: A conceptual framework for scaling up school reforms.* Paper presented at the annual meeting of the American Educational Research Association, Chicago, IL.

Wellman, B., & Lipton, L. (2004). *Data-driven dialogue: A facilitator's guide to collaborative inquiry.* Sherman, CT: MiraVia.

Wiliam, D. (2007). Keeping learning on track: Classroom assessment and the regulation of learning. In F. K. Lester, Jr. (Ed.), *Second handbook of mathematics teaching and learning* (pp. 1053–1098). Greenwich, CT: Information Age.

Zuman, J. (2005). *Interim summary report: Using data project.* Unpublished report, Cambridge, MA and Arlington, VA: Technical Education Research Center and Intercultural Center for Research in Education.

AINSLEY B. ROSE

Ainsley Rose is the former director of education, curriculum, and technology for the Western Quebec School Board in Gatineau, Quebec. As an education leader, he incorporates his expertise in a wide range of principles, practices, and concepts that have been proven to improve schools, including Effective Schools, Professional Learning Communities at Work™, instructional intelligence, and standards and assessment. He also conducts peer mediation for schools and has presented at the International Effective Schools Conference. Ainsley has experience as an elementary and secondary classroom teacher and principal, as well as an instructor of graduate-level courses for administrators and preservice teachers and presently acts as a senior leadership coach. He has served as chair of the Committee for Anglophone Curriculum Responsables and the Implementation Design Committee, and was named to the Advisory Board on English Education by the Minister of Education of Quebec. Ainsley has also received the Outstanding Achievement Award from the Association of Administrators of English Schools of Quebec. He is a contributor to *The Teacher as Assessment Leader* (Solution Tree, 2009) and *The Collaborative Teacher: Working Together as a Professional Learning Community* (Solution Tree, 2008).

The Courage to Implement Standards-Based Report Cards

Ainsley B. Rose

The advent of standards-based assessment has been an area of great interest and activity in recent years. Most provinces and states have endorsed standards-based assessment and reporting practices. Despite this commitment, standards-based assessment still languishes as schools struggle with the implementation of such methods of assessment and reporting. While some schools and teachers are experimenting with these new methods, many school personnel have serious reservations, not the least of which is, If teachers use the new assessment methods to judge students' progress, how can they convey their judgments by means of traditional report cards? Report cards, after all, have been the primary means to correspond about a student's progress that parents have known and understood over the past several decades, aside from parent teacher evenings and more recently student-led conferences. Thomas Guskey (2004) says that one of the greatest challenges that we as educators face today is "describing students' level of academic performance in meaningful ways to parents and others" (p. 326). To change the current instrument and the type of information it contains—to make a significant departure from traditional practices of grading and reporting—is fraught with danger that requires a rare kind of courage. Parent support will be the Achilles' heel of any assessment and reporting reform. We have not been successful in engaging parents in understanding how these new assessment methods work or how they convey useful information parents can use to gauge whether or not their child is being successful.

A second challenge, one that continues to elude a solution, is the automatic association of grades with report cards. Carole Boston (2003) suggests that grades on report cards are used for many reasons, including selecting and sorting students for university entrance and programs and communicating to parents and students about achievement, effort, attendance, and even attitude. Given the many purported uses of the traditional grades on report cards, is it any wonder that changing this method of communicating student achievement has so many ramifications?

Although much has been written about grading and reporting, there are few compelling or helpful accounts of what is really required to develop a thoughtful, reasoned, and sustainable process for designing and implementing a new report card—an integral part of a systemwide approach to standards-based assessment and reporting. The general school public needs to see exemplars of what an appropriate report card can look like. Research needs to be conducted to determine whether the new formats have the intended effect of communicating with parents in a more effective manner or prove to be just another initiative that will slowly fade as enthusiasm for standards-based methods gives way to the detractors and doomsayers of educational change. The challenge will be that we will need to be able to educate the general public that there are better methods to "do" school, ones that are different from what has been the norm for decades. To do so we will have to provide the public with examples of successful innovations before they will be willing to tolerate those that I will suggest in this chapter.

Principles of Effective Reporting

While most of the new literature on assessment, evaluation, and reporting supports, even extols the importance of common

formative assessments, frequent monitoring of student achievement, and the delivery of written, descriptive feedback that is
timely, frequent, and accurate, little mention is made of the most
effective methods to communicate about achievement to parents.
In fact, Guskey points out, "the communication challenge of
issuing progress reports and report cards that describe students'
performance with regard to . . . standards, however, remains
before us. It's also proving to be a more difficult challenge than
most educators ever anticipated" (2004, p. 326). There are many
other challenges when examining the issue of standards-based
reporting. Certainly, the greatest among them is the manner in
which the actual data are derived and what the final mark means
to the student or parent. There are, however, many other considerations in this rather complex method of communicating,
including whether or not a student is progressing or meeting
the standards outlined in curriculum documents.

Thomas Guskey and Jane Bailey (2001) outline the following
guiding premises that school districts should follow if they are to
achieve the goals of communicating about student achievement
clearly to both students and parents:

1. The primary goal of grading and reporting is communication.

2. Grading and reporting are integral parts of the
   instructional process.

3. Good reporting is based on good evidence.

4. Changes in grading and reporting are best accomplished through the development of a comprehensive
   reporting system. (p. 2)

Schools, school boards, and school districts across North
America have a significant challenge ahead of them.

The traditional report card based on norm-referenced
approaches has been the most widely used method of

communicating with parents at the end of each term (Marzano, 2006). To change this to better reflect standards-based education, teachers and administrators will have to take a careful, reasoned approach to the assessment system. A significant step is a new style of report card that will serve as *one* of the communication methods with parents within a comprehensive assessment, evaluation, grading, and reporting system. Furthermore, evidence suggests that we must very carefully consider the differing perceptions of the various parties in the assessment, grading, and reporting process (Guskey, 2002). Following is one documented example of how parents can perceive the shift to alternative report cards:

> In Gloucester, Mass., a record turnout of parents at a school committee meeting in 1995 forced administrators to abandon a new reporting system that had replaced letter grades with student portfolios and narrative reports written by teachers. Kim Norman, school committee chairman, called the parents' response "very political," adding, "People wanted to be able to tell their children's grandparents, 'Johnny got all A's.'" (Pardini, 1997)

Parental concerns brought the introduction of new reporting systems to a halt in Florida as well:

> In Pasco County, Fla., Sandra Ramos describes the elementary report card revision as a "volatile issue—one of the most controversial in recent years." Ramos, assistant superintendent for curriculum and instruction, says the proposed report card met strong resistance, even though it was designed by a task force of teachers, administrators and parents and had been piloted at several schools. Angry parents showed up at school meetings, armed with petitions signed by thousands of their peers. Some teachers resisted a grading system that did away with the percentage-based letter grades they had used for years.

The result: The school district reinstated letter grades in grades 3–5. (Pardini, 1997)

There are more stories like these, and no doubt some that the reader may have encountered personally. Suffice it to say that despite taking a reasoned approach, there is no guarantee that implementing a standards-based report card will solve more ills than it ultimately may create for the recipients of that communication tool. And yet, this should not deter schools from embarking on this courageous course of action, as it is still *the right thing to do*. Literature suggests that assessment, to be effective, should *encourage* students to improve, give them an idea of their progress toward their learning goals, and finally show how they might close any gap between both their progress and the expected outcomes. Effective feedback then becomes an essential aspect of this approach (Marzano, 2006: Stiggins, Arter, Chappuis, & Chappuis, 2004a). By implication, assessment should change to reflect this new direction. Therefore, reporting should likewise follow, since present methods would not reflect this new approach adequately.

Understanding Modern Education

While we must be persistent, we must be careful not to dismiss the complaints and concerns raised by parents and others. When people react in this obstreperous manner, it is invariably the result of a lack of understanding: they do not see the benefits of the new versus the old form (Wiggins, 1997). As educators, we have come to see that old ways of reporting student achievement do not complement modern approaches to teaching or learning. The next step is to share our knowledge about how education has changed with the community:

- The actual curriculum is different from what was expected in the last few decades. With the increasing demand for and involvement in all things technological and the accelerated pace of information flow, we cannot prepare our current student generation to make sense of this changed world using arcane curriculum outcomes and expectations.

- The shift from a norm-referenced approach, where we compare students against one another, to a standards-based approach, where we consider where a student is on the way toward meeting the learning standard, requires new measures to determine whether the student is making progress and to what degree and at what rate.

A single letter grade on a standard report card as we currently know it cannot adequately represent this new educational model. Robert Marzano (2006) makes the case more emphatically:

> Obviously, from the perspective of standards-based education, isolated overall letter grades (or overall percentage scores or even average rubric scores) are extremely deficient because they cannot provide the level of detailed feedback necessary to enhance student learning. (p. 125)

The Old Card

The current and common perspective about what a report card should deliver goes something like this: students get a mark for each subject, and that mark *may* represent the average for all the tests, quizzes, homework, class participation, projects, and assignments students were expected to complete in the term. The marks generally are normative and identified by the letters A to F or by numerical scores on a 100-point scale that can be related to the letters A to F (that is, A = 90–100, B = 80–89, C = 70–79, D = 60–69, F = below 60, or some other variation—which in and of itself presents a challenge). The report card may also indicate a class average so that parents can compare how their child has done relative to the rest of the students in the class.

The New Card

The current approach is clearly at odds with a standards-based system of reporting, which, to repeat Marzano's point quoted above, would seek to do what traditional report cards cannot: "provide the level of detailed feedback necessary to enhance student learning" (2006, p. 125). So, a standards-based report card might feature phrases that describe the achievement levels of the student; that is, whether the student is *beginning, approaching, meeting,* or *exceeding* the standards being assessed in the curriculum. Each subject on the report card has descriptions that are broad and include specific standards, worded (in student- and parent-friendly language) to reflect the actual skills or content from the curriculum expectations. Report cards can use numbers to depict a continuum or range (such as 1–4) in which each number corresponds to a *level* on the continuum that can then be converted into a mark or grade such as we presently use. There may also be a statement to inform the student or parent at what *rate* the student is progressing toward the priority standard: possible descriptors include *at level, below level, below level with help,* and *not at all.*

Unfortunately, attempts to make the necessary shift in the look and feel of report cards to reflect changes in teaching and learning often fail. Following are the most common reasons (Guskey & Bailey, 2001):

- Failure to use language that students and parents can understand without a great deal of explanation

- Failure to build a proper system for communicating the changes to students and parents

- Lack of commitment from teachers who were not prepared sufficiently before the new documents became public and view the new approach as significantly more work

- No easy way for parents, teachers, or students to get answers to their questions promptly and effectively

- Failure to make technology an asset rather than an encumbrance to implementation

Any one of the above alone can jeopardize the successful implementation of a standards-based report card. Together they spell certain failure and one that cannot be easily salvaged to any degree of satisfaction to all parties in the educational enterprise.

Change Factors

Given the shortcomings of current reporting mechanisms, let's now consider the actual implementation process to develop a new report card for a school, school district, or school board. In doing so, we rely once again on the work of Guskey, who has written extensively on this subject. Guskey and Bailey (2001, p. 45) suggest that there are three specific factors that have contributed to the difficulties in grading and reporting. They are:

1. Changes focus on form rather than function.

2. Leaders lack understanding of the change process.

3. Efforts center exclusively on report card reform.

I humbly suggest a fourth factor to consider, which is that individuals who undertake these changes do not have the requisite skills or knowledge to adequately conduct the required change and developmental process. This is complex work and not for the faint of heart. Mike Schmoker (2006, p. 30) cites the work of Robert Evans, who says:

> Most administrators learn quickly to accommodate themselves to the status quo, and . . . are untrained for leading [instructional] change. They have been socialized to be maintainers. . . . .Almost everything one learns as

a principal reinforces the old congressional saw: "to get along, go along."

Nevertheless, there is hope that with time, patience, and a lot of thought, the implementation of a new standards-based reporting system can be successful. Priscilla Pardini (1997) provides us with one example:

> Leslie Anderson, director of instruction and assessment in San Ramon Valley, Calif., Unified Schools, says a three-year old assessment system in place at six of the District's 12 elementary schools has been "very well received" once parents got used to it. The new system, in the form of a rubric (a continuum of increasingly difficult skills), does a much better job of tracking student progress. It clearly delineates an "inexperienced" reader as one who "shows little interest in exploring books" and a "competent" reader as one who "seeks out unfamiliar literature independently."

Kathryn Alvestad (1997) describes her experience with the introduction of new methodologies:

> The best way to approach such a situation is with good teaching practice. This means knowing the needs of the teachable population, setting appropriate objectives for them, providing instruction in an appropriate, engaging manner, giving plenty of opportunity for practice and being available when needed after instruction is completed. A planned program of education for parents and the community can help avert many problems.

The next part of this chapter will explore one approach to developing a new report card, one element of a more comprehensive, systemwide assessment and evaluation plan. Having recently implemented a standards-based report card, I hope that my experience can serve to guide others. Some of the many lessons I learned are to be avoided, while others may be adopted and adapted to suit the reader's context.

Key Development Questions

Let us first consider some of the more pertinent questions that arise for schools or school districts when developing a standards-based report card. These questions can form the basis for discussions of the working committee, the membership of which will be discussed later. Be forewarned: a lack of attention to any one of these questions will make or break this initiative, given the complexity of the issue:

- Will the report card reflect assessment *for* learning or assessment *of* learning, or can it serve both ends?

- Who is the primary audience for this communication tool?

- What should the marks on the report represent, and how will they be derived?

- How can we ensure that all teachers understand and implement a common approach to deriving the final grade on the report card?

- How can we make the report card meaningful to both parents and students while still informing other institutions such as colleges and universities?

- In a standards-based system, how do we represent progress toward the standard?

- What symbols (language) should we use to indicate achievement of the standards?

- What kind of language (student- and parent-friendly) should we use to represent the standards to be mastered?

- What role can and should technology play in this new type of reporting mechanism?

- How can we develop consistency between and among teachers of the same students in different subject areas or the same subject areas?

- What role must teacher judgment play in determining the final mark of a student?

- How can teachers with multiple groups of students manage the work involved in more descriptive reporting?

- What process should school districts use to implement the new reporting system?

- Who should be involved in the development and implementation process?

- What training and ongoing support will be required to ensure a consistent approach to implementation and use of the final document?

- Who will be responsible for presenting changes, and how will they present those changes to parents, students, and other school personnel?

Experience in having struggled with some of these questions has led us to conclude that careful planning, full consultation with all affected parties, and experimentation in pilot schools before launching such a large initiative are critical to the long-term success of this kind of venture.

The Process

Given these challenges, I will address the development of a new standards-based report card by illustrating one approach that began in early 2000 in the province of Quebec, Canada. The province moved to a standards-based, cycle-based model; initially, individual districts (called "boards" in Canada) developed their own report cards. In addition to adopting a new standards-based curriculum, the Quebec school system moved from the single-grade-level system that exists almost exclusively in North

American schools today to a cycle-based model, in which students were grouped together for two years. That is to say, cycle one is equivalent to grades 1 and 2 together, cycle two is grades 3 and 4, and so on. As this was a significant departure from the previous structure of grade levels, all aspects of teaching and learning needed revision, not the least of which was the report card. In order for the reader to appreciate the level of complexity this process demands, you should know that from start to *pilot* implementation, it took three years of monthly meetings to develop an actual prototype report card.

Establishing the Working Committee and Team Norms

Our district began by first engaging the teachers' union, asking that they nominate teachers from elementary and secondary levels and from different subject disciplines to serve on a central committee. At this early stage, the committee was composed of all partners (elementary and secondary teachers and principals, parents, and school commissioners) other than students. We took advantage of the provisions contained in the Education act that gave authority of developing the report card to the local level. Indeed, schools even had some discretion to adapt the school board framework for the report card with certain limits. We clearly intended to make this one of the strengths of our reporting system and therefore the format of our report card.

We agreed, among other things, that this committee would not vote. Rather, we would work to achieve consensus on all fundamental issues throughout the process of developing and implementing our reporting system. Furthermore, they would also consider other aspects of assessment policy and assessment techniques for classroom teachers. We agreed to the frequency of meetings, how the meetings would be conducted, who would facilitate them, our goal(s), and our timeline. Establishing norms is a crucial first step that cannot be overemphasized. The work of Richard DuFour and Robert Eaker helped to guide us; they suggest the following questions that teams need to address to be clear as to their purpose:

1. What are our expectations for how our team will operate?

2. What are our two or three most important goals this year?

3. What indicators will we use to assess the effectiveness of our team?

4. What process will we use to resolve conflict? (DuFour & Eaker, 1998, p. 126)

Establishing Guiding Principles

Using various facilitation techniques, we then set about to develop our guiding principles. We recorded these in a policy mindful of the most current literature on assessment, evaluation, and reporting methods (Marzano, 2006; Stiggins, Arter, Chappuis, & Chappuis, 2004b; Guskey & Bailey, 2001), as well as the work of other school districts in North America and around the world. Deciding to write policy was strategically significant, as it shaped the rest of our work throughout this process. The policy outlined the values, expectations, methods, and philosophical approaches to assessment and evaluation that were to be adopted by the school board for all schools and teachers. Some of the issues that were addressed were how we would treat special-needs students, what other documents could be added to the report card, the number of times that the report card had to be issued, and what latitude each school had to modify the basic document.

Our next challenge was to clearly understand how what we were about to develop met the conditions of the provincial policy on assessment and evaluation. The provincial policy required the use of certain generic scales, common across the entire province, for each cycle. There were clear guidelines about the frequency and nature of reporting, using what each school board/district had developed. Concepts such as the difference between assessment *of* learning and assessment *for* learning were pivotal. The provincial policy required that reporting learning during the cycle was intended to support learning, whereas the reported learning at the end of the cycle was intended to decide whether the student was ready to move to the next cycle or should continue in the current cycle until he or she mastered those competencies.

We focused our thinking around what we wanted to communicate, who our audience was, and how we should go about developing our report card, bearing in mind that this document was only one part of a comprehensive reporting approach. Communication could take several forms, as allowed for in the provincial policy. The actual report card was one of those means but clearly the most important in terms of providing written communication to parents at specified intervals over the course of a cycle. Our guiding principles stated that our new report card:

- Must reflect the provincial Ministry orientation and guidelines

- Must use student- and parent-friendly language

- Must reflect progress

- Must be districtwide (also called "boardwide" in Canada) but allow for local needs—in other words, all schools in the district were obligated to use the same document but could adapt it to reflect a particular project locally.

- Must illustrate progress using graphics rather than only numbers or letters

- Must be electronic

- Must represent only one measure of progress—on achievement—and that different means would reflect other aspects of student learning such as effort or behavior

We further decided:

- The report card would have a one-year trial period beginning August 2005 before full implementation.

- Schools would discuss and create a marking scheme to show effort separate from academic progress.

- Schools would propose suggestions on the report card through cycle teams (teams of teachers teaching the same two-year grade groupings) and schoolwide teams. The law required that the final professional judgment be reached through decision-making teams of professionals, and in our district, we wanted to encourage principals to build the team structure implicit in the new organization of learning.

- Rubrics and exemplars would be developed by subject and by the two-year cycle specified in the law (as opposed to a grade-level cycle) on a districtwide basis.

- Parents and students would be surveyed for feedback on the new report card.

Each of these items was strategically considered to respond to what the literature tells us are important ingredients in the process of developing a report card and an assessment and evaluation system (Wiggins, 1997; Guskey & Bailey, 2001). For example, consider the item "Must use student- and parent-friendly language." After all, if students and parents are our intended audience, we need to ensure that they receive and understand our message. Marzano (2006) suggests one approach when he states, "The logical way to begin changing report cards is to create a report card that provides traditional letter grades along with final scores for each measurement topic addressed in a grading period" (p. 125). Marzano's point is that we need to scaffold the changes for a time so that parents can make the transition over time rather than going "cold turkey." If you remove the letter grades, you run a huge risk of taking away the only point of reference that parents understand about how their child is doing. It is very much like the change from Imperial measures to the metric system that Canada went through. I for one had a great deal of trouble equating temperatures and speeds with the new measurements, as they had no meaning for me initially.

Guskey and Bailey (2004) address this issue when they suggest that often parents find that the labels we use in a standards-based approach to describe teachers' judgments of reading progress (such as *pre-emergent* and *emergent*) are meaningless or confusing. Their advice is to "choose labels that are expressive, precise, and meaningful" (p. 328). We can follow four guidelines to create such labels:

1. Avoid comparative language. Parents all have gone through a school system built on norm-referenced approaches, and that has become their frame of reference when interpreting grades on a report card. They are used to understanding their child's performance relative to other students in the class. In some new reporting systems, the language still tends to be comparative (such as *good, better, best, superb*). The challenge is how to be clear about each student's progress toward the standard without making comparisons to other students or generating class averages in each subject. We chose terms that described stages of development and performance along a continuum of learning toward the outcome or standard: *beginning, approaching, meeting,* and *exceeding.*

2. Provide actual examples (exemplars) based on student work at various levels of performance. If parents can see what *beginning, approaching, meeting,* and *exceeding* look like in terms of actual student work and can then compare the examples with the work their own child

has produced, these terms will have more meaning for them.

3. Distinguish between levels of understanding and frequency of display. *Levels of understanding* refer to what students are required to do, whereas *frequency of display* refers to how often they demonstrate what is required of them in the performance of a task.

4. Be consistent, as parents will translate labels into what they know best—letter grades. The moment we replace grades with other sorts of symbols to represent quality of performance, parents will try to convert those symbols into letter grades. Levels 1, 2, 3, 4 on a rubric, for example, will mean A, B, C, D to parents, and therein lies the challenge of being consistent. Parents will be confused if students get rubric scores on homework assignments or projects, but the report card displays terms such as *beginning, approaching, meeting,* and *exceeding.*

If we pay attention to many of the assessment and evaluation experts, we come to understand that it is essential that we report achievement separately from behavior, attendance, effort, and attitude. Wiggins (1997) suggests that among other considerations we should avoid euphemisms; offer more information, not less; and link grades to work samples when communicating with parents. The reference to euphemisms means that in education we often are uncertain about what we want to tell parents about their child's progress or lack thereof. Because we don't want to harm student motivation, we use fuzzy or unclear terminology to lessen the impact of negative results. The advice about offering adequate information relates to the fact that we tend not to provide parents with a clear description of how we arrived at our professional judgment about a student's mark. Too often even the student is unable to explain how he or she got a certain mark. We must also take into account that in a standards-based report card, another essential ingredient is to show progress over time, as well as whether a student is progressing at an acceptable rate given the degree of complexity and level of independence he or she should be demonstrating for the grade level.

As we developed the new report card, one of our real challenges was how to represent for parents the difference between assessment *for* learning and assessment *of* learning. We decided to use two different but similar documents to represent this important distinction. Our assessment *for* learning report card showed the degree of growth or progress using the following symbols:

++   Progress above expectation

+   Progress at expectation

+ – Progress at expectation requiring support

–   Progress below expectation/experiencing great difficulty

Checking off one of the following identified effort, which was a separate section and not part of the achievement section:

❏ Eagerly engages in all learning activities; fulfills all requirements for learning tasks

❏ Willingly participates in classroom and homework activities

❏ Participates with some encouragement

❏ Requires continual encouragement and seldom completes classroom tasks

Our team considered effort and participation synonymous, but a school or district may choose otherwise so long as it is clear to the students and parents.

This formative report card (for learning) did not include marks or grades of any kind; to report progress in each of the competencies (outcomes), it used symbols exclusively to place students on a continuum represented by the labels *beginning, approaching, meeting,* and *exceeding.*

The formative report card *(for* learning) was complemented by a *summative* report card *(of* learning), an end-of-cycle (end-of-grade-level) report card where teachers could show their final professional judgment on the student's level of achievement (competence). Given that a cycle lasted two years, there were eight reporting periods, seven of which were for formative reporting; only the last was used as a summative report. The summative report expressed a final judgment on whether the students were able to demonstrate competency and therefore were ready to move to the next cycle. (Visit **go.solution-tree. com/assessment** to view the report card.)

Reporting for Students With Special Needs

Our next challenge was how to indicate differentiation in programs and achievement of students at the same grade level, as this is an important distinction for schools with special-needs populations. These students are unique in ways that require us to acknowledge and account for their special needs in the teaching and reporting process; differentiated instruction requires differentiated reporting. Guskey and Bailey (2001) provide a very complete and helpful analysis of this area of reporting; the reader is encouraged to take particular note of the background they provide. Suffice it to say that we took this into account by identifying students according to their category of learning need given their placement in a cycle (grade) as well as the program strand they were following. As the final document was electronic, we were able to include drop-down menus from which the teacher could select the level of program the student was following in an inclusive classroom and then mark the student according to that level of instruction. (Visit **go.solution-tree.com/assessment** to view the report card.) We also provided a section that allowed the teacher to indicate if additional documentation was attached to the report card to give further explanation, such as the child's IEP (individualized education plan or program) and other similar documentation.

There are many more interesting elements to the document we produced, but let us now turn our attention to the critical implementation process of this journey.

Implementing the New Card

So often, good intentions fail because of poor implementation. Certainly, we had some challenges to overcome. Nevertheless, we gave careful thought to this matter. Focus groups provided feedback and input. We designated one of the district schools as a pilot school. This pilot school played a critical role in refining the implementation process. Its staff members were the only teachers who had the opportunity to give us firsthand feedback on all the shortcomings; there were many at the outset, for sure. We then added four more pilot schools, one in each part of our district. Our idea was that each pilot school would have responsibility as an "expert" school to train teachers from designated partner schools within its vicinity. Teachers talking to teachers is a far better approach than having someone come from outside the classroom, and the credibility of the trainers is enhanced when they have firsthand experience with what their colleagues will face.

We developed a plan to expand the implementation and analyzed the technological requirements of our new document as well as the technology training needs of both principals and teachers. While this issue has not been addressed extensively in this chapter, one must be very cautious about how the technology impacts both completing the report card and the transmission of the report card to the parents. Again, I turn to Guskey and Bailey (2001), who write that "technology presents educators with innumerable options when it comes to communicating information about students' achievement and performance" (p. 133). A word of caution, however: we cannot allow technology to determine our final product, since too often the existing products force us to compromise function for form. Programmers too often drive rather than support the final process. We cannot sacrifice what the educational experts tell us needs to be in place to properly communicate the achievement of students to parents in a helpful manner for what is just convenient for the programmer to develop:

> Technology does not alleviate the need for sound and intelligent professional judgment in the grading process. While technology makes record keeping more efficient and numerical tallying easier, it doesn't alleviate teachers' professional responsibility to carefully weigh the various aspects of that evidence in determining the mark or grade that best summarizes students' achievement or performance. (Guskey & Bailey, 2001, p. 133)

With all these considerations in mind, we decided to create a report card and reporting process that met our policy guidelines and then turned to the technological dimension. Our goal was to convert the look and feel of the paper product into an online document that allowed the teachers to interact with it as though they were working on a paper version, rather than having an algorithm translate their words and comments into symbols that we could then replicate on the final print version of the report card.

Conclusions

While there are so many other aspects to consider in the long and somewhat convoluted process of transitioning to a standards-based report card, the process described in this chapter will give school teams ample information with which to begin. In developing a process to create a new report card format, leaders face many competing points of view that will require a measured response and applicable solutions. Consider the following competing paradigms:

- "Take your time" versus "Make haste slowly"

- "Don't reinvent the wheel" versus "Constructing your own will build commitment to the final product"

- "Parents need to be partners" versus "Parents are not the pedagogical professionals"

- "It is one thing to know what you have to do . . ." versus "Get 'er done" (Larry the Cable Guy approach to change)

- "Leverage the technology" versus "Don't let technology drive your final product"

For each of the options just listed, my advice is first to initiate an intentional conversation to address these competing paradigms. Second, one paradigm will drive your decision with respect to one or more of the others on the list. For example, if you are faced with urgency to get a new report card into place, it is less likely you will be able to engage parents in the process, and this will be at your peril. It is one thing to "get 'er done," but if you make mistakes, some will not give you the latitude to try again. The urgency to get a new system in place militates against involving all the partners in the process of creating something that is unique to your school district. There is great merit in creating your own report card, as it clearly is the best way to build ownership, an essential ingredient in ensuring successful implementation.

The Role of Leadership

Despite the work done at the district or school board level, the report card must be owned by the school. Therefore, the responsibility will surely fall to the school principal to lead, support, and communicate the function and process of this important document. While the report card is an essential ingredient, it is only one part of a much larger aspect of assessment and evaluation and instruction. As Stiggins et al. (2004b) argue, "Leadership in the pursuit of excellence in assessment begins with a guiding vision, clearly showing how assessment fits into effective instruction. All school leaders must understand the importance of quality assessment at all levels, and must put forth the standards that will guide assessment practices in every classroom" (p. 67).

Ultimately, communication is a two-way process. How can we be sure in our reporting, as in our teaching, that the message we send is indeed the message that is received? It is incumbent upon us to realize that to be effective communicators with parents and students about effort, progress, and achievement, a report card is certainly necessary, but not sufficient. The challenges of creating and implementing a new report card and a new reporting system are huge. However, with a thoughtful, well-managed, inclusive process, it is possible to achieve a successful and beneficial conclusion. We have learned that accurate, timely, descriptive feedback can improve learning. Thus the time, effort, and energy required to complete this arduous process are certainly warranted, as the results will benefit students and their parents, our partners in learning.

> For additional examples of standards-based report cards, please refer to Marzano, 2000, 2006; Guskey & Bailey, 2001.

References and Resources

Adam. (2008, September 16). *One response to "Grading and Reporting Systems."* Accessed at http://challengebychoice.wordpress.com/steps-for-developing-a-tiered-program/grading-and-reporting-systems/ on September 16, 2008.

Alvestad, K. (1997, December). Communicating new assessment initiatives. *School Administrator.* Accessed at www.aasa.org/publications/saarti-cledetail.cfm?ItemNumber=4362&snItemNumber=950&tnItemNumber=1995 on February 5, 2009.

Boston, C. (2003). *High school report cards.* College Park, MD: ERIC Clearinghouse on Assessment and Evaluation. (ERIC Digest No. ED481815)

DuFour, R., & Eaker, R. (1998). *Professional learning communities at work: Best practices for enhancing student achievement.* Bloomington, IN: Solution Tree (formerly National Educational Service).

Guskey, T. R. (2002, April 1–5). *Perspectives on grading and reporting: Differences among teachers, students, and parents.* Paper presented at the annual meeting of the American Educational Research Association, New Orleans, LA.

Guskey, T. R. (2004). The communication challenge of standards-based reporting. *Phi Delta Kappan, 86*(4), 326–330.

Guskey, T. R., & Bailey, J. M. (2001). *Developing grading and reporting systems for student learning: Experts in assessment.* Thousand Oaks, CA: Corwin.

Guskey, T. R., & Bailey, J. M. (2004). Communication challenges for standards-based reporting. *Phi Delta Kappan, 86*(4), 326–329.

Marzano, R. J. (2000). *Transforming classroom grading.* Alexandria, VA: Association for Supervision and Curriculum Development.

Marzano, R. J. (2006). *Classroom assessment and grading that work.* Alexandria, VA: Association for Supervision and Curriculum Development.

McColskey, W., McMunn, N., & Schenck, P. (2003, April). *Standards-based grading and reporting in classrooms: Can district training and support change teacher practice?* Paper presented at the annual meeting of the American Educational Research Association, Chicago, IL.

Pardini, P. (1997, December). Report card reform. *School Administrator.* Accessed at www.aasa.org/publications/saarticledetail.cfm?ItemNumber=4363&snItemNumber=950&tnItemNumber=951 on December 1, 2008.

Reeves, D. B. (2003). *Making standards work: How to implement standards-based assessments in the classroom, school, and district.* Englewood, CO: Advanced Learning.

Schmoker, M. (2006). *Results now: How we can achieve unprecedented improvements in teaching and learning.* Alexandria, VA: Association for Supervision and Curriculum Development.

Stiggins, R. J., Arter, J. A., Chappuis, J., & Chappuis, S. (2004a). *Classroom assessment* for *student learning: Doing it right—using it well.* Portland, OR: ETS Assessment Training Institute.

Stiggins, R. J., Arter, J.A., Chappuis, J., & Chappuis, S. (2004b). *Assessment* for *learning: An action guide for school leaders.* Portland, OR: ETS Assessment Training Institute.

Tucker, M. S., & Codding, J. B. (1998). *Standards for our schools: How to set them, measure them, and reach them.* San Francisco: Jossey-Bass.

Wiggins, G. (1997, December). Tips on reforming student report card grades. *School Administrator.* Accessed at www.aasa.org/publications/content.cfm?ItemNumber=4359 on December 1, 2008.

PART THREE

Assessing Students at Risk

MARK WEICHEL

Dr. Mark Weichel became the director of curriculum for Papillion-La Vista Public Schools in 2009. Prior to that, he served as a high school building administrator and junior high school social studies teacher. He received his undergraduate degree from Midland Lutheran College in Fremont, Nebraska, and masters degrees and a doctorate degree from the University of Nebraska at Omaha. Following the completion of these degrees, he has been active with the University of Nebraska at Omaha and Peru State College as an adjunct professor.

NINE

Lowering High School Failure Rates

Mark Weichel

Grades have been a fundamental part of the traditional education landscape for years. From the moment we enter school, we are taught that an A is good and that an F likely means attending summer school, retaking a class, or enrolling in other remedial programs. Historically, it was acceptable for schools to allow some students to fail and to let students choose for themselves where they fell within the grading continuum. In the 1980s and 1990s, however, this way of thinking began to change as our society and job market began to look entirely different. In our highly technological, diverse, and global world, students without an education have fewer opportunities than at any other time in history (Stiggins, 2005).

This new landscape and new set of expectations for educators have created an interesting challenge. As educational leaders, we have been called upon to make changes to the way schools look at underperforming students who receive the dreaded F. Instead of playing the "blame game"—in which teachers blame the students, students blame the teachers, and parents blame the teachers and/or students—we are asked to find a solution that is win/win for all stakeholders. This new challenge poses the question, How should an administrator respond when data coming from a classroom indicate that a large number of students are failing?

Solving this problem as a surface level issue could be quite easy: principals could take the authoritative approach and tell all teachers that they can't fail more than a certain number of students. If teachers choose to comply, fewer students would fail. However, this is obviously *not* what any educator would suggest. The real way to lower failure rates is to get more students to *earn* passing grades.

Having worked in various secondary buildings that have faced this problem, I have learned that improving assessment scores and reducing high failure rates take a commitment to ongoing collaboration, implementation of best-practice assessment and grading strategies by all teachers, schoolwide intervention plans, and continual follow-up by the administrator. While these are time-consuming tasks, my experience has shown me that they are worth it. This chapter will explore six steps a principal can implement to change the culture of a school in which low failure rates are the norm.

Item 1: Develop a Committed Team

When confronted with a high failure rate, principals may be tempted to take a top-down managerial approach. I have seen many examples of this strategy. In one school, administrators gave teachers a specific failure rate that was the official "line in the sand." Teachers came to know that as long as they didn't exceed 10 percent failure, they would not be asked about their grading or assessment practices. However, if the failure rate was higher than 10 percent, they could expect to have a one-on-one meeting in which they'd be expected to justify the failing grade of each student. In a different school, teachers who had failed more than a certain percentage of students (again 10 percent) faced a different type of scrutiny. Grade-level counselors interviewed the students who had failed to find out why they failed and who was to blame. Once the results of these individual meetings were conducted, principals shared findings with the teachers in the "failure zone" and suggested they find ways to improve.

As this example shows, top-down management of assessment results and grading practices can create tremendous pressure. The principal placed the blame for high failure rates solely on the shoulders of the teachers. Administration intervened, but only to require the teachers to change their practices. As one might suspect, teachers who took part in these "assessment conversations" were not typically proponents of this plan. In fact, many teachers became very negative after these meetings and shifted their energy toward resisting the administrator rather than improving their assessment results and grading practices.

While these strategies had a negative impact on culture and climate, I have found that there are ways to improve failure rates that don't alienate staff. One effective way of implementing change in assessment and grading practices or any other task is to start by establishing a committed team or guiding coalition (Kotter, 1996). While it may take longer than holding a one-on-one meeting or issuing a reprimand, it is extremely effective; James Kouzes and Barry Posner (2003) studied thousands of organizations from all sectors of professions and found that there was not one example of a successful organization that didn't have active involvement and support of a team.

A guiding coalition who will develop and implement strategies that will impact student learning is critical. Examples I have been involved with are described throughout this chapter. Most principals can easily identify the teacher leaders in their building. They could be formal department chairs, school improvement team members, or informal leaders. Whom do teachers seek out when they have a question? Whose opinions at staff meetings seem to get large numbers of staff members nodding their head in approval? Who "holds court" in the hallway where the teachers hang out during passing time? Leaders implementing assessment and grading policy change will want those people standing next to them when they share new plans for implementation.

One major change process I was involved in was led by a team that included fifteen hand-selected teacher leaders. This team worked together throughout the summer and developed major changes to the school's assessment and grading policies. (Much of the work this group completed is described throughout this chapter and outlined in the six steps.) In the fall, at in-service meetings, attendees were divided into five groups. Each of the five administrators worked with teacher leaders from the planning team to copresent various policies described in the sections that follow. When this team of teachers and administrators worked together and answered questions together, the rest of the staff voiced very little concern or opposition. This was very surprising as teachers were asked to reconsider how they grade late work and work with students, and to use new school structures and interventions. The guiding coalition had poured their hearts into this project, and the staff weren't about to minimize their work. Knowing the impact this team had on successful adoption of new policies, I couldn't imagine attempting this type of a change effort without a team.

Item 2: Develop a Buildingwide Best-Practice Grading Philosophy

When developing a plan to confront high failure rates, you and your team must become knowledgeable regarding best-practice assessment and grading strategies. As a team, make it a priority to attend conferences and workshops; take part in learning teams that meet on a regular basis to discuss current journal articles and books on assessment.

After providing key leaders in the building with assessment information that will help guide future decisions, develop a policy that represents the school's policies regarding grading. By having a policy statement that is systematic for all teachers in the building, commonly discussed, and in the faculty handbook, you can have some assurance that best-practice grading practices are being implemented in every classroom. Ken O'Connor (2002) describes this type of policy as one that supports learning and encourages student success.

There are many excellent resources to use with your team. Teams I have worked with have leaned heavily on the work of a few key assessment researchers and authors that are referenced in this section. Within the work of these authors, the following topics emerged as focal points when developing our grading policy statement. These short briefings do not intend to provide a thorough background on the following topics; they simply represent some of the important concepts administrators may consider to engage his or her team in developing a grading philosophy.

Eliminate Use of Zeros

Many schools and districts have begun questioning the traditional purpose of the use of zeros. It has been argued that assigning zeros does not accurately reflect what a student has learned, inaccurately magnifies negatively low scores, and simply doesn't work. In fact, not one study has shown that assigning a zero is effective in improving student achievement (Guskey, 2004). There are numerous strategies to use in place of assigning zeros, such as calculating averages in different ways, assigning incomplete grades until satisfactory work is completed, reporting nonacademic factors separately on grade reports, and changing grading scales to A, B, C, D, and F instead of percentages. This last technique puts each grade distribution on an equal seven- or ten-point scale as opposed to the disproportional scales when, for example, 0 to 59 percent is a failing grade (O'Connor, 2002; Guskey, 2004). Other methods of limiting the number of zeros students receive include simply mandating that zeros are the last resort and can only be assigned after specific interventions have been employed

(Weichel & Schonewise, 2007) and making 50 percent the lowest grade a student can receive (DuFour, 2005).

In one discussion about the use of zeros with the guiding coalition, the team determined that staff would simply not support 50 percent as the lowest grade a student would receive. The team knew that suggesting this component could put the entire change process in jeopardy. Teachers were told that they could still assign zeros to students who made the choice to not do their work, but only as the last resort, and only after the teacher had employed specific interventions (Weichel & Schonewise, 2007). The allowance that teachers could still give zeros in the worst-case scenario seemed to make this plan acceptable to even the most resistant staff. In reality, very few students do receive zeros after having the interventions. Knowing the staff and being creative with this concept was a major advantage to the team's ability to implement this concept.

Calculate Final Grades in New Ways

Consider the guidelines for nontraditional grading practices developed by Ken O'Connor (2002). Some examples include not including all scores, always providing multiple assessment opportunities that require "grading in pencil," using the individual grades from the semester as a "body of evidence," and avoiding use of the mean.

Many teachers can't imagine not using the overall percentage to determine a final grade. Some teachers prefer using a percentage because it takes the human element out of explaining a poor grade to students and parents; they can simply pull out the list of scores for the semester and show how the final grade is calculated. Looking at those same grades as simply a body of evidence to use when determining a grade that indicates the student's knowledge of the subject area is much more difficult.

I have yet to work in a school that has been able to make a schoolwide policy and effort to accept these changes. In fact, it would be hard to make this type of change without other major changes as well. Currently, a single grade is intended to communicate many things such as attendance, achievement of goals, attitude, class participation, behavior, and work completion. Leaders in the field have suggested that if a school would truly be able to give a grade that reflected only student achievement towards the goals, there would also need to be a place to give grades for other measures, such as progress towards the goals and work habits (Tomlinson & McTighe, 2006).

While whole-school changes may be difficult, it is important to remind teachers that they do have flexibility in assigning grades. It is not uncommon for teachers to "ask permission" from administrators if they can assign a student a different grade from what the calculated average might show. For example, a teacher may share a story about how a student had medical problems at the start of the year and really struggled. However, in time, the student made major progress, understood the concepts, showed evidence of learning, and aced the final. The teacher wants to know if he or she can assign a better grade than what the overall average computed. This is an excellent example of how an administrator can encourage innovative types of grading practices. While a schoolwide policy with major changes in computing grades may be difficult to implement, giving permission and having discussions about these types of themes can "plant a seed" for future thought and implementation.

Accept Late Work

Thomas Guskey (2004) has identified the purposes of grading as to communicate, provide evidence that demonstrates the students' effort levels or inappropriate responsibility, help discover educational paths, provide incentives, and evaluate the instructional programs. If a teacher doesn't accept late work, she will accomplish none of these goals. Many students would probably prefer that teachers don't accept late work, and some teachers might suggest that allowing students to turn in late work for credit is "too easy on them," "letting them off the hook," and "not teaching responsibility."

Others would say that the school shouldn't punish students for not learning what they are expected to learn. This type of punishment is counterproductive if our goal is that all students learn (Guskey, 2004). Allowing late work teaches students what life is like in the adult world. If we don't file our taxes by April 15 every year, we don't just "get a zero" and move on to the next year; we get sanctions and penalties until we file. We still have to do the work. To gain acceptance among teachers in implementing a change in late work, I have found it very helpful to incorporate a "loose-tight" management system. In one school, departments were given some basic parameters with regard to the percentages that would be taken off for late work and asked to determine their policies. In time, because the departments were so close, schoolwide practices were eventually agreed upon and adopted.

Reduce Extra Credit

O'Connor (2002) states that grades should be directly related to learning goals and reflect individual achievement toward those goals. They should not reflect effort, participation, attitude, or other behaviors. Extra credit does not reflect academic progress toward a learning goal and should be used sparingly, if at all.

This has perhaps been the concept that teachers I have worked with have most easily accepted into their practice without concern. It seems that traditionally, students who continually ask for extra credit opportunities are the ones who aren't doing the work that is originally assigned. In a system where students are expected to do the work and are given interventions when they don't, extra credit isn't needed; students simply complete the original assignments. Having a schoolwide policy of little to no extra credit supports teachers and gives them permission to answer the question failing students ask with a commonly accepted answer of no.

Rethink Homework

Teachers should assign homework that is designed with a clearly articulated purpose and outcome and assign an amount of homework that is in congruence with the grade and level of the course (Marzano, 2001). Additionally, teachers should be very clear with parents and students on the homework policy regarding grades and comments. It is acceptable not to grade or make comments on every piece of work that students complete; Harris Cooper (2007) suggests periodic grading and commenting can be just as effective as when it is done with every homework assignment.

A principal can monitor homework policies through attending teacher collaboration meetings and talking with kids. In teacher collaboration meetings, instructors talk about assessment, grading strategies, and assignments. This is an excellent time to ask probing questions. Additionally, in a school that has a strong intervention system, the principal will talk with students every day about their homework and what they need to do, and will be able to see the actual homework. In these settings, you can also learn a lot about homework by asking students, "How will your work be judged? What do you do to get an A versus a C?" Student responses will reveal whether or not the teacher is communicating the goals and expectations in a clear manner when assigning homework (Richardson, 2008).

Interestingly, when teachers are sending students to administrators for incomplete work, there seems to be a natural "check and balance" system that weeds out "busywork." From my experience, teachers seem to ask themselves if the work that they are assigning is worthy of applying the intervention system. They don't want to send a student to the principal for not having completed, for example, a crossword puzzle. Only meaningful work deserves intervention; and if it isn't worthy of enforcing, it may not be worthy of assigning.

Use Formative Assessments

Formative assessment has been described as "a planned process in which assessment–elicited evidence of students' status is used by teachers to adjust their ongoing instructional procedures or by students to adjust their current learning tactics" (Popham, 2008, p. 17). It would be an understatement to say that quality formative assessments are a good idea for teachers to use in the classroom: "Research has suggested that the use of formative assessment, or assessment FOR learning, can double the rate of learning" (Clymer & Wiliam, 2007, p. 36). When teachers provide transparent learning goals, give timely and meaningful feedback, and engage students in a day-to-day reflective process, they are using formative assessment correctly. To promote assessment *for* learning, schools should consider reviewing any grading policies that require grades on every piece of homework (Black, Harrison, Lee, Marshall, & Wiliam, 2004; Clymer & Wiliam, 2007; Stiggins, 2005).

It seems that many teachers do some very good things in the area of formative assessments, while others could do more. Principals, however, should be careful when determining how to implement professional development activities. James Popham (2008) contends that principals need to consider the level of adoption they want to encourage. At the first level, the principal looks to make changes in teachers' instructional adjustments; by the fourth level, the principal looks for schoolwide implementation. A first step for a principal and his or her team would be to determine the level of implementation that will best suit the school. A principal can take first steps without trying to do too much at once and causing everyone to lose interest (Popham, 2008).

One way to begin increasing formative assessment awareness is to have staff share specific ways they are using formative assessment in their classrooms. Having one department in charge of this sharing each month can be an effective way to organize this event. In one such meeting, a new-to-the-building science teacher shared an activity he had just learned at a workshop. After he described how he checks for understanding by having students hold up a colored cup (red, yellow, or green) to indicate how well they understood the material, the building's leadership team had to go out and order a box of colored cups because so many teachers wanted to incorporate this easy-to-use approach in their classrooms.

Use Summative Assessments

Summative assessments are sometimes described as tests administered after the learning has taken place. For your policy, consider items such as summative assessments being the main criteria for grades (O'Connor, 2002; Tomlinson & McTighe, 2006). As a team reading about summative assessments and determining criteria for how much summative assessments should make up a final grade, be open to an honest discussion. In one school I observed, each department met to determine these questions for each of their levels of courses—regular, honors, and advanced placement. They ultimately determined that the advanced placement and honors classes should have higher percentages than the others, in some cases as high as 85 percent (with the remaining 15 percent coming from project or homework grades). While none of the departments went as far as to say 100 percent of a grade would consist of summative assessments, teachers made major changes to their thinking. Starting with departmental agreed-upon percentages was a major step toward alignment to what the researchers mentioned earlier would advocate as a schoolwide policy.

Item 3: Develop an Intervention Plan

Leading education authors and researchers seem to agree that certain characteristics will raise levels of student achievement. These include having a sound and viable set of standards that are taught in classrooms (Schmoker, 2006), effective teachers (Marzano, 2003), ongoing and planned formative assessments (Popham, 2008), and a collaborative culture (DuFour, 2007). A school with *all* of these features may not have a high failure rate. However, what if, despite all of these positive features, students just refuse to do the work? A school needs to have a plan when students aren't learning the intended curriculum—for any reason—and are failing because of it. Additionally, the plan needs to have interventions and be systematic, timely, and directive (DuFour, DuFour, Eaker, & Karhanek, 2004).

In short, an intervention plan impacts learning and classroom assessment practices on a daily basis. In the past, some students were allowed to not complete the classroom work and were not able to be evaluated or assessed by the teacher. Without the ebb and flow of student work and teacher feedback, learning is simply not going to be maximized. A schoolwide intervention system is a great way to ensure that more students are receiving feedback from all of their teachers because more students are turning in their work.

In a school without an intervention plan, conversations with teachers about how to improve failure rates put the sole authority for students' success on the teachers developing and implementing their own strategies for improvement. With an intervention plan, teachers have a "system" and can rely on a team of educators working together. A solid system at the secondary level should consider what happens when students come to class with incomplete work and when students continue to fail classes. Additionally, best-practice examples allow for what Rick DuFour has termed "loose-tight" management by setting clear expectations while allowing for teacher individuality.

There are many excellent examples of intervention programs. Papillion-La Vista South High School in Nebraska has a two-level intervention system. Students who don't complete classroom work are on level one, and students who are failing a course are on level two. Based on their level, students receive interventions and support by an administrator and/or counselor until their academic difficulties are remedied (Weichel & Schonewise, 2007).

At Margaret Mead Junior High in Schaumburg School District 54 in Illinois, another two-tiered approach has been successful. Students who are missing homework assignments receive systematic intervention regardless of their grade level or teacher. Additionally, students who do not meet the 80-percent proficiency benchmark on common assessments receive extra time and support based upon the academic department's intervention system. Principal Steve Pearce (personal communication, September 3, 2008) states, "Our students are performing at the highest levels in the 27-year history of the school. This can be directly linked to our systemic pyramid of interventions."

As assessment leaders, principals must ensure that assessment results lead to changes in instruction. As leaders, we can lead in the creation of a systemic solution to what appears to be a classroom problem. Under a clearly described and utilized intervention plan, teachers have the responsibility to involve the team when a student is underperforming in class. When such a system exists, there are no surprises when a student does fail because he or she would have been receiving extra help and support all along the way. Naturally, these support mechanisms for the teachers and the students lead to improved learning and lower numbers of students who fail classes.

Item 4: Use Technology to Facilitate Frequent Dialogue

Assessment technology can save time in managing a school's failure rate. One common mistake that I have seen principals make is to wait until the end of the semester to run reports and determine which teachers needed to improve student achievement. By then, there is no time to give further assistance. With technology, a savvy administrator can monitor this issue throughout the year and provide needed information to all stakeholders.

In my experience, many computer systems can generate a weekly report indicating important information such as which students are failing, the classes they are failing, and their current percentage grade in the class. This list is helpful to everyone when distributed every Monday morning. Classroom teachers can check the list and see which students are failing. Coaches can see which athletes from their teams need help. Study hall supervisors can check on who needs to be studying—and *what* they should be studying—rather than "hanging out." Counselors get a clear picture of which students they should offer interventions. Administrators can use this information to begin having meaningful dialogue with teachers.

For a moment, envision yourself as a classroom teacher. Consider how you might feel and respond in the following two conversations that you might have with a principal:

1. [At the end of the semester] *I noticed that twenty students failed your class this fall. Can you show me what you did for each of these students to help them pass and tell me how this will be corrected in the fall?*

2. [Three weeks into the semester] *Hey, I noticed that you had quite a group of students on the failure list that came out today. I also noticed that there were a few students on the list that I hadn't seen in the office yet. Do you want to send the students to me so I can get them going on interventions?*

The first scenario contains what might be traditional dialogue between an administrator and a teacher when failure rates are higher than the administrator would like. The second scenario represents the type of proactive dialogue that can happen when ongoing conversations take place. In stark contrast to the top-down management structure, this process is collaborative in every sense of the word. In a collaborative school, it only makes sense to engage in behaviors that are consistent with what you are asking others to do.

Jeffrey Pfeffer (1998) has written that there are certain traits that leaders of an organization need to have in order to be effective. He writes that leaders must build trust, encourage change, and measure what matters. The system of interventions and collaboration that takes place with teachers just described is an excellent example of this type of leadership. There is a clear *encouragement for change* when the administrator is talking to the teacher about students who are struggling and mutually deciding strategies of how they can have interventions arranged for them. There is a clear effort *to measure what matters* when the administrator can look and determine which students are not meeting learning targets and what teachers might need extra support on a weekly basis. Additionally, by being able to focus on the results throughout the semester, the administrator can repeatedly check back with the students and teachers in order to determine if the interventions are working or need to be changed. There is a clear effort *to build trust* as the administrator and teacher exchange ideas in a nonthreatening manner that focuses on what is best for each student.

Item 5: Have Formal Discussions as a Last Resort

In a traditional setting, having a formal discussion with a teacher about his or her respective failure rates at the end of the semester could be item number one. In this checklist, it is number five. At this point, if many students in a particular teacher's classroom are still failing, further conversation is needed—but it would only occur after numerous other discussions about individual students, interventions that seemed to work, interventions that didn't work, and other solutions to problems that came about during the semester. As a result, the teacher won't view the conversation as a once-a-semester reprimand, but rather as a normal step in the process of improving learning for all students in the building.

In these types of meetings, it is important to give the teacher an opportunity to reflect upon the various possibilities and develop a plan to make improvements. It is not automatically the teacher's fault. After all, there are many reasons that a student may fail a course. Rick Stiggins (2008, p. 48) pointed out five reasons that a teacher might have for why students might not have learned:

1. They lacked the prerequisites needed to achieve what I expected of them.

2. I didn't understand the target to begin with, and so could not convey it appropriately.

3. My instructional methods, strategies, and materials were inappropriate or inadequate.

4. My students lacked the confidence to risk trying— the motivation to strive for success.

5. Some force(s) outside of school and beyond my control (death in the family, for example) interfered with and inhibited learning.

After discussing these possible reasons with the teacher, engage the teacher in reflective dialogue, and direct the meeting to focus on possible solutions and strategies. As a collaborative team, discuss possible future goals (SMART goals) and a plan that can be used to see better results. SMART goals are goals that are designed with a very clear purpose and are intended to be Strategic and Specific, Measurable, Attainable, Results-oriented, and Time-bound (O'Neill & Conzemius, 2006). A SMART goal gives teachers and teams a very clear direction about what needs to be accomplished. An example SMART goal for a teacher with a high failure rate might be, "to decrease the failure rate in my classrooms by 50 percent for second semester." Remind the teacher that a goal such as reducing his or her failure rate by a specific percentage would likely contribute to the progress toward departmental, school, and district goals (DuFour, DuFour, Eaker, & Many, 2006). As the assessment leader in the building, the principal needs to work with those teachers who don't understand how to make students successful in their classroom and challenge progress.

You may never change the most adamant resisters. However, if improving learning and the assessment results for students in the building and not allowing high failure rates are important, this is the hard work that you must do. Some teachers, despite all of these steps, will not fulfill the school leader's vision. At that point, the administrator will need to respond accordingly to these resisters. Rick DuFour (2005) suggests the following approaches:

- Assume the resister has good intentions and wants to succeed.

- Identify specific behaviors that are essential to the success of the initiative.

- Focus on behavior—not attitude.

- Plan for small victories.

- Confront incongruent behavior with specific concerns and communicate.

These steps demonstrate the commitment you have as an administrator working towards a goal. By continually communicating and sharing specific goals, the resister will have little option but to make progress toward school goals.

Item 6: Make Low Failure Rates the Way We Do Business

John Kotter's (1996) model for leading change highlights a common mistake made by corporations and businesses: often, once the founders of a change consider the change complete, the efforts cease. A leader in the change movement has to consciously remind staff of the new approaches, practices, and attitudes and make sure future staff and managers understand and continue with the effort.

In this assessment-change scenario, there are many steps to take to ensure that the new way of thinking becomes the culture of the building. Continue to work with the guiding coalition to monitor the programs and assessment and grading policies in place, and don't be afraid of making changes if it becomes necessary. Continue to review the school's intervention program and required actions for failing students with new and veteran teachers, and continue to implement the plan, no matter how time intensive it gets. Hire new staff members who are "on the same page" philosophically with what the school is doing. In interviews, provide a glimpse of the school's assessment and grading policies and practices so that a potential hire can determine if the culture is a good fit. Continually reinforce the principles of collaboration and the need for frequent formative assessments, and never stop measuring what matters. By following through with these items, improved teaching and learning and low failure rates will become the way your school does business.

Final Thoughts

This chapter has outlined some strategies for how an administrator should respond when student achievement data coming from a classroom indicate a large number of students are not learning and subsequently failing. The six key steps outlined offer an alternative to top-down management and ways to incorporate strategies that are ongoing and unintimidating.

A generation ago, it was considered acceptable for large numbers of students to fail a given course (Stiggins, 2005). This practice is no longer an option. As school administrators, if we see students not learning and failing, we need to confront the brutal facts of our building and determine strategies for dealing with these issues. We must learn from those results and support teachers in their work to help students meet our high expectations. By using key teacher leaders to help develop policies and interventions, using technology to monitor results, and continually working with teachers, a principal can do much to ensure a strong assessment and grading program is in place that results in low failure rates.

References

Black, P., Harrison, C., Lee, C., Marshall, B., & Wiliam, D. (2004). Working inside the black box: Assessment for learning in the classroom. *Phi Delta Kappan, 86*(1), 9–21.

Clymer, J., & Wiliam, D. (2007). Improving the way we grade science. *Educational Leadership, 64*(4), 36–42.

Cooper, H. (2007). *The battle over homework: Common ground for administrators, teachers, and parents.* Thousand Oaks, CA: Corwin.

DuFour, R. (2005, February 8). *Whatever it takes: How professional learning communities respond when kids don't learn.* Presentation at Educational Service Unit #3, Omaha, NE.

DuFour, R. (2007, July 25). *Making the case for professional learning communities.* Presentation at the Solution Tree Professional Learning Communities Institute, Council Bluffs, IA.

DuFour, R., DuFour, R., Eaker, R., & Karhanek, G. (2004). *Whatever it takes: How professional learning communities respond when kids don't learn.* Bloomington, IN: Solution Tree (formerly National Educational Service).

DuFour, R., DuFour, R., Eaker, R., & Many, T. (2006). *Learning by doing: A handbook for professional learning communities at work.* Bloomington, IN: Solution Tree.

Guskey, T. (2004). Are zeros your ultimate weapon? *Principal Leadership, 5*(2), 49–53.

Kotter, J. (1996). *Leading change.* Boston: Harvard Business School.

Kouzes, J., & Posner, B. (2003). *The Jossey-Bass academic administrator's guide to exemplary leadership.* Indianapolis: Jossey-Bass.

Marzano, R. (2001). *Classroom instruction that works: Research-based strategies for increasing student achievement.* Alexandria, VA: Association for Supervision and Curriculum Development.

Marzano, R. (2003). *What works in schools: Translating research into action.* Alexandria, VA: Association for Supervision and Curriculum Development.

O'Connor, K. (2002). *How to grade for student learning: Linking grades to standards.* Glenview, IL: Pearson Education.

O'Neill, J., & Conzemius, A. (2006). *The power of SMART goals: Using goals to improve student learning.* Bloomington, IN: Solution Tree.

Pfeffer, J. (1998, Spring). The real keys to high performance. *Leader to Leader, 8*, 23–29.

Popham, J. (2008). Formative assessment: Seven stepping stones to success. *Principal Leadership, 9*(1), 16–21.

Richardson, J. (2008). Evidence of learning: A conversation with Jay McTighe. *Principal Leadership, 9*(1), 30–35.

Schmoker, M. (2006). *Results now.* Alexandria, VA: Association for Supervision and Curriculum Development.

Stiggins, R. (2005). From formative assessment to assessment for learning. *Phi Delta Kappan, 85*(4), 324–328.

Stiggins, R. (2008). *An introduction to student-involved assessment for learning.* Upper Saddle River, NJ: Pearson Education.

Tomlinson, C., & McTighe, J. (2006). *Integrating differentiated instruction: Understanding by design.* Alexandria, VA: Association for Supervision and Curriculum Development.

Weichel, M., & Schonewise, E. (2007). Pyramid of interventions: A progression of academic support. *Principal Leadership, 8*(4), 28–31.

CHARLES HINMAN

Charles Hinman, EdD, has seventeen years' experience as a high school administrator and is assistant superintendent of secondary education in the Newport Mesa Unified School District. Dr. Hinman is committed to ensuring that *all* students leave the K–12 experience with options for success that include a high school diploma, access to the work force, community college, technical institute, and/or college and university. Dr. Hinman developed a passion for educational intervention and safe school programs during the seven years he spent working in an inner-city environment. He drew from that experience to develop and implement a "Pyramid of Success," which involved strategic interventions, credit recovery, and the launching of a voluntary drug-testing program. Several of these strategies are embraced by school districts and their surrounding communities, the Orange County Sheriff's Department, and the White House Office of National Drug Control Policy.

TEN

Assessing the Student at Risk: A New Look at School-Based Credit Recovery

Charles Hinman

It is long past time to take a hard look at the relationship between student assessment and student achievement. Failure to do so will only perpetuate a "silent epidemic": the U.S. high school dropout rate (Silent Epidemic, 2007). One could go as far as to say that such an analysis should be an obligation, considering these education statistics from a report by Civic Enterprises:

- Every 29 seconds another student gives up on school, resulting in more than one million American high school students who drop out every year.

- Nearly one-third of all public high school students— and nearly one half of all African Americans, Hispanics and Native Americans—fail to graduate from public high school with their class.

- There are nearly 2,000 high schools in the U.S. where 40 percent of the typical freshman class leaves school by its senior year.

- The dropout problem is likely to increase substantially through 2020 unless significant improvements are made.

- Dropouts are more likely than high school graduates to be unemployed, in poor health, living in poverty, on public assistance, and single parents with children who drop out of high school.

- Dropouts earn $9,200 less per year than high school graduates and more than $1 million less over a lifetime than college graduates.

- Dropouts were more than twice as likely as high school graduates to slip into poverty in a single year and three times more likely than college graduates to be unemployed in 2004.

- Dropouts are more than eight times as likely to be in jail or prison as high school graduates.

- Dropouts are four times less likely to volunteer than college graduates, twice less likely to vote or participate in community projects, and represent only 3 percent of actively engaged citizens in the U.S. today.

- The government would reap $45 billion in extra tax revenues and reduced costs in public health, crime, and welfare payments if the number of high school dropouts among 20-year olds in the U.S. today, which numbers more than 700,000 individuals, were cut in half. (Silent Epidemic, 2007)

While these statistics are extremely alarming, many educators believe the percentages are actually much higher due to the liberal and often confusing dropout criteria of many districts and states. Since the enactment of No Child Left Behind (NCLB), states have been under pressure to improve graduation rates, and calculation methods vary from state to state. This reporting process has often hid more information about school performance than it disclosed (Winters & Green, 2008). The issue becomes even more critical when we find that the highest rate of dropout occurs in the ninth grade—when the student is only a fourteen- or fifteen-year-old child.

Unfortunately, educational pedagogy still remains steeped in a culture where it is the role of the teacher to teach and the student to learn. But what happens if the student does not learn or actually chooses not to learn? Do we allow these students to fail and eventually become dropout statistics? Whether the cause of failure is being educationally ill-prepared, experiencing culture shock, or being in an educational environment that emphasizes student responsibility over student learning, a single disrupted semester can put a student so far behind in credits that he loses all faith in himself and the educational system. For that student and others like him, graduating on time with a high school diploma from their neighborhood school seems like a lost cause. They often just drop out or are shipped to a traditional continuation school to recover lost credits, where they are required both to find the motivation for independent study and to put in the "seat time" that is too often accepted as a proxy for learning.

Common sense should tell us that traditional continuation schools use a preposterous approach; these students have already shown they don't have the capacity to succeed in a comprehensive setting. Students who are sent to these alternative education centers often have learning disabilities, problems at home, mental health issues, or a combination thereof (Esch, 2008). These students need an intensive program that provides social/ emotional support as well as academic intervention. Although limited, research on alternative schools reveals that students in these programs receive low expectations, haphazard instructions, loose grading policies, and ineffective teachers (Esch, 2008). They usually spend less time in school, receive less instruction, and have less contact with adults.

There comes a time when we as educators must acknowledge the fact that while our goal is for every child to learn at high levels and to have postsecondary opportunities, our educational, environmental, and cultural systems are flawed, and these systems are failing over 30 percent of American children. Policy should not determine the fate of a child; rather, the fate of a child should dictate policy. The proposal offered here for school-based credit recovery is not an argument that standards shouldn't continue to rise in our schools and the bar shouldn't be held high. Nor should credit recovery be seen as a substitute for a system of interventions or high-quality instruction. The purpose of credit recovery is to provide a student with a second chance to graduate with a diploma from his or her neighborhood high school, having options for the future.

A New Concept for School-Based Credit Recovery

At a conference in 2004, Richard DuFour, author and advocate of professional learning communities, commented on student assessment as follows. He asked, "If a student studies for his driver's license and fails the test, does that mean the student can never get a driver's license? Does it mean he has to retake the entire driver's education class? No—it simply means he has to go back and restudy the areas where he was not proficient and try again."

In 2006, the Newport Mesa Unified School District Board of Education directed the superintendent to do an audit of all educational programs in the district to check for both academic/ social effectiveness and fiscal responsibility. The program that sent credit-deficient students out of the district to continue their education was a concern on both accounts. It was not cost effective nor did it return students to their original ("home") school on track to graduate at a significant rate. Based on this finding, the staff began to explore and initiate a concept that allowed students to stay enrolled in the district and "recover credits" by showing proficiency in a subject area they had failed—even if the timeline for the course had expired. As this program developed, the traditional practice of assessing student performance (including factors such as attendance) shifted to *assessing what the student had learned.* This shift suggests a fundamental question that educators must begin to ask as we address the dropout rate: what is more important, teaching responsibility or ensuring learning? And more importantly, should we consider both of these factors in academic assessment?

The audit's initial findings were revealing and suggested that although a student scored below 60 percent in a high school course, which would traditionally indicate failure, he or she might have actually learned a higher percentage of the required standards. Teacher and student interviews made it clear that it was likely that a high percentage of student failure was based on assessments of *responsibility* (such as homework, attendance, behavior, and participation) rather than assessments of *content knowledge.*

The grading process is regarded by many as the last frontier of individual teacher discretion: "The same school leaders and community members who would be indignant if sports referees were inconsistent in their rulings continu[e] to tolerate inconsistencies that have devastating effects on student achievement" (Reeves, 2008, p. 85). But why not treat student learning on content as we treat student learning on a driver's test: if the student did learn a percentage of the required standards, why not give a diagnostic exam to indicate deficiencies and provide the opportunity to "fill in the gap" rather than force the student to retake the entire class? Until a paradigm shift occurs in academic assessment and teachers stop determining grades based on indicators of responsibility rather than learning, a school-based credit recovery system can give students a second chance to "fill the gap" before having to leave their home school.

While the reasons for student dropout are complex, in a survey done by Civic Enterprises (Bridgeland, Dilulio, &

Morison, 2006), 35 percent of students said failing school was a major factor for dropping out, and 32 percent had been required to repeat a grade before dropping out. If we take a new look at school-based credit recovery, we can give students a second chance beyond the traditional classroom to make up lost credit in a much shorter period of time and thus avoid the endgame of failure. This process allows a student to be concurrently enrolled in his or her home school schedule and a credit-recovery program. Through credit recovery, a student can go from "probable dropout" to "comprehensive high school graduate."

Four Tenets of Credit Recovery

Rick Stiggins (2003) suggests that the first rule of the education profession should be "Do not deprive of hope." The first rule of credit recovery should be "Restore hope where hope is lost." However, for a school-based credit-recovery program to work, administrators, teachers, parents, and students must come to some shared assumptions, understandings, and agreements.

> 1. The purpose of school-based credit recovery is to allow a student to make up credits by showing basic proficiency in a content area where the student previously received a failing grade.

Subject-level teachers must collaboratively develop a baseline assessment tool—a "challenge exam" that will show proficiency—and arrive at consensus on what the minimum learned standards are for earned credit. Ideally, content teams have already developed common summative assessments that can serve as a reference point for this process. As in a driver's license test, if a student does not meet the minimum threshold, a diagnostic of the assessment is done and areas of deficiencies are remediated, guided by the credit-recovery instructor. Not surprisingly, in some cases, students will be able to show competence on their first attempt at a credit-recovery assessment and receive immediate credit. This would be a direct indicator that student learning was being assessed by many factors other than content standards.

> 2. The social/emotional issues that led to student failure must be addressed. School-based credit recovery is intended to be a semester program; the cycle of failure will continue if the core reasons for failure are not addressed.

A school-based credit-recovery program must provide an alternative method of continuing learning in an atmosphere that is sensitive and suited to the development of the intellectual, physical, and social capabilities of our students. Beyond the creation of an educational environment that is healthy, safe, caring, and trusting, school-based credit recovery must incorporate a social developmental program. Time needs to be dedicated to covering societal norms such as dealing with peer pressure, the development of character, goal setting, and decision making.

By the very nature of the program, students have smaller classes in which staff members and their peers recognize them as individuals. (While smaller classes suggest an increase in staffing, a slight reprioritizing of the master schedule can make the program almost cost neutral, as shall be shown later.) Students should feel connected to the staff and know that an adult figure is concerned about their successes and accomplishments. Students need to believe the school values and appreciates that they are creative individuals who do not always fit in the box. It is imperative that administration select the right instructors in the credit-recovery program. Some teachers have a calling for students at risk, and their skills need to be recognized and maximized. These individuals are usually easy to find as they are already having a great deal of success with students at risk somewhere on campus.

> 3. Teachers who gave the original failing grade must be aware that two options exist in a school-based credit-recovery system: (1) the teacher can change the grade to passing, reflecting the level of assessed competence, or (2) the failing grade will remain on the student's transcript from the original teacher, and a new course number will be given for the subject area with only pass credit awarded.

There is a natural pushback to changing the tradition of the "independent contractor" grading system. Institutional practice suggests that a student must perform at a certain level within a certain timeframe and that the results of the performance are final. This is ironic, since most educators will agree that children learn in different ways and at different paces.

To change a student's grade or issue credit after the fact seems to go against the very core of our educational system and the life experiences of our teachers. Accordingly, school leaders must work collaboratively with all stakeholders to ensure that a credit-recovery assessment system remains vetted and authentic. In other words, there needs to be a faculty-supported belief that if a student can pass the collaboratively developed challenge assessment, he or she has in fact *earned* the credit for the course.

It is important to be aware that even after consensus has been reached on credit-recovery assessment, some transformational teachers will allow final grades to reflect those assessments, but other teachers will insist that the original fail grade remain and only credit be given.

This is one of the greatest challenges to developing a credit-recovery system. Tradition, board policies, and education codes often give teachers the autocratic authority to base grades on independent criteria that include many factors beyond academic assessment and traditional timelines. For example, the California Education Code (2009) states:

> 49066. (a) When grades are given for any course of instruction taught in a school district, the grade given to each pupil shall be the grade determined by the teacher of the course and the determination of the pupil's grade by the teacher, in the absence of clerical or mechanical mistake, fraud, bad faith, or incompetency, shall be final.

School leaders and teachers need to begin to discuss why students who achieve similar scores on state standards tests can receive significantly different grades from teachers within the same department. As stated by Thomas Guskey (2008),

> Despite numerous calls for reform, based on our growing knowledge of what works and what does not work in grading, the policies and practices used in most schools today have remained largely unchanged for decades. We persist in using these antiquated practices not because they have proven effective, but because they are steeped in long-held traditions. When asked about the rationale behind these policies and practices, the typical response is simply, "We've always done it that way." (p. 2)

Without a structured assessment system, "students' learning experiences . . . with weak teaching cultures are akin to an instructional lottery, in which their learning opportunities depend heavily on which teacher they draw, from class to class and year to year" (McLaughlin & Talbert, 2001, p. 64). If learning is to become the focus of our educational system, rather than teaching, then academic assessment of learning must be the only indicator of achievement. Assessment of responsibility (for class rules, attendance, homework, and so on) must be reflected elsewhere. These are examples of what Marzano (2000) calls *nonacademic factors* and, while important, should be reported out separately from academics.

> 4. Parents and students must acknowledge, through a contract, that entry into credit recovery all but forfeits acceptance into a four-year college immediately out of high school. However, success in the program and achieving a high school diploma will qualify a student for community college, from which he or she can transfer to a university at a later time.

There are many credit-recovery options open to students who are only a few classes behind or who want to improve a grade for college applications. While the most common venue is summer school, students can also take classes through a local community college, university, or private school, or even through an ever-growing selection of online opportunities. District-approved classes through this pathway generally will replace a failed grade with a new one and recalculate the student's grade point average.

School-based credit recovery is not designed for those students, but rather for students who are severely deficient on credits. Traditionally, when students are severely deficient on credits, they are removed from the home school to attend an "alternative" education. Few of those students ever return to their home school; for them, the alternative program is the last stop before becoming a high school dropout (Esch, 2008). For the students who do return, little or no creditability is given to grades that are made up in an alternative education setting. The home school teachers were most likely not involved in the curriculum development for the alternative site and probably believe that if the student couldn't pass their traditional class, any makeup grade would be substandard. This is all the more reason for credit-recovery assessment to be developed collaboratively at the home site.

Since most teachers will opt not to replace the failing grade, but rather to add a pass credit for graduation purposes, the school needs to hold a straightforward conversation with students entering the school-based credit-recovery program and their parents to emphasize that the program will scarcely affect the student's grade point average. The only goal is to recover credits and graduate from high school. Once the student has received a high school diploma, he or she can address other goals.

Sample District Operating Rule and Regulation for Credit Recovery

Credit/No Credit is an important part of the Credit Recovery Center (CRC). Students in the CRC may earn credits on a Credit/No Credit basis when making up a failed class. Through teacher assessment, students may demonstrate competency in the curriculum they have previously failed and have the missing subject-area credits restored without a letter grade. In this system, the original F grade would stay on the transcript and be included in the student's GPA; the recovered pass/no pass credits would have no impact on the student's GPA, but the credits would count toward graduation. The Credit Recovery Center credit replacement is based solely on work produced and/ or demonstrated competency, and there is no limit to the number of previously failed courses a student could recover by attending and studying in the CRC.

Program Design

The first step in program design is to determine if a dropout problem exists in the district and, more importantly, to determine what is the school board and community threshold of institutional failure. Some administrations hold to the conscience-clearing belief that the torch of responsibility has been passed once a student "leaves" the school for an alternative education setting; this philosophy is inadequate to solve a dropout problem, however. Collect data on how many of those students returned to your district to graduate, how many graduated from the alternative education setting, and how many never graduated at all. National figures indicate that most districts should have serious concerns (Bridgeland, Dilulio, & Morison, 2006). Administrators need to make public what is traditionally private and work with school boards to approve internal credit-recovery systems.

Enrollment

School-based credit recovery should be designed for students who are 25–75 credits behind (that is, between one full semester and a full year behind). The counseling department should run credit search queries at the end of each semester to identify deficient students. Students with fewer than 25 credits deficient can still replace failing grades through traditional avenues, and students who are over 75 credits should be working toward a high school challenge exam or placed in an adult education program. Student placement priority depends upon grade level and entry point. *The priority students for credit recovery are sophomores and juniors*; however, in some individual cases, a senior could be permitted to enter the program. Freshmen should not be admitted into credit recovery because all other interventions need to be exhausted; credit recovery should be seen as a last resort, since it does not replace failing grades. A freshman can still be put back on track through traditional credit-recovery systems such as retaking the full course during summer school or later in his or her high school career. That being said, districts cannot just discount the fact that data suggest the highest dropout rate occurs in the ninth grade (Bridgeland et al., 2006) An assumption has to made that if a district is going to develop a credit-recovery system, it is also being proactive in developing a system of interventions so that students don't get into this situation in the first place. In such a system, eventually there would be no need for credit recovery!

Newport Mesa uses three entry points into credit recovery, each with a separate criterion:

1. **Spring/Summer Semester**
   Priority—Second-semester juniors and second-semester sophomores who are 25–75 credits deficient (between one full semester and a full year behind)

2. **Summer/Fall Semester**
   Priority—Second-semester juniors and second-semester sophomores who are 25–75 credits deficient (between one full semester and a full year behind)

3. **Fall Semester**

   Priority—First-semester juniors and first-semester sophomores who are 25–50 credits deficient (one full semester
   or more behind)

Ideally, a student can catch up on credit deficiencies over a
semester, but being enrolled concurrently with a summer session will allow more time for credit recovery. If the program is
successful, the number of students enrolled should decrease over
time. In addition, the very nature of having a credit-recovery
program at the home school lends itself to continuous conversation regarding student learning and ensuring that all students
are successful in the general education program.

Transition

The transition into and out of a school-based credit-recovery
program is vital to a student's success. The role of the school
counselor is paramount on both sides of the program. First and
foremost, the counselor must complete an intensive review of
the student's academic performance, identify the factors that led
to significant academic failure, and implement an academic plan
as well as one that meets the student's socioemotional needs to
ensure success. When a student leaves the program, a modified
schedule needs to be put in place to allow the student time to
make the transition and to continue receiving academic and
socioemotional support. If one of the factors contributing to
failure was teachers' insistence on grading responsibility, it must
be assumed that this will continue to be a problem when the
student returns to the traditional program; addressing the assessment model that caused the original failure must be a priority
in the support process.

Schedule

In a school-based credit-recovery program, students remain
at their home school and take an additional course during their

school day or substitute credit recovery for an elective. This schedule allows students to stay concurrently enrolled and not fall further behind while making up credits. In the section reserved for credit recovery, students who failed a required class can pass it through a challenge exam or by retaking a course through approved online software.

District teachers must develop challenge exams that represent the basic level of required student-learned standards, remembering the program is designed as a pass/fail, not for grade point average enhancement. If the student does not pass the exam on the initial attempt, a diagnostic is done to show standard areas that need to be remediated, and instruction is provided. The diagnostic results should be simple to obtain since the assessment tool was collaboratively developed by subject-area teachers. Remediation only needs to be done where the student did not meet with success. Depending on the subject area, remediation can be done through the credit-recovery teacher or through an online or a traditional tutorial. The number of attempts on the exam is limited only by the length of enrollment in the program. Online courses should also be approved by site teachers to ensure accountability. Subject-area teachers could also collaborate to develop partial online course recovery to meet the minimum requirement proficiency. Any course offered by the school can be recovered through this program, provided the teachers develop the assessment tool.

Staffing

Obviously school budgets can be the biggest determiner of staffing, but a school-based credit-recovery program can be implemented with as little as one teaching section. Students can be enrolled in NCLB-qualified teacher sections, and credit recovery can be done as a pullout section. However, in a comprehensive high school, a minimum of one full-time teacher equivalent should be assigned to implement the program. By doing a teacher rotation throughout the day, most subject areas can be covered.

The credit-recovery staff should include an academic counselor and a counselor who focuses on student social and emotional growth. If funding permits, the staff should include a specialist in youth at risk who can encourage family involvement by making home visits and conducting family classes. Since the program is school-based, counseling services probably already exist at the site. If additional funding is not available, a prioritization of assignments can be made to support the program. After all, these are still the school's own students!

Results

First-year data from the Newport Mesa Unified School District were extremely impressive in terms of meeting the goal of putting students back on track toward graduation:

- Total students enrolled in program—263

- Total credits recovered—10,447

- Average credits recovered per student—40

- Students not successfully caught up toward graduation—11

- Total students sent to alternative education—19

- Total students back on track for graduation—233

While it was still a pilot program, 86 percent of students enrolled in the Newport Mesa Unified School District school-based credit-recovery program were successful in making up lost credits and were back on track to graduate. It can only be speculated what would happen to these children if this program had not been put into place, but the research suggests that they would probably have dropped out of school and therefore be more likely than their peers who graduated from high school to be unemployed, live in poverty, receive public assistance, go to prison, and live an unhealthy lifestyle (Bridgeland et al., 2006).

There are also qualitative data that suggest a school-based credit-recovery program can change lives. Consider this farewell note from student Katie:

> Today, as I wake up and look at my diploma, it still has not hit me that I have started a new chapter in the story of my life. Every single one of you has made a major impact on my life, and all of you helped push me over that bump in the road. I remember I was ready to throw everything away. I just wanted to give up because I didn't think I could make it. I went to the Credit Recovery Center with little hope and not a lot of dreams. I left there a whole new person. I am the person I am right now because of what all of you have done. I will be thanking you for the rest of my life.

Or this note from Alex:

> I started at the CRC with nine credits as a 10th grader. I was from a broken family and had many personal challenges during my freshman year. After getting caught up on credits, I was put in regular classes where I received A's and B's. I plan on joining the football team next year.

There is a dropout epidemic in America. Every year almost one third of all public high school students succumb to educational Darwinism—*nearly one half* of all African Americans, Hispanics, and Native Americans (Bridgeland et al., 2006). Are we as a society so blind as not to see the toll of this epidemic on our communities— the loss of productive citizens and the high costs associated with increased incarceration, health care, and social services?

The cycle to produce a high school dropout is not a well-kept secret and yet seems to continue without interruption. A student who is not successful in a comprehensive high school setting becomes a "not my problem" child and either drops out or is moved to an alternative education setting to clear the conscience of those who failed him in the first place. More often than not, this is just a short holdover to the street. We must not abandon these children. It is incumbent on us as education professionals to develop a system of interventions in which the responsibility for student success remains with us, at our students' home schools.

While this chapter offers a path for students who are severely credit deficient to graduate from their home schools and have a second chance for success, it also suggests a more deeply rooted problem—the inequities of student assessment in our traditional school systems. That is, unless a school is committed to developing both formative and summative common assessments and a grading rubric that focuses on learning rather than responsibility, it will remain likely that two students in the same course doing the same level of academic work with two different teachers could have a different and possibly dramatically significant grade differential. Through the development of credit-recovery programs, educators can begin to dialog about the true indicators of student learning and to confront the inconsistencies that exist between assessment in the individual classroom and assessment in a learning-focused system.

References

Bridgeland, J., Dilulio, J., & Morison, K. (2006, March). *The silent epidemic: Perspectives of high school dropouts.* A report by Civic Enterprises in association with Peter D. Hart Research Associates for the Bill & Melinda Gates Foundation. Accessed at www.silentepidemic.org/epidemic/statistics-facts.htm on September 9, 2008.

California Education Code. (2009). Accessed at http://law.justia.com/california/codes/edc/49062-49069.5.html on May 8, 2009.

Esch, C. (2008, March). *Dropout factories.* Accessed at www.newamerica.net/publications/articles/2008/dropout_factories_6854 on August 24, 2008.

Guskey, T. R. (2008). *Practical solutions to serious problems in standards-based grading.* Thousand Oaks, CA: Corwin.

Marzano, R. (2000). *Transforming classroom grading.* Alexandria, VA: Association for Supervision and Curriculum Development.

McLaughlin, M., & Talbert, J. (2001). *Professional learning communities and the work of high school teaching.* Chicago: University of Chicago.

Reeves, D. (2008). Leading to change/Effective grading practices. *Educational Leadership, 65*(5), 85–87.

Silent Epidemic. (2007). *The silent epidemic: Statistics and facts about high school drop out rates.* Accessed at www.silentepidemic.org/epidemic/statistics-facts.htm on September 9, 2008.

Stiggins, R. (2003, July). *New beliefs, better assessment.* Presentation at the Professional Learning Communities at Work Institute, San Diego, CA.

Winters, M., & Green, J. (2008, April 8). Reforming drop-out rates. *New York Sun.*

TOM HIERCK

Tom Hierck is assistant superintendent of School District No. 46 (Sunshine Coast) in Gibsons, British Columbia. He has served with the Ministry
of Education, where he worked with
pilot districts on the development of a
funding model that is school-based
and connected to student success. He
also served two years as president of
the British Columbia Principals' and
Vice-Principals' Association and was
president-elect for the Canadian Asso-
ciation of Principals before assuming his current role as an
assistant superintendent. With twenty-six years of experience
in public education, Tom has presented to schools and districts
across North America on the importance of positive learning
environments and the role of assessment to improve student
learning. He was awarded the Queen's Golden Jubilee
Medallion by the Premier and Lieutenant Governor of British
Columbia in a ceremony at Government House for being "a
recognized leader in the field of public education." He is a
contributor to *The Teacher as Assessment Leader* (Solution Tree,
2009).

ELEVEN

Formative Assessment, Transformative Relationships

Tom Hierck

You can enhance or destroy students' desire to succeed in school more quickly and permanently through your use of assessment than with any other tools you have at your disposal.

—Rick Stiggins

Robert Marzano (2007, p. 150) observes, "If the relationship between the teacher and the students is good, then everything else that occurs in the classroom seems to be enhanced." Assessment is particularly reliant upon the establishment and cultivation of positive and effective relationships. Schools of the twenty-first century are challenged to meet overwhelming expectations related to academic, socioemotional, physical wellbeing, and behavioral outcomes while preparing students for an ever-changing future. These challenges are shared by all partners in the education system: leaders, teachers, support staff, students, and parents. After all, students are expected to show positive growth at the end of the ten-month academic year. For some students, growth is incremental and fits that pattern. For others, the results may be farther down the road. The Chinese proverb "The one that plants the tree rarely gets to enjoy its shade" is very apt for our profession. Every child that enters every classroom in September will be different in June. How they change rests, in part, with the experience they have during the year. If the only objective is to get one year older, then little is required of us. Fortunately, more is expected—and delivered.

School administrators may not be directly responsible for the assessment of student learning, but they are responsible for the environment in which learning occurs—and accountable for the results. Leaders must create the conditions that connect assessment outcomes with the commitment all educators make to be catalysts in improving the life chances of every child. How do leaders help teachers build strong relationships with students, and what impact do those relationships have on our formative assessment practice? How do we focus our assessment conversations with teachers on learning results, not teaching intentions? How can we ensure that every student is a success story waiting to be told?

Taking the time to build relationships with students may be time-consuming initially, but this investment reaps benefits throughout the school career of students. The development and nurturing of positive and productive relationships enables educators to improve the life chances of every child, especially those at risk. Consider that in Daniel Goleman's (2006) study of students identified as being at risk, he found that those placed with cold or controlling teachers struggled academically—regardless of whether their teachers followed pedagogic guidelines for good instruction. But if these students had a warm and responsive teacher, they flourished and learned as well as other kids. These stunning results show that quality of relationship, above all else, is the springboard to success.

This chapter will examine the powerful impact that positive assessment relationships have on student success and explore how school leaders can model those relationships with teachers and facilitate teacher growth in assessment practices. Quality assessment practices and relationships can transform our traditional view of school from a place for teaching students to a contemporary view of school as a place for creating learners. As school leaders bring their learning communities together to articulate a vision of student success in the age of standards and accountability, we must always remember that as James Comer has often said, "No significant learning occurs without a significant relationship."

Forming Relationships Through and for Formative Assessment

Relationships are critical, and in assessment, we build relationships by helping students ask and answer questions about their achievement. In doing so, we launch them into success.

Effective formative assessment practice has been proven in countless studies to improve learning (see, for example, Leahy, Lyon, Thompson, & Wiliam, 2005; Black, Harrison, Lee, Marshall, & Wiliam, 2004; Chappuis & Chappuis, 2007/2008; Popham, 2006; Stiggins & Chappuis, 2008). As we look to utilize formative assessment practices to help students close the learning gap and maximize their learning opportunities, we must build our practices on the foundational belief that kids don't care what we know until they know that we care. Struggling students display a surface attitude of "I don't care" that belies their lack of target clarity. As Allen Mendler and Richard Curwin (1999, p. xx) remind us, "We are responsible for teaching all students"—not just the easy to reach, easy to teach. Students may not be excited at the outset to do this deep thinking about their learning, but they become extremely motivated once they have experienced success in new ways. They will take risks if they know we won't think they are "dumb" because of mistakes along the way.

Perhaps the words of Deborah Stipek (2006, p. 46) are a good starting point: "Learning requires effort, and one of the best predictors of students' effort and engagement in school is the relationships they have with their teachers." The more engaged our students become in conversations with teachers about their learning, the greater the likelihood that they will experience success. Royce Sadler (1998) poses three questions that frame this conversation: "Where am I going? Where am I now? How can I close the gap?"

The role of the classroom teacher, then, is to help each student bridge the gap between where that student is and where that student needs to be. This requires specific assessment practices, such as differentiating instruction, reteaching certain targets, or re-sorting students to allow for small-group work connected to teacher strengths. For example, an analysis of the results of students on a common assessment may reveal that although some students struggled with certain concepts, Teacher A had great success with that concept with her class of students. Teacher A can then reteach the key concept to the struggling students while the remaining teachers in the departmental or grade-level team move forward with the other students. To ensure that struggling students don't miss new instruction and fall further behind, reteaching may occur outside of class time.

Changes in teacher practice require administrator leadership. The example of Teacher A reteaching struggling students requires, for example, a principal who supports flexibility in teacher and student timetables. Administrators can further support teachers' effort to close the gap by providing common preparation time for teacher teams or subject-area specialists, ensuring that professional development is aligned with the goal of improving student success, and providing time at staff meetings for a focused look at results of recent assessments (perhaps by subject area as a starting point).

As teachers engage students in dialogue about their learning, the guiding principle must be looking at how student involvement in each teacher-created assessment reflects a bigger plan for involving students in their own assessment. The success of formative assessment practices depends upon the level of student involvement in assessment (Black & Wiliam, 1998), which is also one of Stiggins' five keys to quality assessment (Stiggins, Arter, Chappuis, & Chappuis, 2005). Administrators can evaluate whether teachers are involving students in the assessment process through an examination of the following:

- How teachers make learning targets clear to students

- How teachers give descriptive feedback to students

- How teachers involve students in self-assessment, tracking progress, and setting goals

- How teachers involve students in communicating about their own learning

Clear Learning Targets

How clear are the outcomes in the classrooms of teachers in your school? Do students know the endpoints of a lesson or unit, and is the intent of the instructional phase to ensure they all reach these endpoints?

Students often express confusion in regards to teacher expectations. Well-developed rubrics help students see exactly what the teacher is requesting. George Hillocks (1987) determined that the use of scales (another term for rubrics) was a significant factor that led to improved writing skills and trailed only the quality and design of the assignment in terms of impact on results. Rubrics can also help students reflect on what they already know and what they still need to learn. They help both teacher and student understand what is required and move towards higher degrees of quality.

Departments and teams need to have conversations to develop quality rubrics that minimize student confusion about expectations. Administrators can model this approach by engaging staff in a sample rubric development process. You may want to use a lighthearted topic such as developing a rubric for the faculty lounge refrigerator to ensure that everyone is engaged. From this initial step, you can then move to establishing expectations for classroom rubrics and developing the common language necessary to ensure their use.

When teachers go one step further and involve *students* in the design of the rubrics, students are more likely to understand what tasks are being evaluated and how. Often it is the collateral learning—what students learn beyond the topic being covered, sometimes without realizing it—that helps close the gap. As one student in seventh grade remarked to her teacher, "When you are given an assignment, you need to look at its requirements. Sometimes there are things on the rubric that I have overlooked. I can change, and know what to change, by the rubric guidelines." By investing time in establishing the requirements and working with students on meeting them, we continue to build effective relationships that lead to increased student learning.

Descriptive Feedback

Descriptive feedback is essential for students to understand how they can respond to Sadler's three questions; it is also one of the key components that lead to significant gains in student achievement (Black & Wiliam, 1998). This kind of feedback:

- Describes features of work or performance

- Relates directly to learning targets and/or standards of quality

- Points out strengths

- Gives specific information about how to improve

Ruth Butler (1987) reports on another study that examined the effects of four kinds of feedback (comments, grades, praise, and no feedback) on divergent thinking tasks with fifth- and sixth-grade students. The post-test results showed that students who received *descriptive* feedback (comments that fulfill Black &

Wiliam's criteria) reached the highest levels of achievement, one standard deviation higher than the others. Clearly, this type of feedback allows for teacher and student to work in partnership and to bridge the gap between what has been demonstrated and what is required.

Self-Assessment and Goal Setting

As Anne Davies (2007, p. 31) states, "When students are involved in the classroom assessment process, they are more engaged and motivated, and they learn more." Administrators should engage teachers in a conversation about using assessments to gauge the level of student involvement and understanding. Questions that can lead to a deeper level of comprehension about what is occurring in classrooms include:

- Is the assessment designed so that students can use the results to self-assess and set goals?

- Will students be able to use the results to reflect on their learning?

These questions reinforce the important notion for your teachers that students need to be active participants in their learning. The essence of formative assessment is that it helps students develop the ability to set informed and appropriate learning goals on the path to achievement.

Communicating About Learning

Does your school have a mechanism in place for students to track their own progress on learning targets and to communicate their status to others? Davies (2007, p. 50) suggests that "communicating evidence of learning to others compels students to step back, reflect, and assess their efforts." This sharing of results provides an opportunity for both the students and their audience (teachers, peers, and parents) to gain further insights and supports future learning. As an administrator, use your conversations with students to have them reflect on their learning and share their goals.

Relationship Leadership

The building of relationships does not occur in a vacuum, nor does it occur without strong leadership modeling expectations. Roland Barth (2006, p. 8) states, "The nature of relationships among adults in the school—especially between teacher and principal—has a greater influence upon the character and the quality of a school and on the accomplishment of students than anything else." The formalized positions of school and district leadership are responsible for setting the tone and creating the conditions that foster positive relationship building throughout the system. In other words, the processes and resources that are needed for professional teachers to build quality relationships with their students must also be evident in the relationships they have with leaders and must be built into the learning environment.

Barth goes on to suggest, "How it goes between and among administrators and teachers invariably dictates how it will go between teachers and their students and between educators and parents" (2006, p. 8). He describes four scenarios that are evident in schools today:

1. Parallel play—Teachers focus on their own classrooms at the expense of the broader school goals.

2. Adversarial—Conflict abounds, and common ground is difficult to find.

3. Congenial—Teachers show surface and social politeness, but no deep conversations about kids and learning take place.

4. Collegial—All educators show genuine concern about the welfare of each other and their students, as evidenced

through discussions around practice and craft, as well as through peer observation and support. (Barth, 2006)

To resolve some of the challenges facing educators, Barth suggests that we state expectations explicitly, model collegiality, reward those who behave as colleagues, and protect those who engage in collegiality. He states:

> I am certain that empowerment, recognition, satisfaction, and success in our work—all in scarce supply within our schools—will not stem from going it alone as a masterful teacher, principal, or student, no matter how accomplished one is. Empowerment, recognition, satisfaction and success come only from being an active participant within a masterful group—a group of colleagues. (Barth, 2006, p. 13)

Becoming a school of collegiality can be difficult and may require some educators to unlearn bad habits picked up over a career. No one went into education to be marginal or ineffective. If some educators are, it may be necessary to examine why the behavior exists and what supports they need to move forward.

Larry Ainsworth and Donald Viegut (2006) outline some of the expectations for school leaders. With regard to sustaining relationships, leaders must ask themselves the following self-reflective questions:

- How adept am I at fostering and maintaining relationships based on mutual trust and respect?

- Have the changes I have made in the past damaged or strengthened professional relationships?

- Am I the most qualified person to be leading this initiative?

- What success have I really had in bringing about significant educational change?

- Am I willing to do everything that it is going to take to make this implementation effort a success? (p. 128)

Effective leaders are routinely challenged to balance time invested in building and nurturing relationships with staying current in curriculum, instruction, and assessment. The workday does not seem to stretch enough to maintain this balance while also overseeing school operations and supporting continuous improvement. In fact, "the ability to foster and maintain good relationships while navigating the unpredictable waters of change may be the most difficult challenge any leader faces" (Ainsworth & Viegut, 2006, p. 129).

Robert Marzano, Tim Waters, and Brian McNulty (2005) conducted a meta-analysis of sixty-nine leadership studies that investigate the relationship between a school's principal leader and student achievement. They clearly articulate that principal leadership *does* have a discernable effect on student achievement. They found twenty-one specific leadership responsibilities that significantly correlated with student achievement. The behaviors included in their list that parallel what has been referred to in this chapter include knowledge of curriculum, instruction, and assessment; visibility; focus; communication; affirmation; and relationship building. Ultimately, "strong leaders need to focus their attention and their school's efforts on practices that are likely to improve student achievement" (Waters & Marzano, 2006, p. 7). The creation of these positive, focused environments allows staff conversations to center on what needs to happen in order for all students to be successful.

Positive Assessment Data Conversations

Some of the most challenging conversations in education occur around data analysis. It's hard to look at low results and keep the focus on learning while also looking for solutions. How do we use results to engage in conversations about student learning and not teacher performance? One of the first steps might be to look at the data as what they truly represent—our students. The critical conversation is not about numbers or percentages, but instead about what we need to do to ensure every student has a viable future. Mike Schmoker (1999, p. 39) says:

> Why do we avoid data? The reason is fear—of data's capacity to reveal strength and weakness, failure and success. Education seems to maintain a tacit bargain among constituents at every level not to gather or use information that will reveal a clear need for improvement: where we need to do better, where we need to make changes. Data almost always point to action—they are the enemy of comfortable routines. By ignoring data, we promote inaction and inefficiency.

Principals occasionally get caught up in the seeming dichotomy of focusing on the results *or* building relationships. Fortunately, it's not an either/or choice. Highly functioning schools are led by principals who understand the importance of blending these two pursuits. Charlie Coleman is one such leader. Principal of an award-winning elementary school, he'd be the first to credit his school's success to the quality of the teaching staff. As a leader, he's found a way to engage conversation around results while maintaining positive relationships. His successful leadership style resulted in a move to the middle school where he's continued to engage educators in conversations about student learning. Following is his account (personal communication, 2008) of leading the delicate dialogue that needs to occur as educators delve into the data piece and are challenged by what they see:

> It was the end of the first report card term and a week before our faculty meeting, where we would discuss data and analyze results for the first time. We had spent time in the first few months of the school year talking about how we would analyze our results. As I consolidated the

data into a manageable document, one particular class was a major cause for concern as it had an 85% failure rate! This stood out in stark contrast to the rest of the school. While we would not be sharing the data with individual teacher names attached, it would be quite easy for all to assume which class and teacher these results came from. I did not want this first delving into data to derail our new approach, so I took some proactive steps.

I called the individual teacher in to have a conversation and told her that while reviewing the Term 1 results, one of her classes really stood out as a cause for concern. I suggested that this must be a very tough class with a number of students who had obvious learning challenges. This set her at ease and alleviated any need to feel defensive. She shared a number of her concerns and challenges with this class in a positive way that set the tone for a productive conversation. I asked her how I could help support her and her students, and we brainstormed some possible solutions. I reminded her that we would be sharing all our data at the next faculty meeting and that we would use the dialogue on data as a solution-seeking opportunity, not a finger-pointing exercise.

Following that conversion, I spoke to our Learning Assistance Teacher about ways we might support the teacher and her students and suggested they talk before the next faculty meeting to see if an intervention plan could be put in place. The two of them worked on this in collaboration with our Student Support Team. By the time we met as a whole faculty to review the Term 1 results, there was a plan in place, and the teacher felt comfortable sharing with the whole staff both the troubling results and the resulting support plan.

The response plan put in place made a dramatic difference in terms of results. The class went from 85% failing at the end of Term 1 to 85% passing by the end of Term 2. This was cause for celebration! The process we followed also enhanced trust and collaboration. Staff now knew that a focus on results did not mean punishing teachers. They also saw that from the results flow responsive intervention and improved student achievement.

The quick turnaround in these results may seem miraculous, but it occurs often in schools across the country where educators are willing to get together to engage in the conversations guided by a leader who exhibits a commitment to student success.

As Schmoker (1999, p. 77) points out, "If we want [our results] to improve (and who doesn't?), we need to focus on short-term results and feedback that tells us how we are doing in reaching short-term sub-goals and long-term goals." The gains made in the short term serve as springboards to leverage even greater levels of success moving forward. In the early stages of data analysis, it may help to collect and analyze data collaboratively and anonymously by team, department, grade level, or school. Distribute a set of anonymous data for teams to look over and make decisions about. Make sure that one of the sets of results reflects low scores, and let the group develop a plan for remediation.

In doing this, leaders establish a protocol that governs how the team will engage in dialogue about data and what pitfalls the team will avoid when the discussion turns to more challenging data. Educators need to believe that there is neither an undercurrent of manipulation nor a subversive plan to control behavior of some members of the team by rewarding others: "they must see praise and recognition as an extension of a leader's character" (Schmoker, 1999, p. 113).

Just as students benefit from meaningful, valid feedback from teachers, so professional staff benefit from and appreciate a principal's efforts to provide that feedback. If teachers feel they are being watched for any mistakes or evaluated behind closed doors, then administrators lose the opportunity to start meaning-ful conversations about how "all of us" can fix any problems and close the gap for students. If nothing else in the environment has changed in recent times, then "doing things the way we always did" will suffice. But the old "best practice" may no longer suf-fice. Fortunately, though gaps in teaching practice are likely to occur, they are not fatal. Mistakes are a part of the professional learning process. Effective administrators help teachers embrace the challenges that come with new learning.

Critical Leadership Questions

As part of staff development work that Charlie Coleman and I have done with schools that want to combine the work of assessment and leadership, we pose ten questions to school leaders that they should be able to respond to in the affirmative:

1. Does everyone in your school agree on why they are there?

2. Does everyone really believe they can make a differ-ence for all kids?

3. In terms of making a difference, is there a common schoolwide vision?

4. Are there clear and specific schoolwide systems in place to make that happen?

5. Are there classroom plans in place to match the school-wide systems?

6. Are there individual student support options in place?

7. Do procedures in the office support the school, class-room, and individual plans?

8. Does every adult talk about these plans openly, regularly, and systematically?

9. Do you know, with measurable evidence, that the plans are making a difference?

10. If it's not making a difference, are you willing to try something new?

If you ask yourself these questions and give negative responses to some of them, before you decide that your school is not "making the grade," examine where you may be falling short. Use this as the starting point for your staff dialogue on assessment, learning, teaching, student success, and staff fulfillment. Remember that gathering the data is the first step and interpreting the results follows shortly thereafter. As Schmoker reminds us, "Data makes the invisible visible, revealing strengths and weaknesses that are easily concealed" (1999, p. 44). Just as students need to close their achievement gap, so do schools: a greater understanding of where your school is makes the steps to where you'd like your school to be clearer and more manageable. This understanding also provides the foundation from which staffs may generate further conversation around what needs to occur for those students who are not experiencing success.

Action Research

Carl Glickman (1985) defines the five tasks of supervision that have direct impact on instructional improvement as direct assistance, group development, staff development, curriculum development, and action research. Rest assured that these are shared commitments that are best met when the leadership is also shared and taps into existing expertise. Strong relationships are central to effectively enacting any of Glickman's five tasks. The first four items on his list—direct assistance, group development, staff development, and curriculum development—tend to be part of a regular professional development program. The fifth item, action research, offers a unique opportunity for school administrators to engage in conversations with staff about students, assessment, and learning. Examples of this are numerous, but let me share two from my current school district—Sunshine Coast in British Columbia, Canada.

The Network of Performance Based Schools (www.npbs.ca) provides an opportunity for schools across the province to engage in an inquiry process around formative assessment practice and to follow the effects over time. The network is a voluntary action research community that has as its objectives the improvement of student learning and the strengthening of public education. A cross-section of the diversity of educational facilities in British Columbia, the network represents small rural schools and large urban schools, schools serving the most vulnerable students and those in areas of highest affluence. The work is teacher-driven, but administrators play a strong role as a team member. For example, at West Sechelt Elementary, Principal Carolyn Spence and staff asked: Will guided reading increase reading comprehension in our students? Their strategies included expanding the leveled resources and assessing each student to establish baseline data. They met three to five times per week with each group of students at each level and built in flexibility for students to move between groups when their reading levels improved. The results spoke to the value of this type of staff engagement: all students improved by six to twelve reading levels from September to March. The network then helped the West Sechelt team share their new knowledge with colleagues around the province.

Schools in the Sunshine Coast also formed school teams called Learning Community Teams that examined an inquiry question related to literacy. Some of the school inquiry teams also chose to connect to the Network of Performance Based Schools, but not all. The local context allowed schools within a district to collaborate more intensely and helped the district establish a vision for literacy. For instance, Vice Principal Mark Heidebrecht and his team at Elphinstone Secondary posed this question: Will students at risk benefit from small-group literacy class, and if so, how? A small group of students identified as being at risk met for at least four hours per week with a focus on literacy skills. Elphinstone teachers saw improvement in the areas of focusing (students could read for longer periods of time), words per minute, comprehension, vocabulary, and interest and motivation to read silently and orally. There was also a significant decrease in the anxiety and resistance around reading and defensive and adverse behaviors.

In both of these examples, the power of action inquiry—assessment conversations between principals and teachers talking together about student learning—helped to develop positive relationships that had a ripple effect resulting in improved outcomes for students.

Influence, Not Authority

This chapter opened with a challenge to school leaders to facilitate the positive growth and development of all students while honoring the commitment of all educators to be difference makers. This is a tall order at the best of times and becomes even more so in an environment of numerous external and internal expectations. However, as Kenneth Blanchard notes, "The key to successful leadership today is influence, not authority" (quoted in Tucker, 2008, p. 19). As you consider your role and responsibility as a school leader, reflect on your capacity to engage your staff to take action because they want to and know it's the right thing to do rather than because they feel they have to or fear they will suffer the consequences of noncompliance. Transforming relationships with teachers is the first step to transforming relationships with students.

Leading your staff on the assessment journey provides the opportunity for conversations that closely approximate the work we expect teachers to perform with students. As Dennis Sparks (2005) notes, "Leaders shape conversations by persistently offering their values, intentions, and beliefs to others and by expressing themselves in clear declarative sentences" (p. 157). To effectively help all kids learn, the adults in a school need to come to agreement on these values. They must have conversations around their beliefs about how students learn. They must collaboratively establish group norms regarding how they will work and learn together. They ask:

- What are our common expectations for students?

- What are our common expectations for staff? For parents and other community members?

- What do we know about best practice and high-yield strategies?

- What collective commitments will we make to ensure best practice becomes a reality in our school?

As Albert Schweitzer stated, "Example is not the main thing in influencing others. It is the only thing" (cited in Simpson, 1988, p. 217). Developing and nurturing positive relationships begins in the office of the school administrator. These relationships connect every classroom, educator, and student in a network that has as its prime objective the success to which every one of our learners is entitled.

References

Ainsworth, L., & Viegut, D. (2006). *Common formative assessments: How to connect standards-based instruction and assessments*. Thousand Oaks, CA: Corwin.

Barth, R. (2006). Improving professional practice. *Educational Leadership, 63*(6), 8–13.

Black, P., Harrison, C., Lee, C., Marshall, B., & Wiliam, D. (2004). Working inside the black box: Assessment for learning in the classroom. *Phi Delta Kappan, 96*(1), 9–21.

Black, P., & Wiliam, D. (1998). Inside the black box: Raising standards through classroom assessment. *Phi Delta Kappan, 8*(2), 139–148.

Butler, R. (1987). Task-involving and ego-involving properties of evaluation: Effects of different feedback conditions on motivational perceptions, interest, and performance. *Journal of Educational Psychology, 79*(4), 474–482.

Chappuis, S., & Chappuis, J. (2007/2008). The best value in formative assessment. *Educational Leadership, 65,* 14–19.

Comer, J. P. (2001). Schools that develop children. *American Prospect, 12*(7), 30–35.

Davies, A. (2007). Involving students in the classroom assessment process. In D. Reeves (Ed.), *Ahead of the curve: The power of assessment to transform teaching and learning* (pp. 31–58). Bloomington, IN: Solution Tree.

Glickman, C. D. (1985). *Supervision of instruction: A developmental approach.* Boston: Allyn & Bacon.

Goleman, D. (2006). *Social intelligence: The new science of human relationships.* New York: Bantam Books.

Hillocks, G., Jr. (1987). Synthesis of research on teaching writing. *Educational Leadership, 44*(8), 71–82.

Leahy, S., Lyon, C., Thompson, M., & Wiliam, D. (2005). Classroom assessment: Minute-by-minute and day-by-day. *Educational Leadership, 63*(3), 18–24.

Marzano, R. J. (2007). *The art and science of teaching: A comprehensive framework for effective instruction.* Alexandria, VA: Association for Supervision and Curriculum Development.

Marzano, R. J., Waters, J. T., & McNulty, B. A. (2005). *School leadership that works: From research to results.* Alexandria, VA: Association for Supervision and Curriculum Development.

Mendler, A., & Curwin, R. (1999). *Discipline with dignity for challenging youth.* Bloomington, IN: Solution Tree (formerly National Educational Service).

Popham, W. J. (2006). All about accountability/phony formative assessments: Buyer beware! *Educational Leadership, 64*(1), 86–87.

Sadler, D. R. (1998). Student involvement and summary of key ideas from "Formative Assessment: Revisiting the Territory." *Assessment in Education, 5*(1), 77–84.

Schmoker, M. J. (1999). *Results: The key to continuous school improvement.* Alexandria, VA: Association for Supervision and Curriculum Development.

Simpson, J. B. (1988). *Simpson's contemporary quotations: The most notable quotes since 1950.* Boston, MA: Houghton Mifflin Company.

Sparks, D. (2005). Leading for transformation in teaching, learning, and relationships. In R. DuFour, R. Eaker, and R. DuFour (Eds.), *On common ground: The power of professional learning communities* (pp. 154–175). Bloomington, IN: Solution Tree (formerly National Educational Service).

Stiggins, R. J., Arter, J., Chappuis, J., & Chappuis, S. (2005). *Classroom assessment* for *student learning: Doing it right—Using it well.* Portland, OR: ETS Assessment Training Institute.

Stiggins, R., & Chappuis, J. (2008). Enhancing student learning: Create profound achievement gains through formative assessments. *District Administration, 44*(1). Accessed at http://findarticles.com/p/articles/mi_6938/is_1_44/ai_n28487200/pg_1 on February 14, 2009.

Stipek, D. (2006). Relationships matter. *Educational Leadership, 64*(1), 46–49.

Tucker, R. (2008). *Leadership reconsidered: Becoming a person of influence.* Grand Rapids, MI: Baker Books.

Waters, J. T., & Marzano, R. J. (2006, September). *School district leadership that works: The effect of superintendent leadership on student achievement.* A working paper. Accessed at www.mcrel.org/pdf/LeadershipOrganizationDevelopment/4005RR_Superintendent_Leadership.pdf on January 3, 2009.

Index

A

accountability, 170–171

achievement tests, 97

ACT, 97

Ahead of the Curve: The Power of Assessment to Transform Teaching and Learning (Reeves), 9

Ainsworth, L., 57, 77, 80, 81, 85–86, 90, 253–254

Alvestad, K., 183

aptitude tests, 97

Archer, J., 76

Arter, J., 12, 55, 81

assessment

    See also balanced assessment; common assessment; formative assessment; summative assessment

    balanced system, 54–58

    benchmark, 55, 58

    benefits of, 53

    coaching, 57–58, 60

    collaborative, 40–41, 80–81

    comparisons, avoiding, 64

    cut-score development, 104–105

    data, managing, 44–45, 65–67

    data, used to improve student performance, 67

    defined, 94

    evaluation of, 55–57

    for learning, 55, 68

    frequency of conducting, 58–62

    grading and reporting systems, 67–68

    informed, 93–94

    interim, 55

    large-scale, 81–83

    long-cycle, 95–98

    mid-cycle, 98–100

    of learning, 55, 68

    proficiency level descriptions, 102–104

    providing students opportunity to learn before conducting, 104

    reliability, ensuring, 105–108

    sharing of, 62–64

    short-cycle, 98–100, 109

    skills and knowledge needed by teachers, 79–83

    solutions, focus on finding, 63

    support for, 57–58

    writing good, 60–62

assessment literacy

    in the community, 83–89

    creating a culture of, 12–26, 76–83

    defined, 77

    evaluation of previous models, 16

    feedback, use of, 16–19

goal setting, self-assessment,
and self-monitoring, 19–21
learning targets, establishing,
13–16
needed by teachers, 79
policy changes, advocating,
84–86
professional development
mini-lessons, 21–24
revisions, 24–25
self-reflection and sharing,
25–26

B

Bailey, J., 68, 110, 177, 181, 182,
190, 193, 194–195
balanced assessment
assessment types and purposes,
understanding, 101–102
components of, 94–100
evaluation, 109–110
need for, 93–94
reculturing versus restructuring, 111–113
teacher training modules,
100–110
Barth, R., 252–253
benchmark assessments, 55, 58
Bennett, K., 131
bias awareness, 104
Blachowicz, C., 57–58, 60
Black, P., 1, 53, 58, 89
Blanchard, K., 261
Block, P., 160
Bloom, B., 1
Blue Diamond software example,
123–126
Boston, C., 176
Bryk, A., 33
Buhle, R., 57–58, 60

Buros Assessment Institute, 99
Butler, R., 250

C

*Call for the Development of Balanced
Assessment Systems, A* (Stiggins), 9
Chadwick, B., 156
Chappuis, J., 12, 13, 55, 73, 74, 81
Chappuis, S., 12, 13, 55, 81
Cimbricz, S., 112
Civic Enterprises, 225–226
Classroom Assessment for *Student
Learning* (Stiggins), 62
Clymer, J., 68
coaching, 57–58, 60
Coleman, C., 255, 258
collaborative assessment (teamwork), 80–81
data analysis and, 42–43
formative assessments made by,
38–39
goal setting, self-assessment,
and self-monitoring and,
19–21, 251
guiding, 40–44
interdependent work structure,
creating, 34
trust and respect among colleagues, developing, 32–33
Collins, J., 85, 154
common assessments, 36
collaborative versus individual,
56–57
connections between curriculum and, 77, 79
data, analyzing, 75, 156, 158,
161, 162–163
monitoring student progress
with, 46
promoting team-made, 38–39

purpose of, 38
sources for, 61
support for, 57
community support, obtaining, 83–89
competence, 33
Cooper, H., 36, 211
Covey, S., 35
credit recovery
    description of, 228–230
    dropout rates, 225–227
    enrollment, 235–237
    program design, 235–239
    purpose of, 230
    results of, example, 239–241
    scheduling, 237–238
    staffing, 238–239
    tenets of, 230–234
    transition into and out of, 237
criterion-referenced assessments (CRAs), 95–96
culture of assessment literacy, creating a, 12–16, 76–83
Cunningham, A., 131
curriculum
    power standards, 78–79
    promoting common, 37–38
    response to intervention and, 77–78
Curwin, R., 247
cut-score development, 104–105

D

data
    analysis and collaborative teamwork, 42–43
    collapse, 121–122
    providing and managing, 44–45, 65–67

using, to improve student performance, 67, 254–258
data, meaning in
    challenges of, 151–153
    collaboration, fostering, 153–158
    data literacy, building, 158–170
    data purpose, role, and use, defining, 159–160
    efficacy, promoting, 153–155
    norms for logistics, 156–158
    norms for relationships, 155
    protocols, 161, 162–163
    questions and dialogue, posing, 160–164
    rubric for scoring, 168
    sample data report, 167
    teacher data template, 165
    team data template, 166
    tools for gathering and organizing data, 164–170
data collection tools
    Blue Diamond software example, 123–126
    confidence in using, 138–139
    DIBELS, 129–131
    recommendations, 137–144
    research and feedback, use of, 134–137
    selecting, based on beliefs, 139–140
    spreadsheet applications, Microsoft Excel, 131–134
    student response systems and whiteboards, 126–128
    technical support, 140–142
    time commitments, 143–144
data work, use of term, 151
Davies, A., 251
Deal, T., 90

decision consistency, 107

DIBELS, 129–131

Dillon, J., 109

DiRanna, K., 149–150

dropout rates, 225–227

DuFour, R., 41, 42, 76, 186–187, 215, 219, 228

Dweck, C., 19

E

Eaker, R., 186–187

efficacy, promoting, 153–155

Elmore, R., 32, 145

English, F., 112–113

Erkens, C., 2, 8–28

evaluation

    of assessment literacy models, 15–16

    balanced assessments and implementing effective, 109–110

    of current assessment practices, 55–57

    defined, 94

    feedback and, 16–19

Evans, R., 182–183

expectations, promoting high, 36–37

EXPLORE, 97

F

feedback, use of, 16–19, 134–137, 250–251

failure rates, lowering

    calculating grades by new ways, 208–209

    extra credit, reducing, 210–211

    formal discussions, 218–220

    formative assessments, use of, 212–213

    grading philosophy, developing a, 206–214

    homework, rethinking the purpose of, 211–212

    intervention plans, developing, 214–216

    late work, accepting, 209–210

    summative assessments, use of, 213–214

    teams, development of committed, 204–206

    technology, use of, 216–217

    zeros, eliminating use of, 207–208

Ferrara, S., 99, 111

Ferriter, W., 3, 120–146

Flett, J., 112

formal discussions, with teachers, 218–220

formative assessment

    See also assessment; assessment literacy

    benefits of, 1, 9

    Blue Diamond software example, 123–126

    culture of assessment literacy, creating a, 12–16

    data, finding meaning from, 149–171

    defined, 54–55, 94

    DIBELS, 129–131

    digital tools for, 123–134

    frequency of conducting, 58–62

    grading and reporting systems, 67–68

    lowering failure rates and use of, 212–213

    origin of term, 1

parent support, gaining, 86–89
relationships and, 247–252
report cards, 181–195
reporting, principles of effective, 176–184
research and feedback, use of, 134–137
sharing of, 62–64
spreadsheets and pivot tables, 131–134
strategies for student leaning at the adult level, 12–13
student response systems and whiteboards, 126–128
team-made, promoting, 38–39
team-made versus individual making of, 56–57
time taken away from teaching, worries about, 59–60
trust and respect among colleagues, developing, 32–33
why it works, 12
writing good, 60–62
frequency of conducting assessments, 58–62
Friedman, T., 137
Fuhrman, S., 95, 113
Fullan, M., 15–16, 111

G

Garmston, R., 155, 156
Getting Serious About School Reform: Three Critical Commitments (Marzano), 10
Glickman, C., 259
goal setting, 19–21
Goleman, D., 246
Good, R., 129
Good to Great (Collins), 85

grading and reporting systems, 67–68
   See also failure rates, lowering; report cards
   traditional, 203
Graham, P., 131–133
growth mindset, 19
Guskey, T., 67, 68, 75, 110, 175, 177, 181, 182, 190, 193, 194–195, 209, 233

H

Handbook on Formative and Summative Evaluation of Student Learning (Bloom, Hastings, and Madaus), 1
Harvey, J., 112, 113
Hash, J. R., 95
Hastings, T., 1
Heflebower, T., 3, 92–117
Hierck, T., 4–5, 244–264
Hillocks, G., 249
Hinman, C., 4, 224–242
homework, rethinking the purpose of, 211–212
Huff, S., 2, 30–51
Hunkins, F., 109
Hutchinson, M., 123–126

I

independent work structure, 34
informed assessment, 93–94
inquiry, guiding, 42–43
"Inside the Black Box" (Black and Wiliam), 53
instructional strategies, confirming, 39
interdependent work structure, creating, 34
interim assessments, 55

intervention plans
    developing, 214–216
    promoting, 39–40
item analysis data, 66

J

Jacobs, H. H., 78–79
Jakicic, C., 3, 52–70
job-embedded staff development,
    41, 89–90

K

King, D., 3, 72–91
Kotter, J., 220
Kouzes, J., 205

L

large-scale assessment, 81–83
leadership
    See also principals, roles of
    relationships and, 252–261
    report cards and role of,
        196–197
    response to interventions and,
        40
learning, professional development
    and
    intentional, 75
    ongoing, 75–76
    systemic, 76
learning targets, establishing, 13–16
Linn, R., 95
long-cycle assessment tools, 95–98
Love, N., 149–150, 151, 153

M

Madaus, G., 1
Marshall, K., 55

Marzano, R., 10, 56, 59, 110, 123,
    134–136, 154, 158, 160, 180,
    189, 233, 245, 254
McNulty, B., 154, 254
McTighe, J., 35, 99, 111
Meaning of Educational Change, The
    (Fullan), 111
Measure of Academic Progress
    (MAP), 56
Mendler, A., 247
Microsoft Excel, 131–134
mid-cycle assessment, 98–100
mini-lessons, professional develop-
    ment, 21–24
modified Angoff method, 105
modified contrasting group meth-
    od, 105
monitoring
    products, 48
    reflective dialogue, 46–48
    student progress, 45–46
Mundry, S., 149–150

N

National Assessment of Educational
    Progress, 112–113
National Center for Fair and Open
    Testing, 54
Nebraska Department of Educa-
    tion, 99
Network of Performance-Based
    Schools, 260–261
No Child Left Behind (NCLB)
    Act, 31, 112, 113, 226
norm-referenced assessments
    (NRAs), 95–96

O

O'Connor, K., 110, 207, 208, 210
Overlie, J., 26

P

Pardini, P., 178–179, 183

parent support, gaining, 86–89

personal experiences, sharing, 43–44

personal integrity, 33

personal regard, 33

Peterson, K., 90

Pfeffer, J., 217

PLAN, 97

policy changes, advocating, 84–86

Popham, J., 54, 84, 89, 95, 111, 212

Posner, B., 205

power standards, 78–79

principals, roles of
    collaborative teams, guiding, 40–44
    curriculum, promoting common, 37–38
    data, providing and managing, 44–45
    expectations, promoting high, 36–37
    importance of, 31–32
    instructional strategies, confirming, 39
    monitoring efforts, 45–48
    response to intervention, 39–40
    student learning, focusing on, 35–40
    supportive conditions, creating, 32–34
    team-made formative assessments, promoting, 38–39

products, monitoring, 48

professional development
    coaching, 57–58, 60
    defined, 75
    goal setting, self-assessment, and self-monitoring, 19–21, 251
    goals for, 74–76
    intentional, 75
    job-embedded, 41–42
    learning targets, establishing, 13–16
    mini-lessons, 21–24
    need for, 73–74
    ongoing, 75–76
    power standards, 78–79
    skills and knowledge needed, 79–83
    systemic, 76

proficiency level descriptions, 102–104

psychometric perfection, 62

R

reculturing, 111–113

Reeves, D., 9, 25, 62, 110, 154

reflective dialogue, monitoring, 46–48

relationships
    clear learning targets, 249–250
    communicating evidence of learning, 251–252
    feedback, descriptive, 250–251
    formative assessment and, 247–252
    importance of, 245–246
    leadership and, 252–261
    self-assessment and goal setting, 251
    use of influence rather than authority, 261–262

reliability
    ensuring, 105–108
    versus validity, 106

report cards
 developing standards-based, process of, 185–193
 developing standards-based, questions to ask, 184–185
 implementing new, 194–195
 leadership, role of, 196–197
 principles of effective, 176–179, 187–193
 reactions of parents to new, 178–179
 sharing with parents the concepts of new, 179–180
 standards-based, description of, 181–184
 students with special needs and, 193–194
 traditional, problems with, 175–176, 180
 working committee and team norms, establishing, 186–187
respect among colleagues, developing, 32–33
response to intervention (RTI), 39–40, 75, 77–78
restructuring, 111–113
revisions, 24–25
Richardson, J., 43
Rose, A., 4, 174–199

S

Sadler, R., 248
SAT (Scholastic Aptitude Test), 97
Sattes, B., 109
Schmoker, M., 182–183, 255, 257, 259
Schneider, B., 33
Schweitzer, A., 262
self-assessment and self-monitoring, 19–21, 251

self-reflection and sharing, 25–26
Sherman, D., 152
short-cycle assessment, 98–100, 109
SMART, 20, 219
Sparks, D., 262
split half method, 107–108
spreadsheet applications, Microsoft Excel, 131–134
staff development
 See also professional development
 collective growth, 42–43
 job-embedded, 41, 89–90
standards, promoting, 35–36
Standards for Educational and Psychological Testing, 100
STARS (School-based Teacher-led Assessment and Reporting System), 99–100
Steffy, B., 112–113
Stiggins, R., 9–10, 12, 13, 55, 62, 68, 73, 74, 79, 80, 81, 95, 197, 218, 230, 245
Stiles, K., 149–150
Stipek, D., 247
student learning
 expectations, promoting high, 36–37
 focusing on, 35–40
 monitoring, 45–46
 standards, promoting, 35–36
 strategies for student learning at the adult level, 12–13
student performance, data used to improve, 67
student progress, monitoring, 45–46
student response systems and whiteboards, 126–128
students at risk, assessing. *See* credit recovery

students with special needs, report cards and, 193–194

summative assessment

defined, 54, 94

lowering failure rates and use of, 213–214

supportive conditions, creating, 32–34

Susskind, E., 109

Swanson, E., 123–126

T

tangible products, monitoring, 48

teacher(s)

See also professional development

assessment literacy and use of feedback, 16–19

assessment literacy needed by, 79

coaching, 57–58, 60

comparisons, avoiding, 64

learning targets, establishing, 13–16

self-reflection and sharing, 25–26

sharing personal practice, 43–44

training modules, description of, 100–110

trust and respect among colleagues, developing, 32–33

teamwork. *See* collaborative teamwork

Technical Education Research Center, 150

technology, lowering failure rates and use of, 216–217

testing, defined, 94

Thompson, M., 152

Tomlinson, C., 61

trust and respect among colleagues, developing, 32–33

U

Using Data Project, 149–150

V

Vagle, N., 4, 148–173

validity, reliability versus, 106

Viegut, D., 57, 77, 80, 81, 85–86, 90, 253–254

W

Wacker, J., 137

Wallace, J., 112

Walsh, J., 109

Waters, T., 154, 254

Weichel, M., 4, 202–223

Wellman, B., 155, 156

WestEd, 150

What Works in Schools: Translating Research Into Action (Marzano), 134

Wiggins, G., 35, 191

Wiliam, D., 1, 9, 10, 53, 58, 68, 89, 152

Wolf, K., 93–94

World Is Flat, The (Wacker), 137

Z

Zuman, J., 150

The Collaborative Administrator
*Austin Buffum, Cassandra Erkens, Charles Hinman,
Susan Huff, Lillie G. Jessie, Terri L. Martin, Mike
Mattos, Anthony Muhammad,
Peter Noonan, Geri Parscale, Eric Twadell,
Jay Westover, and Kenneth C. Williams*
Foreword by Robert Eaker
Introduction by Richard DuFour
In a culture of shared leadership, the administrator's role is more important than ever. This book
addresses your toughest challenges with practical
strategies and inspiring insight. **BKF256**

The Collaborative Teacher
*Cassandra Erkens, Chris Jakicic, Lillie G. Jessie,
Dennis King, Sharon V. Kramer, Thomas W.
Many, Mary Ann Ranells, Ainsley B. Rose, Susan
K. Sparks, and Eric Twadell*
Foreword by Rebecca DuFour
Introduction by Richard DuFour
Transform education from inside the classroom.
This book delivers best practices of collaborative
teacher leadership, supporting the strategies with
research and real classroom stories. **BKF257**

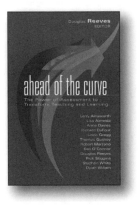

Ahead of the Curve
Edited by Douglas Reeves
Leaders in education contribute their perspectives
of effective assessment design and implementation,
sending out a call for redirecting assessment to
improve student achievement and inform instruction.
BKF232

The Teacher as Assessment Leader
Edited by Thomas R. Guskey
Packed with practical strategies for designing,
analyzing, and using assessments, this book
shows how to turn best practices into usable
solutions. **BKF345**

a division of
Solution Tree | Press
Solution Tree
Visit solution-tree.com or call 800.733.6786 to order.